Viv Graham

&

Lee Duffy's

Parallel Lives
(Omnibus Limited Edition)

Stephen Richards

Mirage Publishing

A *Mirage Publishing* Book

Publishers of Investigative authors
New authors welcome to submit manuscripts

New Paperback

Published in Great Britain
By Mirage Publishing 2002

A CIP catalogue record for this book
is available from the British Library.

ISBN 1 902578 20 1

Mirage Publishing
PO Box 161
Gateshead
NE8 4WW
Great Britain

Printed and bound in Great Britain by

C P Print Ltd, Swalwell, Newcastle upon Tyne, NE16 3DJ, England

© Cover designed by Artistic Director: Sharon Anderson

Contents

In case we forget:
Katieleigh Duffy
Dean & Viv Graham Jnr
Callum & Jodie Annie Graham

Introduction

Pub enforcer Viv Graham quickly earned a reputation on Tyneside as a hard man with a heart of gold. He took every fight with a pinch of salt. His size and boxing skills made him an excellent insurance policy against the thugs and drug dealers who polluted the pub and club scene. Viv's counterpart on Teesside, Lee Duffy, was running a parallel and equally untenable life on the pub and club circuit.

Murder, mayhem, drugs, violence and sex form the backdrop to this modem-day representation of the crime-ridden underbelly of Tyneside and Teesside. This is a book about the rise and fall of the late Viv Graham and the equally legendary infamous late Lee Paul Duffy.

From Lands End to John O'Groats, no city, town or village is without someone who's carved out a name for themselves. Newcastle is no different — London had the Krays and Lenny McLean (The Guv'nor), and the north had Viv and Lee.

Viv, a former amateur boxing champion with a promising pugilistic future that was cut short with 'frozen shoulder', turned pub enforcer; quickly earns a reputation on Tyneside as a hard man with a heart of gold. Always smiling and seemingly carefree, he takes every fight on the cobbles with a pinch of salt, oblivious to the danger that is never too far away.

Starting out as a doorman in the rural outskirts of the city, Viv unwittingly became entangled in the chaotic quagmire of disorganised crime.

After Viv impresses the local under boss by beating up a big-time gangster, he is catapulted to the next level — Newcastle City Centre. There he begins to earn enough money to afford his two favourite obsessions — gambling and women. Women, three to be exact: a blonde (Anna), a brunette (Gillian) and a redhead (Julie), played an important part in his life by unwittingly bolstering up his masculinity. It's like one big happy harem — until the women find out about each other!

Lee Duffy, meanwhile, was also enjoying the benefits of multiple tangled relationships with the women of Teesside. Lee, known as 'The Duffer', was a formidable looking giant of a man. His presence was felt before he had even entered a room, this attracted the opposite sex as equally well as it repulsed his own sex. On the spot sex in pub and club toilets with more than willing groupies was a regular occurrence, conveying Duffy's dominance amongst his peers, this more than bolstered his male prowess.

Viv, like most champs, has a vice; he bets on anything — dogs, horses, football and fights. (And when he doesn't know the fighters, he chooses his bet by the colour of the boxer's shorts!) He is on a rollercoaster ride and enjoying every minute of it, but he doesn't realise where the ride is taking him.

The Duffer is equally on as fast of a rollercoaster ride with his "taxing" of drug dealers along with his 'business' partner, Brian Cockerill. As much as Viv had few confidantes it was the same with the Duffer. Oh, the Duffer's obsession… cocaine!

Viv's infamy attracts the attention of a notorious West End crime family who, it was claimed, controlled most of the drug flow in the city. They try to put him on their payroll. Viv is a lean, mean, fighting machine, but he's insecure about his physique. At fourteen stone he doesn't match up to the beefcakes of Newcastle - so he experiments with steroids and balloons to an eighteen stone Silverback!

However, the side effects of the steroids, coupled with Viv's newfound strength, become too much for him and he nearly kills a late-night drinker. A claim that an iron bar inflicted the damage caused to the victim shows the power of a single punch from Viv! Luckily, the drinker survives and Viv only receives a suspended sentence.

The Duffer too is finding that his strength can also get him into trouble when he fells a club doorman with a single punch. The vertebrae in the victim's neck are crushed! Police refuse to believe one punch could cause so much damage!

Viv is changing from a man who wants to make pubs and clubs safer for everyone to a bully who strikes fear into the very hearts of the people whom he's supposed to protect.

The Duffer has attempts made on his life after he's classed as the bully of Teesside. A drug dealer orders a hit on the man no one dare approach head on!

Soon, both Viv and the Duffer are back in the headlines again — Viv for pummeling Stu Watson, a bouncer at Hobo's nightclub and the Duffer for breaking the jaw of a man who threw petrol over him whilst holding a lighter at the ready! Viv - for this misguided action receives a three-year jail sentence. The Duffer – for his defensive action is charged with GBH for going too far.

While Viv is in prison, two of his three girlfriends; Anna and Julie, temporarily break up with him when they find out about each other, leaving only Gillian, who has just given birth to their second son.

The Duffer is laid up in hospital recovering from gunshot wounds to his leg, as a consequence of yet another attempt on his life, when his girlfriend gives birth to his daughter in a different hospital.

Viv is well received by the prison community, and further enhances his reputation by quelling a cellblock riot that is about to take place in the prison chapel. Meanwhile, Tyneside is burning with riots of its own.

Once again a free man, Viv decides to break all ties with past allies and fly his own flag in the East End, away from the dealings in the West End. With the help of Peter (Anna's brother), Viv becomes a trouble-shooter/minder for pubs and clubs, expanding his business from a few licensees to quite a little empire.

Just as fast as he's raking in the money, he and Anna are spending it — they both crave the high life and the odd bet or two. When it came to blowing cash, Anna and Viv try to outdo each other — easy come, easy go.

Neither plans for the future, believing their good fortune will last forever. Viv has to hide behind the settee when a debt collector calls — he had £30,000 in a bag the day before, but now it was all gone!

Eventually, Viv's concerns begin to interfere with those of the West End criminal underworld. They want to expand their thriving drug enterprise, but the anti-drug Viv is in the way.

Meanwhile, on Teesside, the Duffer is as equally a thorn in the side of drug pushers as Viv is to the Tyneside drug barons. With the Duffer's constant attentions being paid to taxing dealers of their drugs and money he soon becomes a target. The drugs, he gives away whilst showering the ill-gotten money on his friends.

The mobsters enlist the help of a heavy to eliminate Viv in a winner takes all bare-knuckle fight, but the plan fails when Viv is warned about an ambush and doesn't show. The 'heavy' is Viv's counterpart from Teesside, the Duffer!

The daily pressure of the "big time" starts to take its toll. Death threats become the norm for both Viv and the Duffer. Viv suffers from frequent visits to the toilet with loose bowels and suffers frequent headaches. "I'll not see 40," Viv says, predicting his own untimely death. Viv stumbles onto the tiger's back and finds he can't dismount. The Duffer breaks down in tears and tells his girlfriend he "wants out," but doesn't know how! Each man trapped!

Viv and Anna purchase a new house outside of Newcastle, and he tries to legitimise his pub and club protection business. For the most part, Viv's reputation enables him to sit back at home, while his delegates deal with the actual problems. He spends a lot of time in a local pub near to his home, the Queens Head.

Viv Graham & Lee Duffy's Parallel Lives

Lee and his girlfriend, Lisa, take on a council house with the intentions of "doing it up" and maybe, one day, buying it. The Duffer's reputation is growing and now he has the opportunity to reap the rewards that his name can bring him…he uses his reputation to secure what he wants.

A band of locals take an immediate dislike to Viv. One of them is connected to a West End crime lord, and on a dare it is claimed; they plot Viv's murder. "Viv no more for '94."

The whole of Teesside's drug circles are angry at the Duffer's taxations and hit after unsuccessful hit is ordered against him. In a secret meeting, a small gathering of top dealers plans the Duffer's death!

At 3:30am, 25th August 1991 outside of the Afro-West Indian Centre, in Marton Road, Middlesbrough, the Duffer became involved in an argument and was fatally knifed…he died shortly afterwards in the arms of a friend. "Tell Lisa I love her," were his last words.

On New Year's Eve 1993, as Viv leaves the Queens Head, three shots echo through the merriment of the night. Viv is grounded. He summons what is left of his strength, and drags his body along the ground back to the pub. As he lies dying on the pavement, he asks his friend, Terry Scott to lift him to his feet. "I can't let them see me like this," Viv says. One last fight.

Viv Graham and Lee Duffy fiercely resented each other – their names stood for violence - both sworn enemies! Both ran parallel lives as pub and club enforcers, raging their gangland turf wars with a fierce frenzy of brutality and unremitting cruelty!

Engaging each other in a vicious organised brawl would have been the ultimate challenge! Warfare and combat would mean bloodshed and carnage – both men met brutal and violent deaths and as a consequence this battle of the titans never took place! Their violent lives are unfolded.

Starting Out

In order to find out what made such a man as Viv tick we need to examine him from a much closer perspective than that of an outsider's point of view. Here, Sharon Tate, the sister of Anna Connelly (Viv's fiancée), gives an insight into Viv's everyday domestic life. You do not know what makes someone tick until you see him or her unwind. That saying might well be the key to what is being searched for. It would be wrong to assume that those closest to him would reveal anything in terms of skeletons hidden in Viv's cupboard.

Sharon: "I knew of Viv when he was a doorman at the bottom of Shields Road, there was trouble there at that time and he just seemed to come on the scene from nowhere. At that time he wasn't very well known and the people knew he wasn't from this area. I think because of that he wasn't liked; he was from out the area...Rowlands Gill. People were saying things like, 'Who's this?' and 'Who does he think he is coming across here telling us what to do, he's not from this place?' So they didn't like him!

He wasn't from the town, he was from the countryside, he just came in and started telling people they couldn't get in the bar because they were 'worky tickets' and they weren't getting in to cause trouble...the town changed for the better when he was around.

People would come and say, 'Well, who's he? Who's this fellah coming here to tell us what we can and can't do?' So he wasn't really liked when he first came, just because he wasn't known.

I knew him before Anna was seeing him in 1986. We would be having a drink in the bar and things like that when he would come up and buy us drinks, so I got to know him a little bit. As time got on, Anna started seeing him and that was it.

When it came to spotting trouble, Viv could definitely see where the trouble was and if he was there that was the end of it. One word from him and that was it!

He wasn't a townie, but you wouldn't say he was a fish out of water, although I would…because I knew deep down that he was green as grass through the way he would treat people and the kind of person that he was.

He was really soft; he really wasn't what they were making him out to be. But he ended up exactly what they made him. But I don't think he was the kind of person that everybody thought he was.

They built him up, they came and said, 'You can do it.' He could use his fists and he could do it, but that wasn't what he was there for. He was only there doing a job and just maybe seeing that they would drink up, 'Drink your drink up lads, howway!' There's loads of people who do that sort of job and then he just seemed to get bigger and bigger and bigger.

Obviously, if something did start and he had to fettle them, they could see what he was capable of and how quick he moved. He could handle ten people at once if need be, if it come that way. There's not a doorman in the town that could do that. He could do that because he was a boxer and was like a proper fighting man with his hands in that kind of a way.

Whatever Viv's dad said, he did, if his dad said, 'Don't go there, son. They're just enticing you there as their back-up,' or 'They want to use your name,' then Viv would take it all in. This would be voiced over many a thing.

People wanted Viv to go to Spain as their backup in timeshare scams. His father, Jack, would say: 'Don't you get involved, son. You keep away from that.' Viv would go there for his breakfast and he would talk to his father while his mother made the breakfast and they'd ask what had been happening and they'd (Viv and maybe a friend) just have the normal crack. There was never fighting talk, his father would never encourage him by saying 'go on, you do this.' He would just say, 'Keep away, son, nowt to do with you, they're just using you.' Viv would listen and say, 'Aye, father, you're right.' And he would come back and say, 'My father's told me to keep away.' He was quite green, if you would say that was green."

I liked what he did because you respected the way he did it, he never, never, took liberties with people. I've seen doorman do things and I've looked and thought, because there's two or three look how they treat people. You never got that from him because he would come and he would say, 'Howway, lads, howway!' and do it in a nice way or whatever. Even if he was approaching them, if there was trouble he would say, 'Howway, lads, there's no need for this,' and do it in a nice way. He wouldn't run in knowing what he could do with them in two seconds. He wouldn't run in and do it; he'd give them the benefit of the doubt. I liked the way he did it. He impressed me because I thought he was a gentleman and in the job he was in he did it in a nice way.

From when I first met Viv up until his death I saw changes in him, in the end he would hardly ever go out. He would watch videos and ring us up and say, 'Anna's making something, do you fancy coming across at teatime?' They always had their tea on time because Viv trained twice a day. His last training would be around about, maybe, seven, so Anna would have the tea on for him coming back. They would maybe ring here and say there's chicken or whatever '...do you fancy coming across, we've got a good video?'

We would join them for a meal, and then the next minute the video would be on, we'd be in the middle of our tea and then the phone would start. Viv would say, 'Anna, what am I going to do?' He didn't want to pick it up because he didn't want to ruin the night, but he knew in the back of his mind he had to pick the phone up because he had to make sure people were all right wherever they were ringing from.

He'd say, 'Two minutes, two minutes. I'll be back in two minutes!' He'd run, and jump into the car and he would be quick. Maybe he'd be ten minutes or maybe fifteen minutes and he'd be back and sit down and say, 'Right, sorted, let's...' and then we'd start watching the film again and the phone would ring again and this is how the night constantly went on.

As for getting videos and for sitting in with Anna, that was all he really wanted at that time. I'm talking about two years before his death, but prior to that they had their good nights out. Being out late, maybe night clubbing, and that sort of thing, but the last two years he didn't even want to go out. He was happy with his videos.

I think that Anna did him a lot of good because he must have felt happy. His relationship was steady and he was happy with everything that was there. Probably the pressure was a little bit too much at the time and he was glad to just stay in and not be anywhere where things were happening.

There was still the likes of Rob Armstrong and all of them still placed in all the clubs wherever Viv would work. Even then he didn't really work in them, but he knew that if anything was ever said it was always said in his name, 'It's Viv Graham you've got to face.' So although Viv was sitting in the house this news always reached him.

Maybe Viv would get a phone call the next morning saying that two kids were in the previous night acting themselves saying they were going to do this and so on. Viv would know it would be put down to him type of thing. Even though Viv wasn't personally in attendance he still had his finger on the pulse.

Viv used to get splitting bad heads, he suffered them on a near permanent basis in the end. Viv and I used to laugh because we were like two hypochondriacs, both suffering headaches and thinking the worst!

He used to take me training with him and his headache would come back and we used to say, 'Here we go.' We did suffer the same things, I had an abscess and had to have it cut out, then he had an abscess and had to have it cut out. I used to complain and say, 'I'm sure I've got a tumour!' Viv would reply, 'So have I.' He was always complaining about bad heads. When you get an abscess you're run down, it's one of the signs of being run down so it was getting to him, but you would only know it by him saying he had a bad head.

Near the end, he was getting phone calls saying they were going to take his life, but he just used to laugh because he had heard it that many times before. Maybe the first four or five times he'd maybe have been frightened, but after a while he'd heard all what they were going to do to him.

Viv didn't care about his money. Whatever money he had he spent! David, my husband, would try to get Viv to do something with it, he'd say: 'Howway, Viv, do something with it because at the end of the day you're going to get older and somebody's going to come along and knock you out.' We used to laugh about it. He wasn't cared because he lived for the day and he'd say, 'I'm not bothered.' David would say, 'I'm going to get you a lovely diamond ring because you should be wearing a nice ring. You should have a nice watch and a nice house because your job isn't easy, so you should have something that you can say is yours because of what you're doing!' David went and got him a nice ring and he loved it, Viv was over the moon.

He didn't ever get himself a watch, but at the time Viv had said he wanted somewhere nice for Anna to live because Daisy Hill was a bit rough. They loved it there, the people loved them and they loved the people, but David wanted him to do something because he knew Viv was a waster with his money.

He said to Viv, 'You've got to get something under your hat because you're getting on.' This is when they started looking around at little places. David was behind him pushing him into things like that. Nobody else really thought about these things, everybody was only seeing the other side of him. Having a drink, having a bet, doing this, just squandering. David wanted him to make something to put behind, but Viv always said, 'I'll never see forty, man. Live for the day, I'll never see forty.' And now when he hasn't reached forty you wonder what was going on in his mind? He said to us all the time, 'I'll be finished, me. I'll have my leg blown off; something'll happen to me before I'm forty. I'll not see forty.' So obviously something was ticking around in his head telling him that.

He used to talk about what he should have and what he's got and I'd say, 'Look at the life you've got to live, what have you got for it?' He didn't confide in us about any trouble. You would never hear him. He knew he could handle it, but it was only his bad heads that he would complain about.

It used to gut me, I felt like seething because people didn't even know him. Rumours about Viv would get out of hand. It would go from more, one week into the other and the next minute he'd done this and done that, and it used to hurt me because I used to think, 'If they only knew him, if they knew the type of lad he was they would think the world of him, they would have loved him.' Because he was genuine and he was a gentlemen in every way even in the way he sorted his trouble. I respected him for the job that he was in because it wasn't an easy job. The way he did it, he made it look easy.

I remember we were in a nightclub, it was pitch black and we were right at the back. Anna and me were there and Viv was leaning on the bar talking to us, then he just shot from out of our sight. Then I just saw him, he had this man held right up in the air by his neck. I was saying, 'Eeeeh! He's taking liberties, look at the size of that little man.' I said to Anna, 'What's he doing that to him for, he's never done a thing? I'm going to tell him.'

I went across towards where Viv had this man, I saw this lass screaming, Anna was saying to the lass, 'What's happened, what's happened?' One minute Viv's leaning on the bar talking to us and then the next minute he's got this lad up by the neck. Anna thought the lass was screaming because Viv had her lad up by the throat. It turned out that the lad had a knife up to the lass' throat. Viv had seen it from where he was in the pitch black!

That's how unbelievably quick he was. He grabbed the lad and took him to the door, where the doorman was and he says, 'Look at this? He was in here and he's had that knife. He got past you with this.' He took the knife off the lad and kicked him up the arse, kicked the lad out and said to the doormen, 'I'm warning you that you'd better make sure that people are searched properly!'

Some time before this, when Viv was approaching the end of his three-year sentence for an attack on fellow club doorman Stuart Watson, an incident happened in a nightclub. A sex pest in the Studio nightclub glassed a young woman after she had slapped him. The young lady died from the result of being glassed in the throat. Viv had this on his mind when he spotted the same potential fatality that could have happened here, the same nightclub where the glassing incident had taken place. Doormen were supposed to be searching people for weapons and had obviously slipped up. Viv was none too pleased with them.

The lass said to Anna that the lad had a knife held to her throat. The lad was her boyfriend, but she'd chased him and he wanted her back so he was threatening her. The lass was in the toilet with Anna and had been telling her that the lad had been threatening her and he would do this that and the other to her and she didn't think he would be in the nightclub that night, but he was. The lass was very thankful for the way Viv had reacted.

Viv had an uncanny knack to spot trouble and get people out of tight spots. It was as though Viv could read what people were saying by just looking at them. I used to flinch when I could see that Viv had spotted trouble. But you could look and see nothing happening, and then you would see him stepping back and making his way to wherever. The next minute a fist would be thrown. He knew what was going to happen before it actually happened."

The Duffer Starts Out

Having found out what made Viv tick, what about Lee Paul Duffy – The Duffer. What sort of a person was he? Viv was called a wide-eyed country bumpkin, but a bumpkin with insight. What then of Lee, how did he fare in these stakes?

You can take the boy out of the city but you cannot take the city of the boy, which was the comparable difference between Lee Duffy and Viv Graham. What I mean is, Viv was from a little village and even though he tried to make inroads into the underworld scene on Tyneside he still had a bit of the rural villager in him. Duffy though…you could put him wherever you wanted and he could survive because of his streetwise instinct. A true chameleon, adaptable to every facet of life's complications, but still fatally flawed!

If you had never met Lee Duffy and he walked into a pub you would know it was him. One of the stories about Lee Duffy goes like this, one day down the Empire, a box van pulls up with about thirty mountain bikes in it, the driver gets out and asks Lee and another man if they knew where 'Bobby's Cycles' was.

Two other men, who Duffy knew, were standing around. Duffy told the van driver that he does not know where the place is but, he says, 'They'll know in there,' as he pointed to the Empire pub. The driver, leaving the engine of his van running, goes in to the bar and the two men who had nothing to do with Duffy and his friend smartly jumped in to the van and drove off at high speed. At that time mountain bikes were fetching £500 each!

That very night, the man who was standing with Duffy went to his mother's house and she says to him, "Have you heard about your mate, Duffy? A man pulls up from the handicap kids with a load of bikes asking for directions, Lee Duffy knocked him out, broke his cheekbone and took all of the bikes off him that were for the handicap kids." Such exaggerated stories only helped build Duffy's reputation.

Duffy had such a presence about him that it has been said that he could go into a nightclub with 1,000 people in the place and within ten minutes there would only be 100 people left in the building. He would not need to hit anyone with his fists, but his presence was felt.

When Duffy was in prison he was visited by his girlfriend and his friend, when they eventually got in to see him he was walking around on his own in a big caged yard. The reason for him being caged…eighteen people in that prison wanted to murder him! For his own safety it seemed easier to put him in such secure surroundings than the eighteen would be assassins.

A particular story relating to Duffy's time in prison shows Duffy's character. Duffy was brought out through a door leading into a little tunnel; in his mouth he has a joint and one tucked behind his ear. Duffy, puffing vigorously, seems oblivious to the two prison officers at his side. The prison officers escort him into a little room hastily assembled as a makeshift visits area.

Duffy says to the prison officers: "Fuck off!" They reply: "Lee, on a visit we've got to stand over you." Duffy sharply replied: "Look, you've got me out of the cell, but you've got to get me back in the cell, fuck off!" The two prison officers briskly walked out of the room, that is the type of power this man had.

An associate of Duffy's, Neil Booth, decided to climb on to the roof of the Havana club. Booth, off his head with drink, started to throw roofing tiles on to the road below. Duffy was in a house around the corner and the police go to the house to ask Duffy to get Booth off the roof.

"Now then, now then, now then," was Duffy's way of saying 'I'm here.' Sure, Duffy was in an elevated position and had no need to make such grand entrances, but that is how he was. When it came to being involved in running things on Teesside, Duffy could not be bothered with such things like that, he was not business minded, although clever, it was not for him. But making grand entrances was!

Someone who knew Duffy well described him as a schizophrenic and said, "What you've got to remember with Lee is that he was like a schizophrenic. They're all schizophrenics. They've got to be a schizophrenic."

Duffy was always discriminated against from the age of six right up until the day he died, he knew he was not going to see the safe side of thirty so what did he have to lose by being himself. As time went on, the very name 'Duffy' would bring fear and terror to those around Teesside, but only to those with good reason to be feared. All of the people who suffered at his hands had some connection to the underworld, either directly or indirectly. The people who tried to kill Duffy did not know him personally; they were contract killers working for others.

When Duffy was shot the second time, he was hospitalised for a number of days and to help him overcome the pain he would smoke dope. Duffy would scoff and mock his armed police guard: "Come here, do you want a go of this," as he held out a joint.

During Duffy's short enforced stay in hospital it coincided with his girlfriend Lisa going into hospital to give birth to their daughter. Duffy did not get to see the birth of his daughter; he had to be content with friends telling him what his new daughter looked like.

Duffy was a sensitive person and in an extract I have taken from a letter he wrote to Lisa Stockell a lot is revealed about him. Here was a man who had half his foot shot off in an assassination attempt, had his skull beaten with a crow bar and yet all he writes about in this letter, which is written on one side of a greetings card, is the pain and suffering Lisa must have went through, not once does Duffy fall into self-pity for his own predicament.

The Duffer Starts Out

Notice the neat handwriting, an indication of someone who is methodical and artistic. Notice how some of the text slopes down from right to left, an indication he's depressed. The neatness of the handwriting leads me to believe he was a bit of a perfectionist, and as we know perfectionists can become frustrated. Maybe this was the key to it all in how Duffy would sometimes fly off the handle, but regardless of that he was also a great thinker.

① Hello Lisa,   9a.m.

how you doing then, not too good eh? You sounded really low on the phone earlier. It's doing my head in Lisa. (I just want to see you and my new baby daughter). I know how down you are and I can't be there for you... Now I have to wait, untill Monday. Before I can see yous. You were so distant from me on the telephone last night Lisa (You cut it across like I'd forgotten you)! I wrote, I sent a couple of little presents, I got Michelle to order flowers and I telephoned twice, to see how you were. plus I gave Boothy £20 to kim Wendy and Joanne some flowers and I wrote them both a little note saying sorry and thanking them.....

So Lisa, don't think I've forgotten you, Lisa I love the ground you walk on. I'm rock bottom myself Lisa, I'm trying hard to keep my chin up. All I want to do, is put my arms round you and see the baby. I know your in pain, jesus you have just had your tummy sliced open and a 8lb baby dragged out, it makes me ill thinking about it. I know exactly what your going through, I'm doing my head.

Simon Elvin ℗
35 SE 4504 - 2
Printed in England
P.T.O

11

Indicators to the levels of paranoia such a lifestyle can bring are shown when Duffy was on his way to a blues party. He became paranoid and thought the people that had previously shot him were in there. He drove to a house somewhere in Stockton; he went in and within minutes he returned to the car carrying three guns. Duffy said to one of his associates: "Here, get one of them." The man replied: "Fuck you and 'get one of them.' I don't mind having a fight with someone, but if I get caught with this and you shoot someone, the frame of mind you're in, I'm getting 15 years here."

On the way back from Stockton, by the Suite Centre, a police van went through the lights. The driver of the transit van was called Martin Shallows.

An associate of Duffy's takes up the story. "He goes through and misses the car, a Sierra, doing about 60mph. I said to Duffy, 'Go for it, go for it and let's get out of here. He's got to turn around, he's in a transit van, let's offskys.' Duffy says to me: 'Let's fuck fucking offskys.' He pulls up and at that time he's got three loaded guns and ammunition in the car. I'm wiping the guns and the door handles of the car down. Duffy jumps out of the car, goes straight over to the bobby van and he says, 'What the fucking hell do you think you're doing, you?' And Martin Shallows says, 'All right, Lee, what's a matter?' Duffy says, 'I'll tell you what the fuck's a matter with me, you've just nearly crashed into me, you daft cunt.' The reply was, 'Lee, howway, just get yourself out of Stockton, mate, no problem, no problem.'

Another time someone had a load of cannabis resin in the car and the coppers pulled Lee for a routine check because it was Duffy. He went off his head like he was a loony and they brought a squad car out to give the car a full check over. They never found the cannabis, it was underneath the seat. Instead of him keeping his mouth shut he couldn't."

Duffy and his friends, one of them was Lee Harrison, were in a place on Normanby Road and someone went in to tip Duffy off that there was a large police presence outside. An inspector wearing a flat cap and uniform with all the buttons on walked in and he said, "All right, Lee?" Duffy says, "Yeah." "We want to have a word with Lee Harrison over fines," said the inspector. Duffy says, "Fuck off out of here now, before I give you it!" The inspector says, "I can come back..." "Come back with who you want," intervened Duffy.

The man who owned the pub came in and said, "There's fucking loads of them outside." Duffy and his friends knew if they went out and drove away that they would get pulled over so they got a taxi. On their way along Normanby Road, all of a sudden an unmarked squad car pulls in front of the taxi and stops and out of the side of the road armed police ambush them shouting: 'GET ON THE FLOOR FACE DOWN! GET ON THE FLOOR!'

Everyone except Duffy gets down on the floor while he walks around saying, "Fuck getting on the floor, I'm getting on no floor. Fuck you telling me to get on the floor." One of the police officers said to the officer in charge that Duffy wouldn't go on the floor and he was told Lee was "all right." Was this is an indicator of Duffy being considered too lethal to push too far?

Many people have taken what has been said or written about Duffy as gospel, as the definitive guide to what made Duffy tick. I've spoken to the hardest of hard throughout the UK and up to now every single one of these people, with the exception of one, has turned out to be a likable character, why should Duffy have been any different?

Usually it is fear of something that brings out the worst in a man. Duffy had a fear of being bullied so he got the first one in, if you were not a threat to him then fine, if you were not a low life drug dealer then fine, if you were not one of those who had bullied him from the age of six then fine – total strangers who have never met Duffy say he was an evil person. It would seem that the only ones who had anything to fear from Duffy were the evil ones.

Tommy Harrison is one of the elder statesmen of the

Teesside underworld. His reflections on Lee Duffy imply that Duffy was a likable character. "He said to our Lee (Tommy's son), 'I've got something to tell you, something bad is going to happen tonight.' I said to Lee that I said that same thing to myself years ago and it never happened.

Lee once knocked on my door and said, 'I've been shot, I want the bullet taken out,' I said, 'That's not a bullet, it's a shotgun wound, it's lead shot. I can't do it, you'll have to go to hospital because it'll get poisoned.' It did poison because some of his jeans had gone into his leg along with the lead shot. He'd sometimes go missing for days on end up to Newcastle at a pub called the Bay Horse, I used to have to go up and get him.

When the petrol was thrown on him he just whacked the geezer before the geezer had a chance to pull a lighter out. When they had the gun pointed at his belly he just wrestled it to the floor. He was fearless, he didn't fear anyone. How many people in Middlesbrough walk around with guns and knives, the people trying to kill him were out of the area and were paid to do him in. I couldn't have seen anybody enticing him into a blues party so he could be killed, they'd have had to do him in. They couldn't have just whacked him because he'd have come back at them.

When I lived in North Ormsby, he used to go running every day and this day he'd been running and training. He come to my house and said, 'Have you got anything to eat?' Eggs. Sausage, bacon, liver tomato the lot, then he'd be off. He gets round the corner and someone wants to have a pop at him, Lee smashed his jaw, clipped his cheekbone with two right-handers. How do you go and train, have a nice meal and go round the corner and see somebody that wants to have a pop at you, I don't know how you can define that. He used to run up the hills pulling a log up with him.

When he got into trouble at the Speakeasy, he was in there just having a drink when it was a firm from Leeds causing trouble and he was asked for a hand and they all blamed him, the others never got charged and he did. It wasn't in his nature to be used, but it was in his nature to help you. If you were in a bit of bother he'd help you.

I had a bit of bother with someone and he said to me, 'Where are you going?' I said, 'I'm going to go and fight somebody.' 'I'm coming,' he replied. He was barred from the town while he was on this particular condition of bail. But he'd help you straightaway; he wouldn't say, 'How much are you paying me?'

Lee used to love going out with me. 'Half of them are lovely people...' he said, "...and the people in London." He loved it, he didn't swear or anything like that when he was mixing with proper people. He wouldn't swear in front of proper people. Towards the end he started to mix with the wrong people.

He was going to fight Lenny McLean until he got shot. I went down to London with Norman Jones and I had Mick Jagger and a few other people putting money up for all this. He was fit, he was bouncing, then he got shot in the knee! I think Lee would have had the upper hand with Lenny McLean because Lee was young, and don't forget, he was nearly eighteen stone and he could hit hard. I mean, I knew McLean and Frank Warren.

I was going to have a go with McLean in '78 in the Empire Rooms, Tottenham Court Road. Lenny come in with young Frank Warren when they done the back street boxing. I've known frank from being a kid and Ritchie Anderson, I just though if I were four years younger I'd have just been on the boil because now I'm 59. Lenny wasn't as big as that in the 70s, he was on the gear, he wasn't as big as he was when he died.

I said to Frank if ever you want anything then there's my phone number and I said, 'You'll never spend that,' and I gave it to him on a £10 note. He replied, 'I'm not as bad as you, there's my phone number,' and he gave it to me on a £20 note. And Lenny McLean just sat there and we were eyeing each other up, but I don't think he'd have beaten Lee, I don't think anyone could have beaten him.

Everybody knew Lee because every nick he went to he battered the top man. He'd say, 'Who's the gov'nor in here?' Wallop, wallop, wallop and he'd give him it. He just made sure they knew who he was.

Lee did a bit of boxing, but it's what's in you that counts, but boxing does help you. You have to train; a Rolls Royce won't run without petrol. He was powerful and he was a big hitter, if he hit you then something would break. I said to Lee, 'When you're fighting, surprise them.' He had power and he had speed. It's not how heavy you are, it's the speed.

You could rib him and have a bit of crack with him; if he knew you, he wasn't a bully. I loaned him and our Lee £5,000 one day and they dodged me with the money. They were upstairs in the Speakeasy and they were saying, 'Oh, the old man's here!' I said, 'Hey, get here, I want you and I want you,' while pointing at the two Lees, 'Where's that money, I want paying, you bastards and I want the money now.' They said, 'We'll get you it,' and I replied, 'Well I want it and don't dodge me.' We were all laughing, he could have said to me, 'Shut up, you're getting nothing.'

You'd have to get to know him, outsiders couldn't get close to him, but if he took to you he took to you and you'd get a million per cent back off him. He was no fool you know, he was very careful who he befriended.

If he was going anywhere, he'd make sure it was safe, he'd get dropped off a few streets before or be driven around the place. If he was in a taxi, he'd have somebody sitting in front of him. There was a time the police were looking for him, he was out of the back bathroom window and he was off...naked - he ripped all his leg open, but he was off like a shot.

There was a time he got a dodgy passport and flight tickets to go off to Spain to stay out of the road for a bit when he had some trouble, he went to Charrington's garage (Brian Charrington) and they blocked the garage off. Charrington had obviously got on the phone. Lee would take a car off you, 'I'll borrow that car off you.'

The Duffer Starts Out

When mobile phones were first around in the early 90s they were the size of building bricks. Lee would drive around in a soft top and have one held to his ear and it wasn't even switched on! I gave our Lee (Tommy's son) a mobile phone, the bill in the first month was £1,100, I said, 'Give me it here,' they thought it was a trend, the pair of them.

There were never enough hours in the day for him, cars here and there, going all over. They went to the Hacienda and knocked the doors open. I said, 'They've got guns, they'll pop you.' They were all running around looking for him in Manchester, he was hid in the boot of a car. He goes to the doormen. BOOM! BOOM! He knocked them out. Lee wasn't bothered about doormen; it was like going for the title, you go through the ranks BANG! BANG! BANG! Just knocking them out!

Lee was a good conversationalist, but if he were going to be involved in a fight then he wouldn't talk his way out of it, no, no! There's a story about Lee holding a gun to a taxi driver's head in a game of Russian roulette, he never held it up the man's head, it was a lie whoever said it. He just shot a hole in the roof of the taxi before he got out and the man said, 'What have you done to my taxi!'

Lee could drive, but he was lethal! Straight through traffic lights! We lost count of the amount of wing mirrors he broke. He once said, 'Can I have a drive of your Rolls Royce?' I said, 'You cannot! Sit in the back.' He should have had one of those little Daff cars where you put the stick forward to go forward and back to go back.

Lee went to Tenerife with our Lee and they also went to Ibiza, Lee was like a volcano. He needed a rest.

When Lee was with Lisa he was a different Lee Duffy altogether, sitting having a beer, watching telly and having a laugh and then he'd say, 'Right, I'm off to bed now.' When Lee was in company, though, he could take four or five on and when you're young you're buzzing.

I was in Johannesburg and was having a meet with a princess from Kula Lumpur and there's a big bodyguard about 6ft 5in, Greco wrestling champ, the lot, and even he asked me if I knew Lee Duffy!"

17

Respect

Respect is something that played a big part in the old school of the underworld. Long before smack and crack hit the streets there was an unwritten code of conduct that was held aloft. Such an ethos of respect has since long died out, but it still lingers on in some of the last of the old school.

Ernie Bewick has been called a 'gangland killer' and an 'enforcer,' but upon meeting him you would find him to be one of the most forgiving men you could ever meet.

Convicted drug dealer Tony Waters met an untimely end on 7th December 1977 when he started a fight. Waters, 44, lost his life outside of the Eastender pub, in High Street East, Sunderland.

Waters deliberately went looking for Bewick with the intention of doing him some damage over an incident that took place the previous night between Bewick and two other men in Sunderland's Luciano's restaurant.

Ernie Bewick was pursued head on in a confrontation that was designed by Waters, which went against the supposed 'quiet life' Waters was leading since his release from prison some four years earlier. Waters was painted a whiter than white character, but in reality he represented a very different picture to what was painted of him.

Waters left behind a family that grieve him to this day and, of course, the time of year (Christmas) of his death compounds the pain and hurt they must feel for the loss of their loved one, but without fear or favour such sentiments should be put to one side for a moment in order to reveal the depths of Waters' resentment for Bewick. Bewick was, and still is, anti-drugs; Waters was pro-drugs and was well known within the drug fraternity of the north and he saw Bewick as a stumbling block to dealing his drugs in the pubs under Bewick's charge, so any excuse for a confrontation would help in ridding Bewick from the area.

Bewick, not a man to underestimate, was fully aware of the way Waters was dealing drugs and knew that he was the difference between Sunderland being flooded with drugs or being kept relatively drug free and so long as he was in charge of certain pub and club doors it would remain that way. Viv frowned upon drugs, as did Bewick, and just as similarly as others wanted rid of Viv so that they could deal in his patch on Tyneside it looked to be the same way in Bewick's territory of Wearside.

Bewick and Graham had a lot in common, although I would have to give Bewick the slight edge over Graham in his handling of matters and his ability to sense danger.

Waters, a terrier tempered person, met his untimely end as a direct result of his desire to wheel and deal drugs in Sunderland. Although, first here is an insight into Ernie Bewick so as to help you make your mind up as to whether you agree with what is written.

Ernie Bewick unfolds his account of the two fights he had with another northern hard man, Billy Robinson from Gateshead. "That night I was called to the door (the Blue Monkey – rumour has it that Ernie started working there because of trouble with a well known drug dealer selling drugs and because someone had been murdered outside of the club), I was told that Billy Robinson was at the door and he wanted to come in.

On that particular evening, it was the type where everybody had to pay when they came in so I went up, and I really didn't know Billy at the time, and I explained that everybody had to pay to get in. His henchmen standing beside him said, 'Do you know who you're talking to?' I said, 'I'm sorry, you know, but you've got to pay to get in.'

If anybody had of asked me the same thing, I'd have said, 'Fair enough.' So then I was being called a 'little shit' type of thing and there was other abuse like that thrown at me, so

I said, 'Look, you can't come in.' Billy said, 'Right, you little thing, get round the corner, you little shit.' I said, 'Well, fair enough.' So then Billy slapped me across the face and I went forward to go into him, he tried to punch me, I ducked over the punch and gave him a right cross and an uppercut and knocked him out.

Billy's friends were there, his big henchmen suddenly seemed to deflate, and I said, 'Right, get him up and fuck off, don't ever come back here anymore!' They went, but obviously by then all the talk starts to generate. Obviously there were a few scares that they were going to come through team handed at the door and there was a couple of times we had to prepare for what might have happened.

Months later, I heard rumours that I was going to be set up and different things. One day, Keith Bell (Changed his name to Keith Collins – previous mention in Viv series of books.) come knocking on my door trying to go on as if though he was a friend and he says, 'Look, Billy wants to have a go at you and he wants to see you as soon as possible for a one-to-one.' (Known as a straightener.) I said, 'Fair enough, I'll come now,' he replied, 'Well, can you not make it later on tonight, you know where I live, you've been to mine before, can you come through?' We went through and it went on a couple of hours while they were talking, so I got something to eat at Keith's.

Later on, the fight was arranged at a gym in Jesmond, Newcastle, which was owned by Andy Webb (former Mr Great Britain). Andy Webb was a gentleman, Viv was a gentleman, they were all nice and friendly. I went through to the gym by myself.

(Staggering to think that Ernie was fearless in turning up to such a venue on his own, but he did!)

I never brought anyone with me. I walked in their camp on my own; there were a good few of them there. Viv got on the phone to tell Billy I had arrived. I was kept waiting a further hour and half to two hours before Billy arrived.

I remember feeling cold (due to the lengthy waiting

Respect

process), Andy Webb was very good towards me; he gave me a cup of tea to warm me because by the time Billy had arrived they'd been talking for about twenty minutes around the corner. I more or less explained to Viv that if I could sort it out over a cup of tea without any trouble then that's the way I preferred it.

(Again, staggering to think that Ernie was as a calm as a cucumber wanting to talk things out over a cup of tea, obviously the others there might have seen this as a sign of weakness. Ernie is just that sort of person and not for one minute should he have been underestimated – it was not without good reason that his fists were called the 'peacemakers'.)

I didn't want any trouble, but at the same time I went through because if that was the way to solve it! Billy obviously wanted the fight to be on, so fair enough!

I went through to where they had the fight arranged, it was a small compartment, and there was a little bank that went up. I realised then that this was suited more for Billy's needs than mine. With me being a lot lighter he could get me into the corner, or if I ran up the bank I would slip or fall over, which I did at one point when I was fighting, but I got out of that anyhow.

Billy came up to me, and he was a gentleman when he approached me. The first thing he said to me was, 'Ernie, I want to shake your hand now, before we have this fight and afterwards I'm going to shake your hand as well.' I shook his hand and then we got on with the fight.

Billy sort of stood in a boxer's stance. I didn't underestimate him because he's got such a powerful punch and later on, as we became friends, we had a bit of trouble with someone, his powerful punch proved to be awesome!

My strategy for the fight was to wear him out and then go in for it, that was my strategy before I even went through there. I stood there, I jumped about a bit and I was flicking punches at him trying to egg him on to come forward at me. The punches weren't really very hard; to be honest I wasn't even properly warmed up because I'd been standing waiting about all that time in the cold.

Billy was throwing lefts, coming forward with lefts, straight lefts and trying to catch me with them, but obviously I was jumping about a little bit, flicking a punch here and there, getting him to move and at one stage Billy got on top of me, but I managed to quickly escape from underneath his arm and I was back up on my feet in no time. At that time I was only 13½ stone, pretty fit and agile, so I could jump about a little bit.

(Do not be fooled by Ernie's modesty, he is still very fit and looks like he could walk through a barn full of troublemakers.)

We stood, we bounced about a little bit, again, he was trying to get his punches and I noticed he was open for a left hook. But something inside's telling me to hold that left hook back, so now I'm throwing right hands all the time and now I'm warmed up and they're coming over strong. I even said during the fight, as a bit of hype, 'Right, I'm warmed up now. I'm starting the fight off now.'

I don't know how long I was fighting, I cannot say if it was five minutes, but it wasn't half an hour or three quarters of an hour. When you think, five minutes could be a long time for most fit fellahs. Anyhow, I never took any punches, I might have had to a little bit, but nothing really hard and I came in with a right hand all the time. I've thrown a right hand and caught him with a left hook, so now I'm coming in to finish the job off.

Billy's moving around, but as he's staggering over I'm thinking, 'Whoa, I've been caught with an uppercut!' By then I fell over, it was a good punch, one of my hands was on the ground, in fact it was the left hand, and then Keith Bell come around and he got hold of my hand.

I was embarrassed because I thought they were stopping the fight because I'd been knocked over, I thought Billy was now going to run in and kick me because he would have been desperate. I was going to roll around and spring back up, that was the theme that went through my mind. I was confident that that was the way it would go.

I knew I was vulnerable because he could have run at me and kicked me. I got up and that was the point I went berserk! I tore into him, split all his lips and that and literally went mad and shouted, 'COME ONNNNNNNNNN!' I just literally went straight at him, as if to say 'I'm not getting beat off anybody!' I was really hyped up.

Then I went forward and Viv grabbed me shouting, 'HOWWAY, ERNIE! HOWWAY, ERNIE!' and things like that. So they stopped the fight, I was confused because I'd realised Billy had knocked me over, but they said 'Howway, you've beaten him fair and square.' So then Billy went one way and Viv went the other way and I was still confused so I followed the way Viv went.

Remember, walking away from that I'd been involved in a fight and I'd been hit and for a minute my mind went a bit blank. As I walked through the door I remember walking into Viv and he was sitting on the seat and he was saying, 'Look, I want no trouble! I want no trouble in this gym, mind.' I said, 'Look, I'll stand here with you.' I folded my arms and stood beside him. Andy Webb was standing there, his head was bowed down, I didn't know why? I thought it could be because of what Viv had said or he was embarrassed with the way Viv went on because he seemed to be like an honourable type of person and was nice towards me and made me feel comfortable.

I can remember that I went to the toilet, came back and then shook Viv's hand and everything and we were all right. I recall, as I walked towards the door and went out I could feel Viv watching me from behind, without turning my head I knew this.

When I got outside the gym, Billy was at the other side of the door so he must have walked around and out some other way. He come up to me and hugged me and I hugged him back and we shook hands and everything, just like what he said before the fight, he kept his word.

I'd previously boxed Viv Graham and I beat him in the ring, I was too strong for him pound for pound. When I was young I used to idolise Rocky Marciano and when I used to fight in the ring I didn't want to box, I used to think it clever to take punches so I knew I could take a punch even though I'd boxed a few times. At that time I was silly, I was young and it was daft the way I went on at that time. At seventeen to eighteen we go through all sorts of phases when we grow up. Looking up to Rocky Marciano gave me strength. If I wanted to beat anybody I just used to think of Rocky Marciano, he had a head like a bowling ball and you couldn't hurt him and that's the way I thought, so really a little bit of that was still in me.

Getting back to the fight with Billy, as I was getting back into the car Keith Bell said, 'You know, Viv shouldn't have stuck that sly punch on you.' I said, 'Ah, I see what you mean,' and then I realised that it wasn't Billy that gave me that walloping uppercut and it all fell into place.

I got out of the car and went back into the gym and Viv was on the phone and I think Keith was in the other room, although I'm guessing about that. When Viv finished, he came over and said, 'Ernie, look, Billy was like a dad to me he really brought me up when I was younger.' I said, 'Look, it was only a daft punch, forget about it.' Viv said, 'Is it okay if I come through?' (To Sunderland) I said that it would be all right, but I'm always like that, even when I got out of prison I forgave certain people for what they'd done against me.

I can forgive people and I realise everybody's got good points and everybody's got bad points, I try to motivate the good points in people, which isn't a bad thing, but be careful because the bad ones will take over.

Marciano is portrayed as a good man, his mother went to church and prayed for him, he come from an Italian type of family where his mother didn't like him getting into the ring and he didn't like his mother knowing he was getting hurt, so

Respect

I suppose in a way when you're reading books like that as a kid maybe it's been reflected in me and kept me off the drugs and off the streets and got me into the gym training. Back then, people wanted to be like Marciano but now people want to be like Tyson.

After the fight with Billy I maintained some links with Viv and we had a few discussions on the phone about it because I'd heard rumours going about that I'd been knocked out for ten minutes! I'd discussed that with Viv and Viv explained, 'Look, I haven't said anything like that, Ernie.' He told me that he had lots of respect for me and for how I went through there on my own.

Billy Hardy the boxer from Sunderland went through to Newcastle, he met with another boxer, John Davison and Viv and all them and he turned around and said, 'Look, all of them through there, they've got loads of respect for you.' But I was also hearing stories! What happened once was that Gavin Cook was asking me about what went on and he said, 'I've been in his (Viv's) company and he says he knocked you out for ten minutes.' I said, 'Look, if Viv ever wants his go at me...'

I heard Viv was very supportive towards me over a few things because I've had trouble with the Sayers'; we've chased them from Sunderland when they came with guns one night. There's a load of lads will tell you the truth about what happened there. They come barging in; it was Gary Rob who had the 'After Dark' (club). What happened was Gary said, 'Look, they've all barged in.' Ashy (Paul Ashton – now serving a total of 31 years imprisonment.) was there, I said, 'Don't worry, we'll get them out.' I went up to the two Sayers' (Michael and Stephen) and said, 'Look, there's all of us, are you daft or something?'

There were some big hefty blokes with us so I turned around and said, 'If you want trouble we'll do it that way then!' They turned around and said that they had guns so I said we also had guns, 'He's got one there,' I said, pointing to one of the men with me. I was only bluffing, but sure enough one of them did have one, he actually went to his car, came back and told me he had a one, but I never saw it, but I spread that about.

I'm not a bloke that would like to use things like that, but from my point of view it was a bit of bluff and I wanted to get them off the premises and they offered me violence and I said, 'Okay then, I'll have you two together, I'm offering you two violence.' In other words, if that's what you want, but there's loads of scenarios happened like that around the town. Anyway the bluff worked with them and they cleared off.

Some time later there was talk that one of them (Sayers) was going to come through and have a go at me. I heard that Viv went up to him and he turned around and told the lad that was with the Sayers' that he was going to get knackered if he had a go at me. So one night when he comes through to Sunderland, I sat and waited and confronted him and said, 'I hear you're going to have a go at me?' 'Nah, nah, I don't want any trouble with you,' was his reply, so I just left it.

I built up a friendship with Viv and actually went through to his house and had a cup of tea with him and had a discussion over different things. I remember Gavin Cook was working with Viv through there (Newcastle) and he came through and said, 'I've told Viv that you're not bothered about him and I'm keeping out of it so here's his phone number.'

He must have been match making and I said, 'Look, I'm not going to back down from him, Gavin.' So I pulled Viv up and said, 'You're the one going around telling everyone that you knocked me out for ten minutes,' he replied, 'Ernie, I've never said that, I've got nothing but respect for you and all I want is your respect.' I replied, 'Look, Viv, you've always had my respect, I've heard a lot about you although the only thing that put me off was when you punched me, but you've always got my respect, but now you're going around saying you knocked me out.'

Anyway Viv denied saying it to the end. I remember meeting one of Viv's friends called McNally from around where Viv had once lived in Rowlands Gill and he said, 'Honestly, Ernie, Viv Graham had lots of respect for you,' and he went on to tell me that Viv was telling everyone I was 'a man' and how I'd went on my own to the fight. There was another lad training with me in the gym and he said, 'You know something, Ernie, you should never take notice of what some people say, I was training with Viv once and he's got loads of respect for you.'

I ended up getting on well with Viv, but you've always got to remember that there's still a dividing line and you do hear Chinese whispers and all that. I'd heard stories, how true they were I don't know, but he'd come and have a drink with you, he'd take you to the bar when he was ready and as you go in he'll put his arm around you and all of a sudden it's BANG, BANG and he's on you.

Other stories were that he wouldn't take his coat off and stand in front of the man, it would be something like, 'You alright, mate,' and then BANG, so I was advised to be wary of that sort of stroke. I always kept that little bit of doubt in my mind and I was very careful of how I went about it if I ever socialised with him because he did want to come through here.

I'd also heard that Viv liked to have an audience around him when he kicked off with a couple of lads who he might knock out and then the word spreads, 'Viv knacked three lads the other night, you should've seen him.' I mean anybody can go and do that, but that's just the image…but anyway it mightn't be true because you hear all kinds of stories about me, you'll hear some good and you'll hear some bad."

There ends the interview relating to the Billy Robinson fight and it goes to show what kind of a man Viv was in the sense that he broke a code of conduct for his friend and mentor, Billy Robinson, when he punched Ernie in order to give Billy some time. Billy would not have approved had he had time to say so because afterwards he congratulated Ernie on a fair and square win.

Maybe that is not the way it was meant to go, but it did and I believe that when Ernie felt Viv's eyes burning into his back after the fight that Viv may have been overawed at

Ernie's resilience to his punch and it maybe showed Viv that if he ever had a toe-to-toe with Ernie, then as had happened in a past boxing match between them, then it would be Viv who would come off the loser.

Ernie was forgiving towards Viv and this action clearly shows the type of characteristics he learned from his hero, Rocky Marciano. As for Viv spreading rumours that he'd had Ernie knocked out for ten minutes, it fits in with some rumours I'd picked up elsewhere, but of course such bravado helps maintain a hard man image and what better way to perpetuate the hard man image by embroidering on the truth, as Viv seemed to do.

Ernie is the classic hard man; Viv was the new breed, straddling the line between past and present. Viv did not have the inherent safety reflex that is bred into city dwellers and that is what I believe Viv lacked and was to cause his eventual downfall.

The delicate matter of Ernie being on prison licence made it difficult to talk about the Tony Waters murder, but the story I have heard time and time again was that Tony had it in for Ernie and he had made a 'cocked gun' gesture with his hand and pointed it towards Ernie, indicating that Ernie was going to be shot. From a third party I was able to get the picture of the build up to Tony Waters' death. That night, Ernie was hit over the head with a bottle and his head was bleeding. The night before that, Ernie had a fight with Scott Waters when Ernie tried to eject him from a restaurant because he was being abusive.

Word was spreading around town that it had taken seven of them to sort Scott Waters out, a rumour apparently started by Waters. Ernie was in one of the pubs that Waters was in and people were looking to Ernie to see what he would do to scotch this rumour. Ernie was sucked into a vacuum of deceit and lies and reacted in a way that was out of sorts with his character when he decided to approach Scott Waters. Ernie was, maybe, forced into this option in front of the very same crowd that had told Ernie about the rumours that Waters was spreading and because he could not back down he confronted

Respect

Waters head on. Ernie, as a consequence, knocked out Scott Waters.

Further rumour has it that Waters went back and told Tony Waters and a number of others that he was getting the better of Ernie Bewick and in fact had supposedly decked Bewick twice when seven others intervened and jumped him. This twisted story was to be the death of Tony Waters and the following day police intelligence reports suggest that people were walking about with guns looking for Ernie Bewick, looking in all the wrong places it would seem, which gives rise to the fact that they probably wanted word to get back to Ernie Bewick that they were looking for him over the previous night's fight.

They wanted to send a message of strength and into the bargain they wanted to frighten Ernie Bewick into staying away so that they could sell their drugs. Certain people were advised to stay away from the town centre because there was 'going to be trouble'. Ernie being Ernie was not going to stay away. This was Ernie's territory and he had to show others that he was not going to hide away over something like this.

My own intelligence gathering suggests that Ernie Bewick was told that there was trouble in a pub, although there was not any trouble at all, but it was the perfect way to entice Ernie into another confrontation that was designed by Tony Waters.

On entering the Eastender pub Ernie saw Tony and they acknowledged each other and the story goes that Tony asked what had happened the night before and in Ernie's understated fashion he told the truth, but Tony was having none of it and gave Ernie an insult that was designed to cause further trouble, he called Ernie a 'liar.'

Scott Waters was not a fighter and it would go against Ernie Bewick's own code of conduct to hand out the thrashing Waters said he received, but it didn't pull any weight with Tony and Ernie was told to get outside the door. Obviously for a one-to-one, but as Ernie walked towards the door he had a bottle thrown off his head and a scuffle ensued. Ernie then approached the man, Tony's stepson, who had thrown the bottle off his head, but the man's mother got in between her son and Ernie and became protective towards her cherub of a

29

son who had just bounced the bottle off Ernie's head.

The altercation seemed to have settled and one of the doorman, Ritchie Laws, had taken over the dialogue of settling everyone down, but Tony's stepson had now thrown another bottle and this time it hit Ernie square on in his face! It beggars belief that Ernie did not retaliate, he had taken so much and yet here he was still in control, which takes some doing considering the force with which a grown man can throw a bottle off someone's head and face.

My inside source is able to tell me that Ernie pleaded with Tony to go and to forget about it. Surely two bottles smashed off Ernie's head should have been repayment enough, but Tony was shouting at a lot of people and would not leave and he was now making a show in front of people and was walking to go out and repeatedly made to go back inside asking Ernie to come outside with him. Ernie, by this time, was telling Tony's wife the story of how it was only him and Scott Waters that had the tousle and that Scott had been lying about the 'seven' others.

Tony Waters came back in for the third time and during this time Ernie was explaining things to Andrea Chesum and remonstrating that she should ask the man that accompanied Scott about what had actually happened.

During this time Tony was shouting that Ernie was going to be shot and the argument continued down the stairs. When Ernie followed Andrea down, Tony was physically poking his finger into Ernie's face and yet still Ernie did not retaliate.

Outside of the pub…well, Tony Waters met his death in a fight that was ferocious by any man's standards, but when you consider my findings as to how Tony had conducted himself and the provocation Ernie was under I believe that was far more than my words can convey. Ernie did not intend for Waters to meet his untimely ending in such a fashion and was genuinely taken aback when he was charged with murder.

Ernie was Sunderland's 4th Emergency service and the similarities between how he and Viv worked were uncanny, although no doubt every major city in the UK can boast a Viv Graham character I do not believe many can boast an Ernie

Respect

Bewick type character modelled on Rocky Marciano. Where the police could not protect people's businesses from being taxed by criminals, Ernie Bewick could protect them and many a time the services of Ernie were called upon to resolve certain issues that the police stayed away from.

Ernie now faced a murder wrap and his club and pub doors were open to being poached by others seeing this as a power vacuum that they could fill, just as when Viv passed away a power vacuum was also left. Davie Binks was a name suggested as one of the people interested in taking over Ernie's doors, but they were soon won back into Ernie's realm with the help of Ritchie Laws. One of Ernie's men was jumped on by five others and rumour has it that Ritchie stood up to Davie Binks, although for the sake of protecting both from prosecution let us just say this was a fairy tale I was told from one of my Chinese whisperers. We've got two very big men here, as well as a man we shall call Wayne.

Wayne, although young, 23, is very mature and powerful for his age and a fight breaks out where he ends up doing well, and again rumour has it that he told Ernie on a prison visit that no one was taking his doors. Ritchie won some of Ernie's doors back in Sunderland and Newbottle and all of this happened during Ernie's period of prison remand, which was for a period of some 14 months. With such loyalty behind him, Ernie had more support than Viv had when he was murdered and that indicates the difference in terms of Ernie and Viv....yes, Ernie was a lone wolf just like Viv, but when the cards were on the table, Ernie's loyal supporters would always be there for him.

For those interested in further rumour there is a story that Ronnie Bestford went to a pub called the Sun Inn and told Davie Binks that he would have to go and he would not be picking money up anymore and with this, Ernie's friends, continually of their own free will, gave their support to ensure Sunderland was not taken over by outsiders.

Initially, when Ernie was on remand, Joe Freeman and a few others helped secure peace for the city of Sunderland and eventually Graham Potts was brought in to work with Joe as well as Brian Loughlan and many others safeguarded Ernie's doors. Of course Ernie was still on remand while all of this was going on and little did he know what was to be the outcome of his trial where he was to face the charge of murder.

Paul Massey from Manchester (serving 17½ years reduced to 13½ years on appeal) had been able to help avert a gangland war in the city of Sunderland over the death of Tony Waters and because of this Paul Massey must be given credit for his part in smoothing things over in respect how people were fed rumours as opposed to fact.

While the police intelligence were oblivious to what troubles were brewing in Sunderland it was down to Ernie Bewick's ability as a 'peacemaker' to avert a serious takeover of the city from outsiders and with the backup and support of those brave enough to step out into a city ready to burst with violence a very serious situation was avoided.

Ending on a high note it would seem that Sunderland is a pretty well mannered city and things have settled down. Ernie Bewick deserves some credit for how he handled things when he was actively involved in running the doors; his followers deserve some credit for how they conducted themselves and maintaining a calming atmosphere.

Ernie Bewick is the typical understated character from the underworld, he is not a brash and egotistical man, he does not stick his chest out and spit on the path to give himself a hard case image, in fact Ernie is the total opposite to what you would expect such a hard man to be and that is what makes him hard, he does not have to try, there is no need for such dramatics as I have often seen displayed by drug or drink fuelled louts…you can keep the lot of them because there is only one Rocky Marciano in Sunderland.

The Duffer v The Tax Man

Lee Duffy. They say you should not start an opening sentence with someone's name. I have given Lee Duffy his own sentence because the mere mention of his name in the north of England is a statement in itself. The connection between Lee Duffy and Viv Graham ran deeper than the old disused coalmines in Northumberland and higher than the famed Transporter Bridge on the River Tees.

Just as Ernie Bewick and Viv had so much in common so it was with Viv and the Duffer, but Viv kept Duffy at arms length because Duffy had something quite different about his nature and that was something Viv was wary of! Lee Duffy did not want to be upstaged by any man, no matter how big and they do not get much bigger than Brian Cockerill, the 'Tax Man'.

Brian seems to be as big as a barn door and when the sun shines you can imagine him having to stand out of the way of it otherwise the whole of Teesside could be brought in to total darkness! Brian's friendship with the Duffer started in the most unexpected way…as enemies! Undoubtedly, such a force as Brian being meddled with was a foolhardy way to earn a trip to the nearest hospital casualty ward. That is exactly what the Duffer did…he meddled with a force beyond his imagination. Brian tells of the run-in the Duffer had with him.

"Lee was bullied at school the same as me, I was bullied until I was about 13 years old, nearly every day. When Lee was 14 years old he was trained by John Black and eventually Lee started working on the doors for John. Lee got his four stretch and he was doing everything, so he was a lot more streetwise than me. I didn't start working the doors until I was twenty, I trained up until I was 19 years old, but I was quiet. Lee and I knew of each other through John Black.

I was about 25 years old and Lee, the Duffer, was going by in a car, I'd just come out of a restaurant and, I always remember, I had my finger strapped with a metal splint because it was broken.

Lee jumps out of the car with his mate who's drinking a bottle of Pills. Duffy says, 'What do they call you then?' I thought to myself that he was going to say something like, 'Hi, I'm Lee, John's told me all about you.' Anyway, I said, 'I'm Brian.'

So I'm looking at his mate holding the bottle in his hand and as I spoke, Lee hit me on the side of the head with his right hand and I see nothing but stars, I fall into a squat position but I grabbed Lee around the legs and he tried to push me away, but he couldn't, he didn't have the strength. I threw him into the wall and I head butted him a few times and hit him with my forearm.

I couldn't punch him because of my finger, so I head butted him on the floor and he's shouting, 'John, John, get him off me! Failey, get him off me.' He's beaten because I'm 23 stone and I'm sitting on him and he hasn't got a chance then, so his mate hits me with the bottle of Pills! So I grab him and throw him into the car and I walk off.

My mate's with me and he's a bit scared of them so we walk down the road and I'm trying to get to this other lad's house because he was a fighter and worked on the doors. So I thought with the two of us we'd stand a better chance.

I was crossing across a roundabout and pulled one of the metal bollards out of the ground and I rammed it at Lee because they were following us and I pushed it at him and he fell back and John Fail, the other kid with Lee, runs off and I was shouting, 'See John Black and we'll fucking fight it out on the field one-to-one, no problem when my hand's better.'

Lee didn't want to get near me and he was just trying to show off because he knew if I got hold of him that he wouldn't be able to get away from me, so he's standing off and not getting any closer. As I was walking towards him he was backing away from me.

Afterwards, I went to this Mick Storey's house. Mick come out, but they'd gone and then I went to Boothy's house and I said, 'Is Lee in there?' He said, 'No, he's not in,' so I replied, 'Tell him I'll fight him.'

So anyway, I trained, I went to Eston with Mat Johnson, Mat put Lee on his arse years ago. I'm looking for Lee and he's with this Craig Howard, we come up near the police station in Eston, near the garage, and they come around in a green 'A'-reg Sierra and I jumps out of my car and they try to drive off, so I dived on the car and the weight of me starts bouncing the car up and down and this made Craig stall it. They eventually got the car going again and drove off and just didn't want to know, so I'm buzzing then because I've won the fight without even throwing a punch.

About a month later, Lee phoned me in the pub and he said, 'Look, can I met you?' I said, 'Yeah, we'll get it on, me and you, anytime,' thinking he wanted to fight me. So the next minute he asks me to go to his house for the following day. Lisa Stockell (Lee's girlfriend) was there, Boothy and Mark Miller, a kid who knocked about with him. Lee walked in, he was putting his boots on and said, 'Look at the size of him, me trying to fight him, I must have been raj!' He shook my hand and he was all right after that.

After that we ran around with each other for about three months taxing all the drug dealers. There were no drug dealers selling drugs then, it all stopped because we just used to take the money off them."

This is the first indication that Lee Duffy knew he had met his match in someone and that someone was Brian Cockerill, so if he could not beat him then he would work with him as collector of taxes. Duffy had a few losses to his name from fights he had had years earlier, but he was still developing his style and had some more developing to do before he would become a formidable fighting machine.

Together with Brian Cockerill, as a fighting team, this pair could have conquered the world but for Duffy's carefree ways and spending money on his friends like there was no tomorrow.

Yet in direct contrast to the Duffer, Viv did not have the same sort of associates. Sure, Viv had the likes of Rob Armstrong and Rob Bell, but their friendship did not have the core strength to run as deep as that of the Duffer and Brian Cockerill. Viv was a little wet behind the ears in how he apportioned trust. He could fall out with his friends over the quirkiest of things, which may have lost him some of the earlier support he had built up when he was a maverick trouble-shooter.

This fundamental difference between Viv and the Duffer shows the divide between streetwise ability and backstreet guesswork. The Duffer, with his streetwise ability instinctively knew whom he could and whom he could not trust. Viv, with his backstreet guesswork showed his lack of pedigree in what he did.

Duffy, as did Viv, admitted life was for living and at his young age, early 20s, he was going to enjoy it come what may, so any planning for the future was out of the window.

Although Brian was still young, being in his mid 20s, he was to have some run-ins with other hard men in the area. A close associate of Brian's told me of how Brian had a few run-ins with heavyweight boxer David Garside (British title and world title contender).

Cockerill, it is said, was to get the better of Garside in two fights. The first fight took place at a rave club where Stephen and Michael Sayers were present. The rave had gone on for three days and everyone was full of ecstasy.

Garside had made his way to fight Cockerill and it was suggested that someone in the rave was watching Cockerill's movements in order to report them back to Garside. Cockerill left the Rave at 9am, after a heavy three days of raving madness. After coming out from a place that was in total darkness but for the strobe lighting effects, the daylight must have been like looking at a million-candle lamp shining into his eyes. But still, Cockerill was able to stand up to Garside and, it is said, bit half of both his ears off in a fight that lasted some ten minutes. Cockerill did not escape injury and he came away with a broken rib and a closed eye and towards the end of the fight Garside was getting the better of Cockerill.

Cockerill v Garside II took place in a tiny room and this time Cockerill managed to even the score and it was suggested that this is what contributed towards Garside retiring from boxing, although it has been suggested that Garside was retired from pro-boxing already.

Now what I am going to write about next has been gained from information sourced from three very reliable people and given the amount of violence involved I have had to tone it down otherwise I would have to get the local abattoir to stand by to clear the mess up, in fact the mess afterwards did take some cleaning.

Certain names have been withheld, not though for legal reasons! Should anyone wish to instigate litigation then they are wasting their time because there are three taped interviews that back up and corroborate what is enclosed herein.

It is not for me to act as a policeman or to turn such interviews over to the authorities, that is why people trust me because they know when I give my word I keep it and I have given my word that I will not use these tapes to incriminate anyone, however if you want to waste your money, about £150,000, in a civil lawsuit then be my guest.

What follows is on par with the Texas Chainsaw Massacre.

For those of you who have faithfully followed the previous series of Viv paperbacks you will recall the time Viv, unwittingly, took part in a rather unpleasant job of holding a man in a bear hug in order that he could be restrained so his finger could be chopped off for a debt repayment. Viv was horrified at the gory sight and upon realising what had happened he ran off!

Tommy Harrison was put in a very difficult position when

he was facing the twin barrels of a shotgun being poked in his face, Middlesbrough's elder statesman of the underworld pushed the gun away from him and gave the person pointing it at him a few words of friendly advice.

Tommy was ordered to phone Brian Cockerill up and ask him to call around on some sort of pretext. Tommy was not in an immediate position to refuse such a request considering the closeness of the gun barrels to his anatomy!

Some sources say that Tommy did not suspect such violence would be used on Brian. Brian turned up at Tommy's home like a lamb to the slaughter where a posse of armed men with handguns, a shotgun and all sorts of other equipment used in butchering animals lay in wait.

Brian was about 18 stones in weight and had not trained for some time although he was still a very powerful man he could not do anything against such weaponry. A fight took place in which Brin did put up enough resistance to ward off his life being taken.

The ongoing blood letting lasted for some time in which time Brian's legs were so badly hacked and his head smashed to an unsightly mess so much so that Tommy's house was left resembling a house of horrors.

During the sustained butchering of Brian, a man familiar to Brian came in, (not Lee Duffy), and he tried, unsuccess-fully, to break Brian's jaw in an attack of vengeance. Not a single bone in Brian's body was broken but his head and legs were a mish-mash mess and he should have been dead. A lesser mortal than Brian may well have been undertaker's wages. Some time later, one of the attackers paid compensation to Tommy Harrison to cover the cleanup bill for his home.

A number of people were arrested and remanded into custody over this totally unforgivable attack, but although Brian knew his attackers he did not make any statements and as a consequence no one was ever charged with this brutal and savage revenge attack carried out by some of the more familiar mix of underworld characters from Tyneside,

The Duffer v The Tax Man

Sunderland and Teesside.

A story I was told from a dead underworld character's (Speedy) friend indicates that when Speedy was locked up serving time with one of the main players (serving time for a separate offence) in the Cockerill attack he was able to fully explain the side of a story that was withheld and it changed the main attacker's opinion of Cockerill and it made him wish he had never been involved in the attack.

Some time later when Cockerill recovered from the butchery, he was imprisoned for motoring offences ($2^{1/2}$ years) and he met up with his main attacker. An apology was made to Cockerill because it was said they were "misinformed" about the situation.

Brian is able to expand on the rave scene when he says, "I remember how I met Sunderland's Ernie Bewick when Gary Robb had all the rave clubs and Ernie Bewick was brought down by him because I was in Stockton and Gary wanted to open a rave club there. I said, 'You're not opening a rave club down here unless you pay me some money every night to open this club because it's my area so you're not coming down here.

The night come for everyone to go to the rave club and I just told everyone not to go, so only about twenty people turned up. So they brought Ernie Bewick down to fight me, so I went down to fight this Ernie Bewick. I got there and we ended up shaking hands, he was the nicest person I've ever met, sound as a pound, great.

I used to go and see him every weekend up there in Sunderland. Ernie said, 'I haven't come down for trouble, I'm just getting a few hundred quid on the door, it's your door, it's not my door.' They were devastated because they had to pay Ernie a wage and they had to pay me a wage, they used to pay me £1 for every one that went in. Because there were only twenty people in they thought nothing of it, but the next Monday there was over 2,000 people in because I got all the kids to come. I remember it was a Bank Holiday and Ernie used to come down till about six o'clock. We used to mess about on the door with the pads (boxing pads) and things; he was a nice man, Ernie. The night he killed the lad, Tony Waters, he phoned me and I said he should come down.

Ernie had trouble in Sunderland when Garside was brought in, but they didn't fight, Ernie fronted him and then another time the Sayers' come and they tried to beat Ernie, but Ernie had about 200 lads waiting in the car park, he had some pull in Sunderland.

The Sayers' didn't turn up when Garside was there because they were wary of Ernie. I knew Ernie and I knew them so I was trying to sort it out, so I was going up and I would go around the clubs with Ernie to meet the lads and that, I even met Gina G.

Paul Ashton from Gateshead come in to one of my clubs when I was in jail with his mate Monkey Lyons (Paul Lyons), well it wasn't my club, but I was in charge of security and he comes in and says that Paul's putting a wage away for me for when I got out, he was all right with me like that.

Paul had a fight with Viv Graham and he was saying, 'Fucking make him stand still,' because Viv kept jumping around. Viv was only fifteen stone at the time and Paul was over twenty stone! I was inside with Paul and he wasn't strong, I was curling more on the bar than he was benching. Paul, though, could take a good shot on the chin, but he wasn't very clever with his hands.

I remember when the armed police come for me because I was accused of having a couple of people shot in the town. About seventeen cars full of armed police pulled up, I was in my car and I just drove off. They got me for dangerous driving, but I said I was in fear of my life, which I was; they gave me $2\frac{1}{2}$ years! The thing is they would always come with an armed response unit for the likes of me, all what they had to do was be polite…manners cost nothing.

If I never had another fight in my life I'd be happy. I entered the strongest man competition, but three days before I was due to go in for it I pulled my knee out. I often think it's not really worth doing because I'm all right on certain movements, but when I run with the ball and pull the tractors it starts hurting. There's not much money to be made from it, look at Glen Ross in Ireland he's still working the doors and runs around in a little Fiat, he weights 35 stone and he's got it wrecked.

When I go out I try to be nice to everyone, but when Viv and Lee went out everyone would be frightened of them and they loved that. Lee used to love going into a club and emptying it and I think what's the point of that. I like to talk to people and have a good laugh, but when I used to go into a pub with Lee it used to just empty.

He used to give people a punch and I said, 'What will happen is that one day one of those young kids you hit who's 18 or 19 years old now is going to be thirty odd and when you're about fifty, he's going to give you a good hiding.' But obviously he never made that age. The night he died they were spitting on him and saying things like 'Die, you bastard,' it's true that, the lad who was up for his murder, Allo, (David Allison), I beat him up after it, he never come out for six months after that.

What happened was, he was fighting with a lad in a pub and he was hitting the lad in the face with a stool and I thought he was going to get done for murder if he kept it up so I broke it up, as I broke it up he turned on me so I gave him the biggest hiding he's had in his life, I knocked him out, woke him up and knocked him out again and turned him around and gave him a kick up the arse. How it happened was I'd knocked him out inside the pub and I said 'there's no room in here' and we went outside, he run at me and I caught him with two body shots and a left hook to the head and I knocked him out.

I remember Lee and me went to one dealer's house in Eston and there was about seven locks on the door and Lee said, 'Big fellah, get this door open,' and I kicked the door and my leg got stuck in it and he said, 'It's on top! It's on top! ' My leg's stuck in this door, that was his favourite saying and he'd wind me up into thinking the police were coming.

He was a get for borrowing cars off people, he borrowed this car off a lad, a convertible and he's going down to Middlesbrough, flying down the road, when he only goes and opens the hood! As we were driving, it just blows off and blew away down the street and he just kept on driving.

Another time we were in this car and it stalled at the lights and he said, 'Ah, fuck it,' and just left the car at the lights, he done it loads of times. He used to take cars off people and just leave them in the middle of the town, it would run out of petrol, he wouldn't put petrol in, he'd just jump on a bus, he was mad.

What I liked about Lee was that after we had the fight in Redcar, some months later he come over and he sat and as he talked he gesticulated with his hands and he said, 'You know that day we had the fight was the first time I knew I was beaten and for six weeks I couldn't believe I got beat.' Lee had only been out of jail for a few weeks and he was with this John Fail and as they were driving along he said to Lee, 'Look at the size of this fucker, would you have a go at him, Lee?' So it was Lee being wound up by others and it seemed easy for people to do. John Black used to say he was like a clockwork mouse, wind Lee up and he was away.

So when Lee and me got to be friends, Lee said to John Fail, 'I've made it up with the big fellah now, so now it's your problem.' I walked into Fail's house and said, 'And you!' I wasn't going to hit him, I just shouted at him and he went white.

I remember seeing four doormen kicking this young kid on the floor, I went round and knocked two of them out and the police come and grabbed hold of me and the lad punched me in the face, as the police had hold of me they put me in the van and I kicked the van doors off the hinges and I went into a one and I got nicked.

Another time my car got nicked a few years ago when I was in Stockton I was going through Ragworth, Rosewood and Bluehall, all the rough areas, looking for it. I spent a week looking around and every car thief got a good hiding and people were coming up to me in the street and telling me that since I'd been looking for my car there'd never been anything nicked and they went on to say they wished it was me working the streets.

Some time ago, a drug dealer was using my name for six months in order to protect him, he was saying that the heroin he was selling was mine, I took offence to how he was using my name because the police were starting to give me bother over it.

The dealer then had the misfortune to be taxed for a lot of money (£21,000) and people suggested it was me that had taxed him.

I then get a phone call from his supplier in Newcastle and he said he wanted the money back off me and told me I was out of order. I told him to sling his hook, so he went to the best fighter in Darlington and he turned around and said, 'What the fuck can I do with the big fellah, I can't fight him!' He then asked who the drug dealer was and when he found out he said, 'I wouldn't do it for him anyway because he's a grass and his supplier's a grass.' (The supplier in question is thought to have been responsible for the murder of pizza deliveryman Paul Logan.)

I remember when Peter Donnelly and Joe Hunt (10 year for robbery) tried to get me to team up with them. Joe Hunt's a nice lad, I had a rave club down here and they come down and said, 'Are you all right?' I replied, 'No problem.' I'd be in with every firm because everyone liked me and I got on with everyone, but some people tried to use me and they'd say, 'You fight him,' and I'd say, 'No, I don't want to do that.'

With Lee though, he'd be off doing the fighting for others and that was the difference with him and me. People would get him into Newcastle and fill him full of ecstasy and just have him running about taxing people. He might collect, say, three grand and he'd get one and they'd get the other two and it was him doing the taxing, he was just used really.

I think what it was that with Lee being in the jail for four years, he comes out and he was just enjoying himself being in all the clubs and everyone talking about him and he loved to have a fight every night so everyone would talk about it the next day, he loved that.

We used to go on the pads (boxing) with John Black or John Dryden and when you're a big lad you hit the pads hard so the trainer pulls the pads back a bit otherwise it hurts their shoulders over the years. They used to pull the pads back and Lee would say, 'Stop doing that,' because he used to like people being able to hear the big thud of the punch and daft things like that.

When you're young you want to be the best, but when you're getting older you can't be bothered with it and if you know you've got it then you'll use it.

Now if I'm with anybody and I spill their drink I'll say sorry and buy them another drink, but a lot of people take that kindness as a weakness and they think 'He's not that hard, he's not that good.' I'm not being big headed, but down here they all want to talk to me, buying me drinks, saying, 'My car's been pinched, can you sort that out?' and things like that.

I was approached by a man whose 7-year-old son had his motorbike pinched, they'd been to the police, which they're entitled to do, and nothing happened. I got it back for them within three hours and I took nothing for it because I was pleased to see the kid on his bike.

At times when I've had trouble though I've had to handle it differently, Stu Watson come down here with Stevie Abadom, Stevie Hammer and all them, about fifty of them come down, a big bus load of them and they come in to one of the raves where I was and they all stood in the door and I shouted, 'What the fuck are you doing in here?' Stuey Watson was sitting down, he didn't want to know. I went upstairs come down, there must have been about 200 hundred of them, we had all the Sunderland crew come down and the lads in the place and I said, 'If you don't go now you won't be able to walk,' they never come back.

And it was some time later when I went to jail and they were all in there, Stevie Hammer, Geoff Brown and others and they were all right, we had a good laugh. Stevie Hammer was a nice lad, we used to sit in the passageway in prison playing dominoes and the screws would walk by when we were playing dominoes looking at us as if though we were mad.

I've had guns pulled on me and you just have to confront people, 'Come on then, you wanker,' you know they're not going to do it, you just know when it's certain people, it's all bullshit. There was a lad here, Speedy, if he'd have pulled a gun out he'd have shot you, he used to work with me and he got killed, he got shot. I was working it out the other day, there was about ten of us, all top fighters Viv Graham, Lee Duffy Speedy and others they're all dead or in jail.

When I was in jail I was moved around all the time and the police would contact the prison saying I should be in the block because they knew if I was in the block it would stop me getting my cat 'D' (open prison status), which I should have got because I was only in for dangerous driving.

I was being shipped to different jails all over and I remember when I was in Walton jail I had a fight with one of the best fighters in there, he was bullying all the screws and they were frightened of him. He took a copper's eye out and got 10 years. His name was Duckdale, about 24 years old, a tall kid, I knocked him out in there and I got awarded cat 'D' status after that."

Brian is also featured on the underworld hire a Crimebiz star web site of www.crimebizz.com

Working The Doors

This chapter starts off by reminding those of you who are unfamiliar with the incident that took place in September 1989 inside of Hobo's nightclub, Newcastle. In a totally unprovoked attack, Viv attacked Stuart Watson. CCTV video cameras caught the incident, which was also witnessed by two undercover police officers that did nothing to intervene.

As similarly as the Duffer was used like a clockwork mouse, so it was the same with Viv. Point and go! These men were easy to manipulate, but was it their trusting qualities or just their gullibility to want to rise up the ladder that made them so easy to control, we will never know.

Stuart Watson has spoken of the brutal attack and of the circumstances surrounding the build up to it and why he could not retaliate, but even so, he still managed to humiliate Viv by taking some of his best shots without returning any and still not going down. Stu takes up the story prior to the Hobo's incident.

"It went back further than that with me and Viv. We had a bit of a do down at Julie's nightclub about 18 months before the Hobo's incident. Viv comes in and a few words were exchanged, I didn't know he was in the building. He come across and put his arm across my shoulder in a friendly sort of way and he said, 'You're Jobie's pal, aren't you?' (John Jobie) I replied, 'Yes,' and he gave me an uppercut on the chin. (Stories are coming out about Viv that confirm what other people have said.) I've still got a scar on my chin even now after all these years. He didn't drop me, I pushed off him and we had a bit argy bargy and Rob Armstrong and a couple of other kids were with him. We burst out on to the street and a few words were exchanged. We were going to have a fight up the back lane but then all the doormen on the quayside were his mates and more or less worked for him down there, the trouble dispersed. (Where were all of Viv's so called mates when he was murdered?)

It never stopped at that though and I was supposed to meet him up at the bridle path, up at Whickham (Near to the Metro Centre shopping complex.) the next day on a Sunday. Viv ended up actually shaking my hand after the set-to on the Saturday night and said, 'I'd like you to come in with me,' and as he shook hands with me he said, 'I'd like to get all this sorted out.' I met with a few of the lads down at Dunston and it was me and a lad called Stephen Vaughan, who used to be a good friend of mine, and I went up to Whickham to meet Viv, him and Armstrong (Rob Armstrong was once a close friend of Viv's.) and they never turned up, so that was that.

A while after that, Cecil and Reg Levy offered me to do the door at Hobo's. Cecil said, 'Will you do the door?' and he went on to say that he didn't want the likes of Viv Graham or the Sayers' in the place. I said I would keep them out. So the first couple of nights nothing was said, but word got back to me that a few of them were running around the town and were coming up to see me. I told the lads on the door at the time, Joe Quince, Stephen 'Flash' Gordon and a few other lads who were working with me. I said, 'Don't let them in the door; if they come to the door give me a shout. I'm inside and I'll come and sort it out.'

One of the doormen come and told me that Viv and his team were at the door. I said, 'At the door?' So when I went in they said that Viv wasn't at the door but actually in the foyer of the club. I said, 'Who's let the fuckers in?' So I went straight out to the foyer and I went to the door, they were standing in the corner and as I went through the door I actually walked past them. Again I said, 'Who's let these in?'

A voice behind me, Viv's, said, 'WATSON!' I turned around and he gave me a left hand straightaway, I went backwards and the rest of them, five or six of them, stood around me and were saying to Viv: 'Go on, Viv, do him! Kill him! Kill him! Do him!' I knew two or three of them were blade merchants and I knew they'd be tooled up to the teeth.

Soon as he hit me I knew he hadn't done anything with me. I was going to have a shot, but I could see I was in a no win situation with him, especially when the doormen who were supposed to be standing with me fucked off out of the door. They dropped me like a hot pebble. My girlfriend was there and she could be heard squealing in the background when the court played the video footage at Viv's trial. One of the doormen had a hold of her, she wanted to intervene herself – I'm married to her now.

By this time Viv is still giving it to me, batting me and at the finish we burst into the club itself and he still couldn't put me on my arse. Viv, by this time, was running out of puff and he says to me, 'Go down! Go down, man!' The others who were with Viv had kicked open the fire exit doors by this time and everybody had made a big space for them and they were saying to him: 'Get him outside! We'll kill him!' So Viv was still shouting at me, 'Go down! Go down!'

Viv was more concerned at what was going to happen because he didn't have the arse for it, because if they had of killed me or stuck me then he was in the shit with them and he knew it. I didn't go down though, I kept a hold of the spiral staircase, he didn't hurt me, but they were like a pack of dogs and jumped in and started punching and kicking me. Viv stopped it, he was shouting, 'HE'S HAD ENOUGH! HE'S HAD ENOUGH! THAT'S IT!' I was all cut and Viv was looking worried. I said, 'Is that it then, are you finished?'

My then-girlfriend, Sharon, was crying her eyes out. I said, 'I'm all right, they haven't hurt me. I'm all right.' I went to the toilet to clean my face up and gets in the car and went to hospital to have a few stitches put in. That happened on the Friday or Saturday night and I was back at work on the Monday. Davie Lancaster was there, he was the instigator, he's a little man with a big mouth and he likes to throw fuel on the fire. I've never professed to be anybody; I'm just a man off the streets.

I was a one who wouldn't bow down to them, if I was given a job to do and they asked me to do a job and I was being paid to do that job then I did the job and if they didn't want them in the club then I'd keep them out. If you're getting paid to do the job then you do the job, if you cannot then they'll just get somebody else to do it, simple as that.

After that, I was arrested three times for perverting the course of justice because I had a meeting with John Sayers, which the police knew about. And he started out by telling me that I should do this and do that, he didn't ask me at first. I said, 'You don't tell me to do nothing, ask me and then we might get somewhere, but don't tell me,' Dodgy Ray Hewitson was there at the meeting.

What happened on the night of the fight was there were three or four undercover police in Hobo's and when Viv and the others were up in court the police were asked about whether they were supposed to intervene in any sort of violence? They said that they had orders from the top saying that they didn't have to intervene at all; they had to let it go to see what happened. That's why you get people turning against the police, full stop, because they were using me. They were hoping I was going to get killed or if I was stabbed up then they had to do nothing! Their orders were not to intervene at any time!

I said to the police that I threw the first punch, but of course it was on video and they weren't having any of it. I made an affidavit (A sworn statement usually made through a solicitor and sworn to be a true and accurate statement.) saying I'd started the fight. The police asked me if they owed me anything? I said, 'You owe me fuck all, I owe you nothing and you owe me fuck all, I want nothing off you.' (Stuart Watson refused to allow his medical records to be used in court and did not give evidence at the court hearing when Viv and his associates faced charges for assault. It can also be said that the police brought the action without consulting Stuart Watson.)

When Viv comes home on a home leave from his three-year sentence he had a big party. I went down, the whole lot of them were there and I went down and showed my face. Dodgy Ray said, 'He's out, do you want to break the ice,' I replied, 'I'm not bothered about going down.' They were all in Macey's and I went down, as soon as I walked in the front doors you could have heard a pin drop. The whole place went dead quiet.

After that Viv and me were working together at Rockshots nightclub, Dodgy Ray was the go between for Viv and me. Every time Viv and me were there you could cut the atmosphere with a knife. I could tell that Viv was dubious of me and wasn't sure if he could take my shots or not and it was always the case where he was always doubtful and you could feel the atmosphere there all the time and I knew from day one that it wasn't going to work, me and him working together, because he just couldn't let things go at that and he wasn't sure what would've happened if we did have a proper fight.

So when we're working Rockshots together, he was getting X amount of pounds and I'm getting X amount of pounds and he was coming in once every two weeks, three weeks, and I was there like a mug standing on the door and he's getting the same money as me! So they say they want the West End lot kept out because they were making a nuisance of themselves and some of them were doing what they wanted.

So I said on the Thursday, 'Right, no more West End lot in,' to the lads at the door and I said if any names come then I'm inside and they should come and tell me and then I would tell them that they cannot come in. I said, 'You lads on the doors don't get paid enough for that, that's my job.' They were kept out good style and not one of them got in. Viv was half paly with the West End lot at the time, but he said, 'All right.' It was getting to the point that I was fighting nearly every other day on the door and I was getting threats to kill, 'You're going to get shot,' and all the usual shite. Then Viv was away for six weeks and I still had his money and then Dodgy Ray said: 'Viv wants his money!' I replied, 'Tell Viv he's not getting his fucking money!' He says, 'He's not going to be happy!' My reply was, 'Tell him I'm not happy, me doing his fucking work and he's getting the same money. Tell him he's not getting it!' So he says, 'You know what he'll be like!' I replied, 'I don't give a fuck, he's not getting it, I'm not going to do his job on top of mine, I couldn't give a fuck what he says.' Dodgy Ray went to see Viv and he half accepted it and told Dodgy Ray, 'Tell him he can keep the cunt for his fucking self!'

So I pulled a few more lads in rather than me keep his money, so I felt a little bit more secure and I had some decent lads with me. Viv was up at Madison's, say, three or four times a year or so and he'd phone Rockshots up and he'd say to me, 'People's telling me I can't fucking do you!' I said, 'Who's telling you this? He replied, 'People's told me that!' 'Well who the fuck is it?' I replied. He's giving it the big one on the phone so I said, 'Who's saying this?' It turned out it was Mackem Tommy who used to work for me, then he went to work for Viv up at Madison's.

Viv was still on the phone saying, 'He told me I didn't drop you,' I said to him, 'Well you didn't fucking drop me!' 'I'll tell you what, I'm going to come down,' was what he said, so I told him to come down, but 'there's just going to be trouble, but I'll tell you what I'll do, I'm going to come to your house tomorrow.'

I went to his house with Geoff Brown because Geoff knew where he lived. I went there, knocked on the door, he answered all apologetic and shaking my hand and that. I said, 'What the fuck's a matter with you? If you're going to listen to people then we're going to be at each other's throats all the time!' And he'd say, 'Aye, I know, I know.' Three or four months would pass and there he'd be on the phone again, the same fucking scenario! Obviously it was eating him away that he couldn't put me down."

Terry Mitchell, a close friend and associate of Stu gives his account of Viv. "Viv could have a fight, but at the end of the day just say a big kid come in here, he'd have to go over and knock him out for no reason at all just because he'd be feeling that little bit insecure in himself in thinking this kid was bigger than him."

Stu continues, "We were once in Rockshots when we used to work together and Dodgy Ray come across and he says, 'Stu, Viv wants you to go over and knock that kid out.' I said, 'Viv wants me to go and do what?' I wasn't doing Viv's dirty work so I said, 'Tell fucking Viv to do it himself. I'm not his fucking monkey, tell him to fucking do it!' He must have thought I was going to work for him, I didn't work for anyone, I worked with them."

Terry Mitchell sums it all up, "It's not just because he's my pal, anybody can tell you that he…" as he looks in Stu's direction, "…. can have a fight and so could Viv, but one goes round throwing his weight about like that and one's just a normal friend and a gentleman who can sit in the company of his friends and his friends can take the piss if they want. I mean, I should be booted all over the car park the way I talk to him," and again Terry nods in the direction of Stu.

Stu goes on to tell of a further confrontation he had with Viv, "I was at the gym with a friend of mine called Todd, and Viv come in and he said that he wanted to see me outside. So we're standing at the front of the gym and he says to me, 'I want £15,000 off you or Adrian.' He wanted this for his part in keeping trouble out of Rockshots. I said, 'You're getting nothing out of me!' This was two years after he had left Rockshots, he was short of money and he was a gambler.

He sees that you're doing half all right and wants some of it. Todd comes out of the gym and Viv said to him, 'What are you fucking coming out for?' Viv went to throw a punch at Todd and I grabbed a hold of Viv when he went forward to punch him and pulled him back and he said to me, 'Don't you fucking jump on my back!' I said, 'Jump on your back!

Working The Doors

I haven't jumped on your fucking back, it's got fuck all to do with him, it's between me and you.' Viv then says, 'Get round the fucking back with me!' I told him, 'Anything you've got to do with me you can do round the front, I'm going round no back! I don't know who the fuck's round there.' 'I want fifteen grand off you,' Viv said. My reply was, 'You're getting fuck all off me. I'll ask Adrian about it and if Adrian doesn't know anything about it then you're getting fuck all.'

I saw Adrian and said to him, 'Tell Viv he's getting fuck all and that I'm standing by you.' At the time the club was in trouble anyway, it had lost its drinks licence and he wanted fifteen grand out of a club that wasn't making anything.

Then it was a couple of nights after that we went down to The Lion, in Gateshead, it was a Bank Holiday Monday. Viv was coming out of the Lion as we were going in and there was a little bit of animosity, you could feel it and we were having a bit eye-to-eye. He said, 'Are you all right?' I went, 'Aye, I'm all right.' He left a message that he was coming back on the nighttime and he was going to come up to the Malting House pub, just up the road from the Lion.

So we're sitting up at the Malting House and I said to the Hammer (Stephen Eastland), Geoff (Brown) and Terry, 'If he comes in then let me and him fucking get it on and see what the fucking outcome is. I'm sick of all this shite.' And he, Viv, was in a bar (the Lion) about fifty yards away and he never come up. He was threatening he was going to come up, but he never. It was a standoff all the time, I wish it had got off the ground, but it didn't."

Stu is now a prosperous businessman with a string of interests in pubs. His transition from what he was to what he has become must have been difficult? "I think it's hard for the community around me especially the council and the police. I took the kids from the school across the road to see a pantomime because they couldn't raise the money.

They can't understand how a man can change, but give a dog a bad name. I've got two pubs and none of them have a drugs problem, no one is allowed to smoke joints in them and that was made clear from day one. I'm not going to give the police that chance to come down on me.

When I first took this pub over I got a visit from the police, they used to come in here fifteen and twenty handed on a Friday night, a Saturday night and even when the place was being done out, ten or fifteen armed police would be running around the front. Then they'd be coming in and pushing and shoving people about saying, 'It's twenty past eleven and people are still sitting in here!'

They'd come in on numerous occasions, but now they know I run a clean place they don't bother. They used to come around smelling and looking in all the ashtrays looking for joints, but I wouldn't let it happen. The police kept it up for nine or ten months and they would send two vanloads, but it must have been costing them money to do that."

It would seem that the public purse is bottomless when it comes to such tactical operations by the police, but who pays? How much extra goes on to the Council Tax bill because of these police crusades? The bobby on the beat has to do as he's told, but how many more bobbies could be employed by the cost of these, often, worthless operations?

You do not get the likes of Stu Watson causing criminal damage or street muggings. Fear of crime is one of the biggest fears the public have. Protecting the ordinary citizen in the street from crime should be of paramount importance as opposed to 'sting' operations that net little in return for their cost.

Consequential trial costs of major police operations are often hidden from the public eye. Where money is no object for such operations then, equally so, money should also be no object for the safety of members of the public whilst going about their every day duties.

Wagging Tongues Have Empty Heads

For those of you not familiar with Lee Duffy:

Born 11th June 1965: Lawrie and Brenda welcome their newborn son, Lee Paul Duffy, into the world. Duffy was born and raised on a council estate in the South Bank area of Middlesbrough. First school was Beech Grove primary and then he attended Stapylton School, in the Eston area of Middlesbrough.

1971: At the age of six, Duffy was regularly assaulted by much older boys, if you can call 19 year olds 'boys'.

1979: Duffy, now a 14-year-old, was brutally assaulted by a hoodlum gang of older teenagers, he was knocked unconscious – he was awarded the sum of £80 in compensation, but the taste of blood was to start him off on the road of discovering 'boxing skills', which were intended for his defence. Later on, when he became a strapping 6ft 4in and 16 stone man mountain, he dished out vengeance beatings to those involved in the attack. (West Indian, Shandy Boyce is credited with teaching Duffy how to box. Although many say that Lee never really took to boxing.)

In later years, Duffy would go to the gym and train, if you were a boxer he would spar with you. He would turn up off the streets, go into the gym once every two or three weeks and knock someone out. Senior night at the boxing club was usually a Tuesday and a Thursday night, Duffy would turn up on one of these nights

Duffy often recalled the bullying from his early years and it is obvious that this played a part in traumatising him during his formative years. (Psychologists say: 'The bullied become the bullies.')

December 1980: It does not take too long before Duffy is indoctrinated into the rough and tumble that these estates breed into children and he has now got convictions for burglary and car theft. The court sends him to a detention centre for three months.

1981: Duffy leaves Stapylton School with a grade three CSE in woodwork.

1982: Violence lands Duffy in a detention centre for six months.

April 1983: Duffy receives a $2^{1}/_{2}$-year youth custody order after attacking and robbing a nightclub doorman.

1984: Charges of affray and assault dropped when no one would give evidence. Four similar charges were dropped on separate occasions, again, as a consequence of no one giving evidence at court.

1984: When the Duffer is freed from prison he meets single mother of one, Carol 'Bonnie' Holmstrom, a South Bank girl three years older than he is. They spend five years in a relationship, which is turbulent and leads to Carol having a breakdown.

March 1988: Duffy jailed for four years after pleading guilty to a vicious assault on a man in the Speakeasy nightclub (became the Havana club), the attack left his victim, Martin Clark, without an eye. During this sentence Duffy was moved to 18 different prisons. When strip-searched during these moves he would become very aggressive. He would want to take over each jail and to be the 'top man'.

August 1988: His second child, another daughter, Michelle is born whilst he is in prison and mother of the child, Bonnie, tells Lee "it's all over."

May 1990: Duffy released from prison and visits Bonnie in hospital; she had suffered a breakdown because of all the stress. Duffy breaks down crying and then goes on holiday; on his return he breaks the news to Bonnie that Lisa Stockell is pregnant to him.

Lee Duffy's hero was another of Teesside's hard men, Kevin 'Ducko' Duckling. Duffy was infatuated with

56

'Ducko' and, as a child, he idolised Ducko and wanted to be like him when he got older.

As a result of being pushed and as a consequence of hitting his head on the ground, a partially disabled Sheffield man, Paul Dallaway, 21, died at a blues party – Ducko was charged with his manslaughter in June 1988 and received a four-year prison sentence.

Duffy had modelled himself on Ducko and similar hard men and maybe this is what helped mould him into the man he eventually became, although as a family man, undoubtedly, he was a compassionate man and he cared about his two daughters he had from the relationship with Bonnie and his daughter to Lisa, Kattieleigh.

For anyone not familiar with a blues party or what it is: it is a group of people gathering together in unlicensed premises, which are converted, in a spartan manner, from terraced houses, flats or disused commercial premises. Once the pubs and clubs were closed for the night, people would want the party to go on and that is how the 'blues parties' developed. A few cans of booze and a few grams of white powder or cannabis would get things going, but then they became more commercialised and people started to make money out of running these blues where hundreds of people would pack into such premises and usually an old timer would be on the door taking the entry fee.

The kitchen would be serving curry & rice and a plentiful supply of drugs would be on sale to keep the party mood in full swing while reggae tunes blasted out at full power. Frequented by prostitutes and drug dealers - a proper den of inequity where illegal gambling would take place in the quieter rooms either upstairs or out in the back while usually an open fire was left burning continuously so as to consume hastily thrown drugs in the event of a police raid.

Duffy would use these blues parties as his hunting ground for the rich pickings drug dealers could be trawled for. Soon, Duffy's reputation went before him and he was a formidable force second to none in the Middlesbrough area and no sooner was his name mentioned it would make drug dealers run a mile.

Someone once said, "Wagging tongues have empty heads," or something close to that, but at times this rule has to be ignored. 'There is no smoke without fire' is another saying that might well apply to certain claims made about a Newcastle crime family wanting Duffy to be a pawn in their game of chess and, accordingly, used him to their advantage.

Duffy was a fine strapping lad; he had a similar background to Viv. He had made a name for himself in the Teesside area and could handle himself as well as take a good punch. He lived with his girlfriend and daughter in an industrial area. He had attempts made on his life, similarly as Viv had. Both were no strangers to the smell of death they had both been staring death in the face from the barrel end of a shotgun in their pasts.

Viv was a former associate of the Sayers family, but after the Stuart Watson incident that led to his imprisonment, he always blamed the Sayers for being the cause of that. He knew he had been used and after finishing his prison sentence for the assault he went solo. His territory, in terms of being a trouble-shooter for publicans, was off limits to just about everyone and that included the Sayers. It meant that the potential drug territory was closed down.

Viv was the thorn in their side and a plan was needed to oust him from his position of authority in stopping drug dealers from entering his patch in the East End of Newcastle. (John Sayers the North East robbery expert being excluded from this, as he was a totally different kettle of fish. He was the North East's answer to John McVicar - a thinking man's robber.)

Who could be brought in to sort Viv Graham out? There was no one in Newcastle capable, and even if there were they would not want the unenviable position that Viv held. They had to go head hunting outside of the area in their recruiting drive for someone who stood a likely chance of winning a fight against Viv.

Wagging Tongues Have Empty Heads

Lee Duffy was the man drafted in, he had been having a bit of a hard time of it in Middlesbrough because it seemed no matter where Duffy turned there was someone out to get him. He was offered the opportunity to take over things in Newcastle, but there was just one slight problem, he would first have to beat Viv in a fight.

A brief run down of Duffy's past will show he was much more orientated towards violence than Viv ever was and because of this Duffy ended up having his life threatened on a number of occasions in Middlesbrough. Going back to the 1980s when Duffy was in his early twenties he was already well on the road to a life of crime.

Using his boxing skills he thought he could carve a reasonable living out of crime, although to Duffy and anyone carving out a life of crime it is not thought of like that. A life of crime becomes an accepted way of life. Court appearances were an occupational hazard and by time he was sentenced to a four stretch for Affray in 1988 by Teesside Crown Court, Duffy had seen the inside of courts over a dozen times; some of those times for violent crime.

No sooner was Duffy released from prison, he was in trouble again this time though it was trouble of a different kind. He was usually the one to dish out the violence only this time he was on the other end of the stick.

December 1990: Saw the early hours of the morning in Middlesborough disturbed by the noise of a shotgun attack on Duffy. He was, in the typical underworld way, shot in the kneecap. A man was later charged with the shooting, but the damage was not as serious as it might have been and this gave rise to make Duffy believe he was invincible.

Duffy was called many names for what people believed he stood for, the word 'thug' was a lesser word used to describe Duffy's behaviour to others.

Duffy shared a home with his girlfriend, Lisa Stockell, in Eston, Teesside. The 'old school' gangster would often consider the home as a place of refuge and it was considered out of bounds for causing trouble on the doorstep where innocent people could be hurt. That used to be an unwritten rule when the time was that most gangsters had an unwritten code of conduct. Especially where innocent pregnant people lived! That code of conduct may have applied years ago, but it did not apply when two men were looking for Duffy on the last night of **January 1991**: The two heroes who broke into the home of Lisa Stockell were real hard men and to prove how hard they were they wore masks to keep themselves warm from the chilly January weather! Obviously expecting to find their prey, Duffy, they came tooled up and, as in such cases, when cowards are given the job of a real man, they had in their possession some equalisers in the form of a shotgun and a leg breaker. (Iron bar.)

Not finding Duffy, they decided to vent their feelings out on the four people in the house; two were relations of Duffy's pregnant girlfriend. The scene is set, two hairy gorillas wearing masks carrying a loaded shotgun and a bar, breaking their way into Duffy's home where there are three females and one male.

Duffy was not at home and that should have been that, but no! The gorillas decide to rip gold rings from the fingers of Duffy's girlfriend, who is at that stage nine months pregnant...visibly pregnant. Then they start threatening all sorts of things while demanding to know of Duffy's whereabouts.

They then leave in search of Duffy, feeling full of themselves - full of shit no doubt. Again, in the early hours of the morning that Duffy just seemed to love, he was attending a blues party held in a shop that was previously a wedding boutique.

Duffy was unaware that his pregnant girlfriend along with her sister and mother had been the victim of two thugs. Two black men (Advice was taken on this directly from a black person, they said, "Calling them coloured was wrong and the word 'black' was the correct way to describe a black person." SO! Do not go running off to the Race Relations Board.) were involved in a fight with Duffy, a man pulled a shotgun out and leaned over the bar counter, deliberately pointed the shotgun at Duffy, but the gun was snatched by Duffy and it went off, blasting his foot into a gory mess! The consequences do not need any further elaboration.

Eventually, when the gunman was on remand in prison he came out of his cell on association and took a draw on a cigarette, blew the smoke into a trainer he had just taken off and asked people what it was. No one knew until he said, "This is Duffy's foot after it was shot!"

The two black men ran off, as is normal in a case like this, regardless of anyone's colour, they do not wait around for the police to call. A month earlier a gunshot attack on Duffy was meant to kill him, but he dived over a car and it was lucky for Duffy that he was shot in the knee.

The two who confronted Duffy at the blues in the ex-boutique were the same two who robbed Duffy's family one hour earlier in his home. When Duffy, the former club doorman, heard about the incident at his home it was a case of seeking those out who had been involved. Somehow, Duffy had got hold of photographs of those involved in the raid; rumours have it that a police source passed these on to Duffy!

On the surface it may have seemed that Duffy was the most hated man in Middlesbrough and everybody was out to get him. Everyone is entitled to his or her own opinion, but when it comes to the innocent people in the life of Duffy becoming victims of a savage gun threatening robbery, it drives the situation home that these men have no scruples.

The violence that was taking place in Middlesbrough was a campaign to take Duffy off the scene by killing him. Drug dealers were losing a lot of money! In Newcastle it was also thought to be the same with Viv...he was stopping a lot of dealing going on.

The people involved in the attempts on Duffy's life wanted to go all the way - no less than ten men in total on three different occasions faced attempted murder charges relating to Duffy...all were acquitted, see later on!

The onslaught by so many against one person indicated the strength of feeling behind these attacks on Duffy.

April 1991: Three men from Blyth, about ten miles north of Newcastle, were charged with the attempted murder of Duffy in relation to the earlier January shooting. Raymond Palmer, Robert Charlton and Anthony Cole were from the Northumberland town well known for its drug dealing amongst the small population and for the record amount of illegal drug induced deaths.

The drug problem being so bad in Blyth that even the regular market in its town centre bans stallholders who sell any related items to the drug culture. One stallholder was asked to leave the market for selling what are commonly known as hukka pipes. The hukka is usually thought of as a decorative ornament but often used for smoking cannabis from. Charges against Palmer and Charlton were later dropped.

Birmingham has its connections in this story through the involvement of Marnon Clive Thomas of Balsall Heath and Leroy Vincent Fischer of Aston who were charged as the people responsible for the robbery of Duffy's pregnant girlfriend. Lisa was robbed of a large quantity of jewellery only a short while before Duffy was shot in his foot. Fischer was also involved in some other crime in Birmingham, which was thought to have been a robbery of a hotel of about £1,000.

A third man from Birmingham, John Leroy Thomas from Edgbaston was charged along with Fischer and Thomas with conspiring to Murder Duffy in January of 1991. They were all charged within a few weeks of the shooting incident. Later on you will read of how a Teesside woman, Ria Nasir, admits to wanting Duffy murdered.

The web was widening and more were yet to be charged with conspiracy to murder, John Leroy Thomas was given bail, which in a case like this is usually deemed to be in return for the suspect having been co-operative.

This sort of break, if it had of happened in Wallsend,

would have helped Northumbria Police in the questioning of their suspects for the killing of Viv. There was, however, snippets given to the police in the Viv murder inquiry from suspects which lead to some arrests on drug related offences, but no break in those being questioned revealing the names of people involved higher up. This was not a case of them not wanting to say anything, just a case of being concerned about their own safety.

Four more people were pulled in and charged with conspiracy to murder Duffy. Shaun Thomas Harrison of Grangetown, Paul James Bryan, 30, of Eston (the same area as Duffy lived in), Kevin James O'Keefe of Teesville and Peter Corner of Eston (near to where Duffy lived).

April 1991: It could have been a case of third time unlucky for Duffy when another murder attempt was made on his life. If shooting could not put paid to Duffy in what they were trying to do then surely petrol would! In this incident, that had the horror house of the Hammer film set written all over it, underworld sources established that Duffy had petrol doused over him and the offender chased after him with a lighter. Duffy was running scared for his life and it must have looked like a Keystone Cops chase scene.

The Commercial pub was the scene of the attack in South Bank, Middlesbrough. Patrick David Tapping was charged with attempting to kill Duffy. Tapping, in return, did not get off lightly; he suffered in an attack from Duffy in which Duffy was charged with committing GBH on Tapping.

Only a week before this, a judge in chambers freed Duffy who was granted bail with conditions attached that barred him from entering any licensed premises in Middlesbrough. It has since been suggested by certain people in Middlesbrough that Duffy was released on bail so as to be murdered! A claim that, if true, would see the judiciary system itself brought before the courts…but that is all what is, an allegation, perhaps, brought about to help romanticise the memory of Duffy.

Duffy had been remanded for GBH with intent (grievous

bodily harm) on a man called Peter Wilson. It was alleged that Duffy had offered Wilson £2,500 to drop the charges and Duffy was consequently charged with attempting to pervert the course of justice. A further charge of actual bodily harm was brought against Duffy for an attack on Islam Gull, who he threatened to kill.

Amazingly, all the men involved in the charge of conspiracy to murder Duffy from the shooting in January were all eventually bailed! Conditions of bail were strict, but the men had won their freedom. Later, charges were revised against all seven men and they faced a lesser charge of conspiracy to do grievous bodily harm.

August 1991: Duffy was attacked by a group of men that were armed with baseball bats on licensed premises in Middlesbrough. The picture is slowly building up of weapons ranging from shotguns, iron bars and petrol to baseball bats being used to attack Duffy with. From this, it can be assumed that Duffy might not have been unaware that people wanted to hurt him at the very least! By the same token these people were not really any better than Duffy was alleged to have been.

Viv Shooting

Viv did not have as many physical things happen to him by way of attempts on his life with a weapon. But in an incident when Viv was working a nightclub door, Viv refused entry to someone. The person decided to get even. Whatever way you look at it, Viv was becoming complacent with his own security.

The sinister looking black Nissan car following Viv, unnoticed, and later on, was not recognised as the same car when it pulled up and waited for him to get out the car he was in.

The gunman in the Nissan shot at Viv out of the rear window, preferring to stay within the safe confines of this fast car...that is how frightened they were of the power of Viv. They feared that even a pump-action shotgun might not be enough to slow him down.

Wagging Tongues Have Empty Heads

The gunman and his driver were not taking any chances in the way that they carried out this shooting.

Rob Armstrong, who was with Viv, had his city wits about him and he could see what was going on. He shouted at Viv to move. Armstrong dived on Viv, who had his back to the masked gunman, and pulled him down to the ground. For this heroic deed Armstrong paid a price, he was shot in the back while going towards Viv and he was shot at again while lying protectively over the top of Viv on the ground. An emerging clubber suffered slight facial injuries.

The incident was over as fast as it had started. The black Nissan sped off with its occupants tucked safely away. There was no chance these sardines were going to fall out of their protective tin into the hands of Viv. In the time honoured traditional style, the car was dumped and burnt out a mile away with no identification plates on it.

This incident was a foretaste of what was yet to come on New Years Eve of 1993; Viv survived this attempted murder carried out by losers.

Armstrong and the other slightly injured man were discharged within hours from the hospital; Armstrong though in pain was still mobile. Viv was not spatially aware of his surroundings. He took too much for granted and I believe it stemmed from his upbringing in a countryside environment where things could be trusted to always go the same way, usually day in and day out. Compare this scenario to how Duffy reacted when facing such weaponry! Duffy was a street ahead of Viv.

When you see how quickly a huge man like Armstrong moved it was as though he was acting on instinct that most city dwellers have in them, even if it is just the actions of jumping out of the way of a car or running across a busy city road.

These reactions were inherent and a conditioned reflex. That is what comes across when you read the chapter relating to the murder of Viv. Nobody dared to get close to this man if they wanted to kill him. They could not take any chances that his pure physical power might still be able to get them after he was shot, they had to have a means of resisting any attempts he might have of being able to land a one on them. That is how these people carried out this type of attack, from a place of safety. Obviously, if anyone were to make an attempt on Viv's life they could not afford to take any chances therefore it would always be a car that would play a part in any attempt.

I have it on good faith from a member of the criminal fraternity who allege that one of the men involved in the nightclub shooting was party to a vicious burglary of a ninety-year old man's home. This resulted in the man being tied up and then the heating was turned off and he was left for a day until found, nearly dead. He died in hospital a short while after the sadistic attack.

The involvement of the man is said to have been in handling stolen property from the raid in which he alleges he stole it from another address and then he dumped it in a churchyard where police discovered the items.

May 1998: Gary Thompson, 31, was charged with the murder of ninety-year old Thomas Hall along with eleven others who had various related charges against them. Thompson is the alleged gunman who shot at Viv and Rob Armstrong from within the safety of the black Nissan car in 1989. This is on very strong underworld information of the highest calibre. It has been alleged that it was Thompson had the run in with Viv at the nightclub door and simply set out to even up the score!

In a subsequent murder trial, Thompson was found guilty and now serves life in prison. The eleven other charged alongside Thompson were George Luftus; 49; Geoffrey Smith, 39; David Clark, 28; John Douglas Trattels, 39; Christopher Dale, 35; Paul Dees, 28; William Renforth, 27; Allen Sidney, 29; Diane Hemmings, 43, and Lorraine Trattels, 40. All were charged with various offences from conspiracy to rob to handling stolen goods.

William Trory, 59, of Shieldfield, Newcastle was charged

with attempting to pervert the course of justice and assisting an offender. Trory had given Thompson shelter during the time the police had been looking for him.

Chronology of Duffy attempted murder acquittals

December 27th, 1990: First attempted murder on Duffy takes place in Princes Road, Middlesbrough, when he's called out from a club and dives over a car for cover, but still gets blasted in the knee with a shotgun. Spends four days hospitalised, but signs himself out.

When he gets out, he goes to a pub called the Empire, which has then just been fitted with CCTV cameras to stop all of the drugs. Duffy goes up to the camera and blows smoke at it from a joint he was smoking.

(Anthony Cole, 28, of Blyth is acquitted of attempted murder in a trial that took place in **December 1992** when the court hears that there is no real chance of securing a conviction when vital witnesses fail to turn up.)

January 31st, 1991: Second murder attempt on his life in a blues party in Harrington Road, Middlesbrough. Duffy fights with a gunman and deflects the gun downwards away from his torso and gets half his foot blown off. He had to have skin grafts taken from his thigh to close up the hole in his foot. As a party piece, Duffy would show the sole of his foot, which visibly had pellets on view.

An hour earlier, the same gunmen had stalked his girlfriend's (Lisa Stockell) home before storming it and holding a gun to the heavily pregnant Lisa and then demanded to know where Duffy was.

(All seven men accused of conspiring to murder (dropped to conspiring to commit grievous bodily harm) Duffy were acquitted in a trial that took place in **October 1992** when a witness refuses to give evidence.)

April 1991: Third attempt on Duffy's life when petrol is thrown over him in the Commercial pub in South Bank, attempts to light the petrol fail and as a consequence the man receives a broken jaw. Patrick Tapping was later acquitted of attempted murder when witnesses failed to turn up at the trial held in **May 1992**. Ironically, Duffy who was charged with GBH on Tapping immediately after the petrol-throwing incident never stood trial...he was dead!!

October 1992: Seven men acquitted of conspiring to cause grievous bodily harm to Duffy: **John Leroy Thomas**, 36, of Edgbaston; **Leroy Vincent Fischer**, 31, of Handsworth; **Clive Thomas**, 31, Sparbrook – all from Birmingham. **Peter Corner**, 23, of Eston; **Shaun Thomas Harrison**, 25, of Grangetown; **Paul James Bryan**, 31, of Eston and **Kevin James 'beefy' O'Keefe**, 32, of Teesville – all from Teesside.

The main prosecution witness in this trial, Ria Maria Nasir, was a former prostitute and drugs dealer of over 20 years standing from Teesside. She refused to give evidence against the seven men and was advised that she did not have to answer questions that might incriminate her. This in itself is highly unusual for such a serious case and usually witnesses are held in contempt of court if they do not co-operate or, at the very least, a good prosecutor would ask the judge to consider the witness to be 'hostile'.

In the case of a man who was severely assaulted, he was so frightened that he refused to give evidence against his attacker, he was jailed for three months for contempt of court and yet here we have the prosecution led by Andrew Robertson telling the jury he was 'compelled to offer no evidence,' he continued, 'Miss Nasir is the main prosecution witness, but her attitude shows her evidence isn't going to be forthcoming.' With this flagrant breach of court etiquette the trial collapsed and all seven men walked to freedom!

(Author's note: Imagine this, some sex pervert comes along and rapes a little girl and, say, you are a witness to aftermath of this ugly crime and it so incenses you that you carry out the unlawful act of instant retribution by running the pervert over with your car, you can bet that you would be up in front of the court and you would receive the maximum sentence possible because you would have committed a murder and that is regardless of what the reason was behind it or what the person was you had run over. And remember, no one held a gun to your head to force you to do it under duress.

Why then should the attempted murder of Lee Duffy be so different, the very same people who attempted the murder are cold callous people, the very same people kicked in the door of a nine months pregnant woman and stuck the twin barrels of a sawn off shotgun into her mouth in order to find out where Duffy was and they then rob her and her sister of jewellery. This pregnant woman was not Lee Duffy the so-called 'Terminator of Teesside'; she was not a threat to anyone.

Drug dealer Miss Nasir can give an interview to the local press some four months later and tell them that she carried on dealing drugs in spite of threats Duffy had made to herself, her teenage daughter and her grandchild and in spite of a series of alleged sinister attacks on her home, how brave of her to carry on under such pressure, what were the local police doing in all of that time about her claims of being victimised by Duffy?

The top and bottom of it all is that Duffy taxed her, any such threats she says Duffy made against her family are not substantiated and certainly if such threats were made then she did not go to the police. When Ria Nisar ordered the hit she said it was done as a favour, but it is rumoured that she paid £1,500 - £1,150 of that was used by the hired assassins to buy an ounce of cocaine.

Hell hath no fury like a woman scorned, and this particular episode proves that. Miss Nasir put an awful lot of emphasis on her family being threatened, yet when Duffy's own family and unborn child are traumatised the courts can turn their backs with complacency over such an issue. A contract was put on Duffy because he was stepping on the toes of other people carrying out illegal acts – two wrongs do not make a right.)

Duffy and his followers allegedly broke up a blues party,

the party organiser was then told to give the proceeds of the blues party to Duffy and this was the final straw that spurred Miss Nasir on to put a contract out on Duffy and it was claimed by the prosecution to have been organised for her as a favour by her brother-in-law, John Thomas.

On the other hand, we have to look at how Miss Nasir became a prosecution witness in all of this and then her boast of the 'contract' on Duffy and in the same breath claim that "murder wasn't talked about" in relation to the contract on Duffy. Anyone in the real underworld will tell you that a contract is a contract – no messing!

There is, allegedly, a taped telephone conversation in existence where a female is saying that she wants the blood of Duffy and cannot wait!

The Crown claimed the two men allegedly responsible for carrying out the hit were Marnon Thomas and Leroy Fischer. These two men were picked out of an identity parade and fibres from the Crombie coats the thugs were wearing were cross matched with bedding taken from the home of the victims, this is what one of the victims was told by the police.

That in itself, and even less if we look at the evidence Barry George the alleged murderer of Gill Dando was convicted on, would have been enough to bring a successful prosecution, yet against all the odds the case was thrown out of court simply because the victim was Lee Duffy.

A paedophile would have stood a better chance of securing a conviction in Teesside Crown Court against these seven men compared with the name of Lee Duffy.

After the trial collapsed, Lisa Stockell asked the MP for Redcar and Cleveland, Mo Mowlem, to intervene and all seemed well until about a week later when Mo told Lisa that she could not get the paperwork released to her.

Criminal injuries payments for the loss of Lee Duffy were not pursued because Lisa was told that legal aid would not be forthcoming due to Lee having had a criminal record, again there seems to be one law for one and a different law for another. Criminal Injuries payments are meagre, but every little helps.

A top underworld figure, Viv Graham, gunned down and murdered on Tyneside had criminal injuries payments paid out on his behalf to one of his three girlfriends, Anna Connelly, and he had a criminal record just like Duffy had!

Claims have been made that the police and the judiciary of Teesside should be pursued for gross neglect of duty in the case of Lee Duffy's girlfriend being let down so badly and nothing less than a full public inquiry should have been conducted into this affair by the CPS.

If you are to believe Miss Nasir, that at the last minute the gun aimed to 'kill Duffy' (her very own words) was pulled downwards by another one of the would be assassins then what she says is an admittance that Duffy was meant to be killed, but one of them bottled it.

But if you hear the story on Duffy's behalf, it was he that fought and grappled with the gun and managed to get the gun pointing in a downwards direction before it went off, blowing half his foot off.

Regardless of Miss Nasir refusing to give evidence, there was enough evidence to convict the men responsible for robbing Lisa and her sister, Joanne, but the prosecution did not even try to secure a conviction and even though Lisa and her sister were on standby as witnesses, kept nearby in the local police station, they were never called.

One of the reasons given for not calling Lisa was that immediately after the robbery she was asked if she would be able to recognise any of the men, her reply was an emphatic 'NO' and even though she picked the men out a little while later, it was this shocked statement of one word that would be the prosecution's reason for not calling her!

Lisa did not want to say anything to the police until she had spoken with Lee. What if she gave the descriptions of these attackers and it affected Lee's credibility within the underworld, not that he could be much more disliked by certain factions, but being called an informant was pretty bad, as bad goes!

Viv Graham & Lee Duffy's Parallel Lives

Only when Duffy told Lisa to tell the police everything about what had happened on her behalf did she act in more controlled manner. Given the shock she was under after such an attack, none of that was taken into account, yet she DID pick out two of the assailants from an identity parade and her sister was also successful in doing the same.

Duffy's World

April 1991: Wickers World pub in Middlesbrough was the scene for a violent attack on doorman Peter Wilson. The man, a kick boxer, was hit so hard that his neck was broken and many believed Duffy had used a beer can to smash Wilson with, but a private investigation revealed it was caused by the fist of Duffy! Duffy was so powerful that a blow from his fist would probably have caused similar damage.

A quote follows directly from a letter Duffy wrote from HM Prison Durham dated Sunday **2nd June 1991** (8pm):

Now then, I thought I would write and tell you the crack of late. They've let me out of the block and back on the wing, so that's alright. I can get to the gym now and have a crack with the Boro lads. People thought I was on protection, all kinds of stories flying about. Well I'm here now so anybody's got a chance to see me, I'm ready and willing!! Everyone has been to my cell asking about me.

A million "alright Lee mates," half of them were slagging me off when I was down the block!! They make me sick, two-faced cunts...The idiot with the petrol is in here, I haven't seen him yet, if I chin him, I'll only end up in the block again, it can wait. Beefy, Paul and Nipper got bail. My Judge-in-Chambers was knocked back XXXXX!!! Bastards...I'm up at court on Wednesday 5th and Thursday 6th June – (old style committals).

The Wickers World assault is on Wednesday and that (Islam Guul assault) is on Thursday. I should get the Guul assault thrown out, which automatically gives me another shot at bail. And reading between the lines I think that Guul will sack it. We'll see eh? I have just received the statements from the petrol assault charge, they aren't too clever either, some woman says I punched the lad "10" times!! And another one says I went over the top!! What about me soaking in petrol I hear you ask? Fucking right. How can you go over the top when someone's trying to kill you? Let's see what a judge and jury thinks. Not guilty.

Duffy had spilled some lager over a man on the landing below, the doorman came over and 'started being funny with Lee.' Duffy punched him once. A third party was asked to see if Wilson would take a few thousand pounds to drop the charges…Wilson went straight to the police.

(A similar scenario to how Newcastle club doorman Howard Mills was offered money to drop charges against a man who had stabbed him in Bentleys nightclub in 1987. The stabbing resulted from when Mills had intervened when someone had thrown an empty beer can at a fellow doorman. Mills turned down an offer of compensation from the person responsible for stabbing him and people have suggested that as a consequence for turning down the money. That is thought to be the reason Mills had his leg blown off in a shotgun attack.)

As a result of this attack on Wilson, further charges of attempting to pervert the course of justice were fired off at Duffy when he attempted to bribe his victim with £2,500. In all, Duffy had nine court convictions to his credit varying from burglary and motorbike theft to GBH.

April 1991: Duffy was in court for a bail application in relation to the Wickers World incident, his girlfriend, Lisa, attended court to lend her support and while she was walking up the stairs of the court building she was confronted by the men charged with conspiring to commit grievous bodily harm to Lee and for some reason they were attending/leaving court in a pre-trial hearing. They started mimicking being shot in the foot and were singing some sort of song to her. Lisa was so distressed that the police let her see Lee whilst he was in the holding cells.

And, whilst the trial of the seven was waiting to go ahead

some of the men were held on remand in the same prison as Duffy was held in for his attack in the Wickers World incident. Duffy was put into solitary confinement whilst his attackers were free to wander in the mainstream prison. Many might say that it was in the interests of safety for all concerned but in reality it was further punishment for Duffy to endure.

No one would disagree that Duffy had taxed drug dealers and frightened the living daylights out of them, but would you want a drug dealer living next door to you or the enforcer taxing them?

Dick Hobbs And Door Knobs

Where do you start when you want to secure information? You turn to an expert and the expert that was recommended was Dr Dick Hobbs, his name is real enough so please do not start taking the piss out of it, OK. Dick Hobbs was and probably now is even better known in academic circles. Dick had written some articles for the Home Office as well as being some high up personage in Durham University. He has obviously worked hard and spent long nights at it to get where he is and with having the title of 'Dr' before his name lends credibility to his status showing he knows a thing or two about whatever it is he is supposed to be good at. BRRRR! BRRRR! (Phone tones.)

Me: "Hello, is that Dr Dick Hobbs."

DH: "Yes."

Me: "I understand you've written some articles about crime and I wondered if I could arrange to have an appointment to interview you about true crime on Tyneside. You've contributed to an article about gangsters in Newcastle and maybe you could help me with your comments to be included in a book about the late Viv Graham?"

DH: "You really need to speak to someone with specialist knowledge on the subject, I can't help sorry!"

Me: "Oh! I see, well could you recommend someone?"

DH: "You could try Dr Ann Campbell, she's at Durham

University."

That is it! The conversation dried up! It was thought to be strange that Dick Hobbs would not comment since he had done so in some articles that one of our researchers picked up on. They involved his comments on 'bouncers', 'drugs', 'Middlesbrough drug dealing', 'Newcastle's ethnic community' and 'Gateshead's Hassidic community' as well as mentioning 'crack' and 'cocaine' use. Talk about being stuck up!!!

So it was on to Dr Ann Campbell of Durham University. She was stand offish and suggested a forensic psychologist was needed (A 'Cracker' like TV character.) and recommended someone in Leicester University. It was explained that someone from the North East was sought to give comment.

She, Ann Campbell, sidestepped the issue and skirted around it by passing on the name of Bruce Charlton from a university in Newcastle, either Newcastle University or the University of Northumbria. Anyway, regardless of what university it was we were getting nowhere very fast.

Bruce Charlton was as much help as a chocolate fireguard when he could only come up with a doctor from the local psychiatric ward at Saint Nicholas' Hospital in Newcastle. I too was heading that way! The man, he said to contact, was called Dr Swan.

Sure enough, we were up the Swany without a paddle as he could not help either and he was rather surprised we were put onto him, obviously a very good sidestep from Bruce Charlton, touché.

All was not lost at this point, after being on the telephone for quite some part of an afternoon so it was that Sunderland University was eventually contacted and surprise, surprise, they had a Criminology Department!

Telephone numbers of Mike Presdee and Ivan Hill, both criminologists at the University of Sunderland in the newly formed City of Sunderland, were obtained.

Dick Hobbs And Door Knobs

Mike Presdee was as hard to find as rocking horse shit, but Ivan Hill was sensible enough to have an answer machine. Some student might have been trying to get a hold of his or her lecturer and what better way than to have an answer machine to accommodate such students. A message was left asking, in a very polite manner, if he would call in relation to a comment being sought for inclusion in a true crime book (notice the word 'book' is used early on) about Tyneside and the late Viv Graham.

Two days go by, no reply! A second message was left, Ivan Hill returned the call. He suggested that Mike Presdee is contacted and said he would leave an e-mail message for him. Ivan said that if Mike would not make a comment then he would. Great!

It was made very clear that the book was about true crime on Tyneside and about the late Viv Graham who Ivan knew of. The shine on Ivan's voice sort of rusted over at the mention of Viv's name, the Irish lilt of Hill's voice becoming decidedly croaked. It was expressed how important that it was for a comment to be obtained from a North East based criminologist and again he agreed to make comment if Mike Presdee could not or would not.

Mike Presdee's telephone was called for a period of over two weeks with more chance of being hit on the back of the head with a snowball in the middle of Kuwait than getting through to him.

Ivan hill had gone to ground and it was easier finding hen's teeth than finding him in, mind you, his answer machine…that was in perfect working order. The facility to leave a message was used with various messages being left about him promising me to make a comment

Ivan Hill was caught with a telephone call made to his office in which he said that he had been away for some academic reason and that Mike Presdee was off on compassionate leave due to bereavement. That being the case it was respected that Mike would not be at work for a few days Ivan was pressed for a decision on whether he would make a comment due to how long it had been going on. Bear in mind that Ivan had previously said he would make a comment if Mike could not or would not. That is the reason no other academic was sought in the matter after these two were approached, not that there were many left who I had not already tried. That is why I telephoned Hill so often. The research was taking a lot of man/woman hours and this hassle was not needed therefore if he had said something to let me know that no comment would be made I would have been out of there faster than a cork out of a lottery winner's champagne bottle. Ivan asked that I wait a little longer and he would give a decision if he were called again in a few days.

Those few days were like weeks, especially when you have been kept waiting for nearly three weeks and time was precious in this research. The call was made, and sure enough, Ivan was on the other end of the line, surprise, surprise. A date and time was arranged to call through to his office for a comment, at last we were getting somewhere with these prima donnas.

Maybe he was just playing hard to get and liked the attention. It was made plain that a comment was required about Viv Graham and that a number of other academics had been approached including Dr Dick Hobbs so there was absolutely no room for ambiguity or misunderstanding. Travelling from some 150 miles away where further research was going on was no laughing matter so it was made clear what the comment was for.

A car park nearby was used and the ticket from the machine shows a date of WE 01 Apr 98. Week ending 1st of April 1998. April Fools day!

There was no sign of Ivan Hill, I waited for over quarter of an hour and went back to reception that I had called at prior to going up the stairs of the dilapidated building. A message was left there for me saying that Ivan was marking some papers and could I hold on, this man really was playing hard to get. I found out later on, he was really playing for time so he could have the support of Mike Presdee to hold his hand and wet nurse him thorough this daunting experience. If Hill had been marking papers then surely he would be in his office I had just visited? Did he take me for an idiot? Probably!

We eventually met and shook hands. We get to the office door that I had only left about ten minutes before, when Ivan turns around and says he has got to go and get his senior colleague, Mike Presdee? He returned within minutes accompanied by a man in tow who introduces himself as Mike Presdee, we shake hands in a half-hearted way that indicated to me that Presdee's heart was not in what he was doing in life.

I could see small pupils in Presdee's eyes, not a good sign! Let the battle commence. We are all sitting on low level seats that remind me of being back in infant school, my seat nearest the door facing into the light of the window while Presdee and Hill sit sideways on to the window. Out comes my favourite tool, the audio tape recorder! Both Hill and Presdee recoil back as if it was a crucifix flashed at Count Dracula. They wanted to think themselves lucky that I was not wearing the normal apparatus I had become accustomed to over the months of investigating. Maybe that is how you frighten these sorts of people, just pull out an audio recorder! Wow, what power? The conversation now gets underway.

MP: "It, it's not on is it?" (Meaning the tape recorder.)

Me: "No, no."

MP: "Right, before we start we need to establish some ground rules."

Me: I think to myself subconsciously as I speak, 'I hope he's not going to want a game of badminton' and catch myself saying, "Yes, anything you want."

IH: "Mike's here just to oversee everything's above board and he's my senior colleague."
(Wasn't that sweet of him wanting his colleague there with him to hold his hand.)

MP: "Can you just give me a bit of history about how it came about?"

Me: I'm unsure about what he wants to know and stutter through a few muted words. ""@?+#*.""

MP: Seeing this he elaborates by saying, "What sort of a book is it?"

Me: I look at Ivan Hill as if he has got horns growing out of his head, he's dragged me all this way and here he is passing the buck and has not even bothered to explain to Presdee the details of it all. "It's a book about true crime and Viv Graham who was murdered on Tyneside," I say.

MP: "Ah! (Here comes the first attack.) So it's not an academic book then?"

Me: "No, it's a book about true crime based on Tyneside."
(If all else fails keep playing the same record over and over again and parry the blows.)

MP: "Well in that case then, we can't really comment, it wouldn't be appropriate." He goes on to say something fanciful about the book being rather less than he had hoped.

Me: I think to myself that he is taking the piss and feeling full of himself and maybe he had eaten three weetabix for breakfast. "So you'll only make comment in an academic book to be read by academics, you're not cared about those people in Durham or Holme House prison who could be another Viv Graham in the making and their families going

Dick Hobbs And Door Knobs

through all what Viv Graham's suffered?"

MP: "You really need to speak with Dr Dick Hobbs."

Me: I thought he really is taking the piss, until I realised that he was too far gone in the academic way where you just cannot get through to them. This lot are all on a level that is beyond reasonable levels of..."Dick Hobbs put me onto other people who were of no help and now I'm here," I said. I looked at Hill and said, "You said you'd make comment for me." He just looked sheepish and I knew he had lost his bottle about making comment. He could not say anything.

MP: Sat there looking smug with himself, as if he had just told some first year degree student off. Only I was not a first year student and I did not have to suck up to him to get good assessments.

Me: "Dick Hobbs has made comment in a non-academic book and in newspaper articles…"

MP: Interrupted. "Dick Hobbs does Home Office reports and…"

Me: It was my turn to interrupt Presdee and it was like a game of badminton building up to a volley of shots that was getting faster and faster with each return of the shuttlecock between me and Presdee. I pulled out a book as fast as a magician pulls a rabbit out of a hat, whoosh! One of the researchers had armed me with that and it was non-academic, as I pointed out that Hobbs had made comment in that and I showed Presdee the page that was marked by the researcher. Saying, "There you go, here's a book that Dick Hobbs has made a comment in that's not academic."

MP: Takes the book from me, and fingers through it like a lost schoolboy looking at a map. I am standing and he is sitting, as I see no point in sitting down to take this sort of disrespect, 'I can go into any pub for that if that is the case', I think to myself. He flips to the back of the book and says, "This book's got a bibliography in it and it's semi-documentary with an index." (Big licks, so what, he was pre-judging my book before it was even printed and without him seeing it, what was he? Book review of the month club!)

Me: "My book will have an index and a bibliography in as well so what's the problem?" (Referring to the first Viv book.) I have him where I wanted, in a corner, there is no way out for him now and this is negotiating Beirut style.

MP: Obviously now lost for any defence he comes off the ropes fighting and shoots a hard-hitting shot with his badminton racket of a mouth as I am closing my briefcase. "You can take the matter up with someone more senior if you want," he says angrily, illuminating the room with his bright red face.

Me: As I walk towards the door, obviously seeing how much of my time had been wasted by these two plonkers I say, "No, that wont be necessary, but you haven't heard the last of this by no means!"

MP: "Don't come here insulting us," he says in a fake half baritone voice.

Me: This was like a red rag to a bull in fact any coloured rag, as bulls are colour blind. I let go of the half turned knob, turned around flashing a look of contempt at Hill sitting there like a sheep and gave my direct eye contact to Presdee who looked like he needed an outing or two on the badminton court. "Don't you tell me I'm insulting you when I've travelled all this way to be insulted by you." (Here is me arguing about who is insulting who, academics can do this sort of thing to your head; batter it.) By this time my voice

Dick Hobbs And Door Knobs

has raised along with my heartbeat and Hill says something for the first time in a while which shows his sheepish nature.

IH: "I think this conversation's over," he said like a church mouse peering out of its hole asking if anyone has seen the cat.

Me: "I think so as well." And with that I walked out of the door slamming it behind me.

I can tell you that anybody with less restraint would not have taken the shit I did on that day. I have seen steroid filled monsters that would have lost the plot completely. To say I had the piss pulled out of me would be an understatement in this matter. The book is bigger than me so I took it for the sake of others and out of respect to those within

Hill knew what the arrangements were and he had offered a comment and he had bottled out so he got Presdee to do the dirty work for him by coming up with excuses that I had answers for. In the end, Presdee took the areshole's way out by just barefaced piss taking. The time I had spent going up the stairs and waiting outside of Hill's office was obviously the time that he was sorting out arranging for Presdee to be available to do the dirty deed.

I telephoned Dick Hobbs that afternoon, luckily for him the answer phone was on. I left a message telling him that he had took the water out of me by fobbing me off when he had said he could not make a comment for inclusion in the book made about crime on Tyneside. Yet he had made comment to other people and that it was a water take to be passed on to lots of people who in the end referred me back to him exactly where I started! Had I of spoken directly then I would not have held back in my comments?

What gives with these people so called experts who will not give comment just because the ordinary public will be reading the book? They are no different to you and me and no better either. If one person can be prevented from becoming another statistic in a city morgue because of this book then that is one less person's family that can be caused the heartache that Viv and Lee's families went through and are still going through.

Expert analysis is okay if it goes along with what it is you want analysed and agrees with your way of thinking. The moment the experts disagree with your views on the subject though! That is what happened when experts dubbed Newcastle as a 'lesser city'. Experts? (What makes someone an expert?) Experts from the Henley Centre based in the cosmopolitan city of London researched world cities and were using sixty different criteria when assessing an area. What the researchers found was that Newcastle was not likely to become a super city?

Places such as Cardiff and Manchester were placed higher up the ladder as likely to succeed in their bid for worldwide recognition as super cities. The term 'super city' is a bit outdated as it comes from the USA who used that descriptive elevation about forty years ago.

After studying economic trends in nearly 500 local authority areas, the North East was said, by data analysts, to be heading towards decline? They picked out London as a typical example of a city that has global standing and can attract jobs and prosperity from abroad. These people are really clever!

Manchester in comparison to Newcastle has at present a much worse reputation in terms of gang warfare, yet this seems to be overshadowed by the facilities on offer to the public. It has to be said in all honesty that Newcastle does fall behind on this point. Newcastle and Manchester amongst other northern cities that were in decline are now rising out of the ashes.

However, the growth rate Newcastle has in leisure facilities is somewhat behind that of Manchester, but not wishing to take anything away from Newcastle's planners and developers. They have produced new work that should see the city centre become more of an attraction to tourists as well as the facilities giving the local community more choice. It is a case of wait and see what they produce in terms of facilities that can rival other big cities.

The once famous Newcastle quayside market that was once home to hundreds of small stalls has been blitzed by shiny new developments that took no heed of the needs of ordinary working class folk. A Sunday morning stroll amongst the crowd of eager buyers used to be the highlight of the weekend. Developers with no conscience have torn a strip of Geordie culture from the map.

The once busy paddy's market, where nick-knacks were sold, has now gone. The goods would be roughly spread out on a blanket and would awaken a Saturday morning. Pavement artists' pictures mixing in and becoming instant culture. Their lifelike chalk drawings that animated the footpath coming to life like a surreal rainbow only to be washed away by the tears of traditionalists when it all came to an end. Artists like the late Dennis Barrass, who used the name 'Ssarrab Sinned', would be there with their pastels.

Come hail or shine, the hardy stallholders would still be there, their loyalty betrayed by city planners and land buyers eager to line their pockets with money made from selling off bits of Geordie culture by the square foot. Once the longsighted money people knew what was happening in terms that the quayside area of Newcastle was being regenerated they started buying land faster than monopoly pieces so that they could resell to the developers at a nice fat profit. The past and present being at odds with each other!

Estimates of some 50,000 people attending Newcastle's Bigg Market pub and club scene on a busy night may well be underestimated. The eighth wonder of the world, well nearly, or so they say. Classed the sixth best place in the world to be entertained. That is if you like alcohol as your main courses for the start of a culinary weekend that sees most of the ingredients being mainly in liquid form. The traditional bag of Fish & Chips after a good night out on the swill has been replaced by cosmopolitan dishes that your average Geordie would have thrown up against the wall in disgust only a matter of years ago. No matter if the crowd is hungry or not, the smell of freshly baked pizzas wafting gently is enough to get their taste buds working in a conditioned reflex, like Pavlov's dogs.

Catering is a big business in Newcastle, as in any major city. The service industry has had more jobs created within it over the last ten years than most other types of industry. The jobs created by the leisure industry have helped the city's economy. That in some way has helped bail Newcastle out of the jobless plight caused by the closing down of heavy industry.

'Work hard and play hard' used to be the motto of every working class family. It seems as if though that tradition has been retained, which is verified if you walk around the Bigg market on a Friday and Saturday night. Listening for a foreign accent you will be hard pushed to hear many.

With the changes to Newcastle's leisure and nightlife facilities comes a new type of criminal, chameleon like in their versatility to adapt to changes in the environment.

The increase in volumes of people coming into any city like Newcastle, Middlesbrough or Manchester increases the likelihood of criminal activity. Drug dealers need customers to sustain their income, which is used in a majority of cases to help support their dependency and the hope of changing their lifestyles in terms of buying luxury goods that the advertising media has made us believe is an essential part of our everyday lives.

50,000+ people in the evening coming into a dense area of Newcastle's Bigg Market all looking for new and different ways of getting a high, gives the drug pusher an edge that any advertising executive would love to have in their box of tricks. A product that gets free advertising every day around the world in newspapers, TV and radio that is in demand from cash paying punters sounds too good to be true. Drink and drugs is the staple diet for some clubbers. There are two types of patron visiting Newcastle city centre.

Dick Hobbs And Door Knobs

Near the end of Viv's life he had more responsibility for the East End of Newcastle, the Bigg Market and quayside areas. It would be easy to say that Viv scudded the undesirables first, but that was not always the case he would often as not give a verbal warning and if they did not take heed of that then it would be looked at differently. Just like getting a caution from the police, Viv would offer his caution and the next time you would be charged!

Viv will always be remembered as a man who stood for the better part of a bad job and, yes, he loved people and even cried the odd tear now and again.

Who came out to fight for Viv when he was attacked by unfounded lies? Where did all of his mates go with their so-called allegiance that used him like a money machine? Viv's father, Jackie said, "They used our Viv like a money box."

Viv was a part of Newcastle, he helped make it a better place in many respects and those who would libel or slander his character do so only because he is dead and he cannot defend himself. Yes, Viv slapped people about, but those who have been on the receiving end of a crime would have wanted to do the same to those responsible, maybe they had their car damaged, washing stolen from the line or they had been burgled. What would your immediate thought have been if it happened to you?

No matter who you thought was responsible for the crime it might not be appropriate to 'grass' them up to the police because it was not in your nature to get someone into that sort of trouble or if you did and they found out then you would be victimised and have more trouble. So the next best option was to see Viv who would then go and find out if they were responsible and if so it would be remedied and not always by a slap, as he usually gave them an option. He fixed the problem that no court in the land could do based on the available evidence. This was zero tolerance, Viv style!

An Empty MFI Unit

"I first started boxing as an amateur when I was 25, I had nothing else to do, I had just got married, I was living in a flat at Throckley in Newcastle and I had bought an MFI unit," said boxer John Davison. "I had nothing to put on it, a couple of lads said, 'Come to the gym in the West End.' Phil Fowler was the coach there, I said, 'It's a mug's game!' They persisted and said, 'Come down, come down.' So I went down and started punching the bag and Phil Fowler said, 'Who do you box for?' I told him I hadn't boxed and he said, 'You have!' I replied, 'No, I haven't.'

I did some sparring with the lads and knocked three of them out. They just went crazy and I was told I should be a boxer. Again, I said it was a mug's game. Then again, I had this MFI unit with nothing to fill it, so I thought, 'I might as well box just to get a few trophies for the unit.'

After the first year, I fought the world rated number one, a boxer called Paul Hodgkinson, an amateur, a great lad. My first nine fights, I had nine knockouts! They stuck me in the ABA, the national championship at featherweight. I knocked out Paul Hodgkinson in the first round and then I went on to captain England 17 times all over the world.

Then I was picked for the Olympics and I trained for two years. Politics started to come in to it though. I had already fought a boxer called Michael Delaney and I beat him twice, but they sent him to the Olympics instead of me. There is a long story behind that; they just thought I was too aggressive; I'm more of an aggressive style, more of a professional style. When you box for England, they like a tippy-tappy boxer, jab and move. They don't go a lot for aggression and mine was a very aggressive style so they didn't go along with that, amateurs don't really like that.

I travelled all over the world and boxed the world number one; the world number two and the world number three. I won a silver medal against the world number two, Yurri Alexandrov, from Russia, so I naturally thought I was going to the Olympics and I wouldn't have turned pro. I was never at home; every weekend I was always training at Crystal Palace. It creased the wife when I was overlooked for the Olympics and Delaney was chosen instead, a man I had beaten twice!

Delaney got beaten in his first fight at the Olympics, he didn't really seem to try, his heart wasn't in it by the look of it. I thought, 'I'm not going to box amateur anymore.' Kevin, the national coach, kept phoning me up asking me to stay on as an amateur, but it didn't change my mind.

How Viv come in to it was that when I turned professional I was looking for a sponsor and I was looking all over and somebody mentioned Viv's name. I asked him if he knew anybody who would sponsor me. Viv offered to sponsor me to the tune of £1,000, which helped me get all my gym equipment and other items. I had a proper gum shield, gloves, boots, head guard and a gown. Our sparring friendship grew, he used to come into the gym and spar with me. He couldn't believe how strong I was for a featherweight.

Viv must have been around eighteen or twenty stone at the time and he could punch, really punch, his hand speed was very fast, he was tremendously fast for a big fellow. Your hand speed is a lot different from your body speed and it was a natural thing he was doing when he was boxing. You train all the time with your hands, that's how you get your hand speed, but your top half speed you go with the flow. Hand speed doesn't mean the rest of your body is fast. (Author's note: This obviously accounts for Viv's ability to be able to sort two or three men out within seconds.)

Personally speaking, I thought Viv was a great kid, a real nice gentleman. I didn't know anything about his lifestyle. He helped me out, he started me off in boxing, him and Rob

Armstrong, they were the ones that gave me the money.

When Viv was an amateur boxer, he thought about going professional, when we were sparring I said that with his size and strength he could probably beat half the professionals in the country at that time. I used to say to him, 'You want to turn professional.'

I had Viv's name on my gown in the last fight I had when he was alive, as a 'thank you' for him giving me that £1,000. I had '*John Davison, Sponsored by Viv Graham*' put on my gown, but the cameras avoided that area and it was covered over. It was just a friendly sort of thing to do, as he gave me the money to get me started off. I suppose he started my career. It might have seemed that I was advertising thuggery, but it was simply returning the favour. The first gloves that I won the World International title with, I'm sure I gave Viv those gloves.

I was boxing in a booth on the town moor in Newcastle for a while at the beginning of my boxing career. I still have the same mates and when I won my first major title I was car booting on the following Sunday. People were walking past and they couldn't understand why I was selling junk at a car boot sale. I said I'm not going to change just because I've won the title. People automatically thought that because I was the champion I should change my personality.

At the end of the day your friends are more important than anybody else, you stick with the ones who you know. Some that are trying to be your friend are going behind your back calling you names; they're not your mates. So I've never changed, I've still got the same mates I had years ago and I still drink with the same mates.

I remember when I was boxing in Manchester as a professional. I stopped my opponent and this little kid come up to me and he said, 'I'm going to be a champion one day.' I patted him on the head and said, 'Good lad.' It was the first time I met Naseem Hamed! We met years later in the Metro Centre when he made it big and he was fighting up here. I went along to see him and I said, 'Can you remember?' And he said, 'Yes, I remember, come on, let's have our photo-graph taken together.' He's a good kid. The reason he isn't liked on television is because of the way he acts. It's all hype and that's what it's all about now. In real life he's not that person as appears on the television.

I have an interest in training people who want to box. Boxing training is the best fitness training in the world. Nobody has ever done what I have from Newcastle. The last man that won the British title from Newcastle was called Thomas Watson, sixty years ago. It was a job to me and that's it.

I still do what I did all those years ago, antiques, car boot sales, shopping and wheeling & dealing. When I was brought up there were tin baths and outside toilets and that wasn't that long ago. Viv and I were brought together with a common bond and his background was not of any concern to me, we came together as sparring partners and that was my life at that time.

My neighbours accept me as normal and no different to anyone else and that is the way I like it, although people do still come and shake my hand because it was only a few years ago that I retired.

Amateur boxing now seems a waste of time because if you get a head shot now, you get a standing count; it's so strict now because of the dangers involved. As for women boxers, I trained Audrey Godfrey who was the first woman ever to fight in the ring up here. That is another piece of history I made. I do train quite a few women who do it for keep fit purposes, it's great if you want extra stamina, keep fit or you want to lose weight. Athletes should do more boxing training because it's the best training. I help women who want to lose weight and feel good about themselves.

Fifteen years ago, it all started, I was pleased of Viv's help. I was pleased to present his kids with my gown so that his kids could say, 'My dad sponsored John Davison, the first man in sixty years from Newcastle to win two World International titles and a British title.' Thanks Viv."

Riding The Tiger

"Lee wanted a quieter life than the life he was leading because he had kids and he wanted to settle down. He'd been in prison, he'd done it all and he'd had enough. He wanted to quieten down more instead of the fighting and all of the attempts on his life; he'd had enough of it. That's what I wanted him to do, quieten down and move away and I felt as long as we were around here that his life would never quieten down because of what he was. I just felt there would be more attempts to kill him, there'd already been so many," said Duffy's girlfriend, Lisa Stockell.

Just as Viv wanted to move away to a nice quiet place and have the quiet life it was the same with his counterpart Lee Duffy. Neither was to discover contentment!

Lisa continued, "I remember Lee saying to me, 'How do I get out? What do I have to do?' The first time Lee was shot was at a blues party, he was shot in the knee. He drove home and I was in bed, I heard a beeping outside and I went to the car. Lee was in the driving seat and he said, 'I've been shot!' I didn't believe him at first and then he fell out of the car and I just ran in and got my mam. We drove him to the hospital. I didn't think of anything other than getting him to hospital, I didn't have time to be in shock.

The second attempted murder was at another blues party, they'd come to my house, but I don't want to talk about that part, they then went on to the blues and they'd caught him inside. It was when he was fighting with them, that's when he was shot in his foot. Lee wouldn't make statements to the police about these things, but this time he told me to make a statement to the police because of what they'd done to me and he said, 'Tell them everything.' But Lee said nothing and he told me not to worry about it and that he'd sort it himself.

I wasn't surprised to learn that Lee had other women because that's how I ended up with him. He was only young when I met him and he didn't have a name for himself then, he was only eighteen and I was only fifteen. When Lee ended up getting his four-year (1988) sentence for having a fight in a nightclub and doing something to someone's eye he got four years in prison.

At that time Lee had a girlfriend, but at the beginning of his sentence the relationship with her ended completely so then I helped him through his time and when he came out we had Kattieleigh and that's when it all started.

When he was in prison he trained and trained, but when he was released he didn't do much training, he did it all in his four year sentence, which is why he was so big. When he came home he used to keep fit himself, he never had a regular thing, of going to the gym every day or every week. Maybe now and again he'd go with a friend, but it wasn't a regular thing, but he liked going to the gym and keeping fit.

He was only out for a year and a half and then he died, everything had happened in a year and a half. In that short space of time everything happened to him.

I remember we went out for a meal with the Sayers', but I wasn't aware that they were a crime family and I wasn't aware of a fight going to take place between Viv Graham and Lee until after Lee's death, when Lee wasn't home he was completely different.

We lived with my mam for a while because we didn't have our own house and he'd come in and bathe Katieleigh, take her out and do things. Lee was a family man and there was a really nice side to him. We'd take the kids out, including those from his previous relationship, to the park and do things together like a family.

I never ever knew Lee dealt in drugs until it was said in the newspapers, they said he was bullying this one and that one, but when I was with him he was never bullying. The only time I've ever known him to fight with people was with drug dealers and they've always had attempts on him, I've never known Lee go out and pick a fight on someone innocent.

When threats started coming, Lee moved out of my mam's house because he didn't want our lives to be in danger.

We'd go and stay at different houses after that, we'd go and stay at friends. I just accepted it, so everywhere Lee went I went too.

Even though Lee was threatened, he still went out on the town, he still took me to Middlesbrough and still went to all the places he went. He never hid anywhere.

People showed him loads of respect, soon as he went into a pub they'd all come over and sit and drink with him and talk with him. The press said that when Lee went into a pub the place emptied and everybody stopped enjoying themselves, but that just wasn't true.

Lee went to all the pubs and everybody stayed and had drinks with him and played pool with him. If people didn't want to be in his company then they wouldn't have stayed, but they did. He never drank much, he'd drink more coke than anything, he wasn't a drinker.

Once he went drinking in the afternoon and the front door opened...he just fell in, he'd only been out a few hours and he was absolutely legless. All the lads had been drinking and he joined in, but he didn't usually drink.

Lee never had his own car, he'd borrow a car to get around in, if he needed one then he'd hire a car for a week or so if we were socialising and sometimes he'd go to the races and things like that.

Lee loved dancing, he loved a joke and he was really generous to his friends and it's not true that he had lots of enemies. The only enemies he had were the people who dealt in drugs.

When he came home he switched off and he was good to his kids, he had two children to his ex-girlfriend, we used to go and pick these two up and go out for the rest of the day to Redcar or wherever and then maybe we'd go and visit my dad at Liverpool, he remarried and moved there.

I remember that Lee once broke down crying, it was at a time when he was tired and worn out, and he'd had that many attempts on his life and there'd been three this time. I think he needed a rest, but he couldn't rest! He was never ever in fear because he still got up and went out into town after he'd been shot so he can't have been frightened; he'd just had enough.

He just felt like he wanted to settle down, but maybe he thought he couldn't with the attempts on my house and the attempts on his life, he'd just had enough. We wanted to settle down, but everything happened so quick we didn't have time to sit down and talk, we were both young.

Lee once said to me: 'All I want to do is settle down with you and Kattieleigh, that's all I want, get the house together.' We'd got this house and the night before he died for some reason he just wanted to stay in this house so we went and stayed there and slept on the floorboards.

Just the week before his death he was there decorating it, stripping paint, he wanted to do it all form scratch. He had no money, no car, nothing. He didn't even have a wardrobe full of clothes. He used to wear jeans and sweatshirts and his favourite was shorts, he liked to show his legs off, he liked his legs. He'd even go to the nightclub in his shorts."

'He who rides the tiger can never dismount', is quite relevant to Viv and Duffy's plight. Each living off their ebbing and flowing reputations in order to put a loaf on the table. Neither having a real profession that could earn them a living. Okay, Viv at times helped, or so they say, with building work, but what could these men offer in terms of skill to any potential employer?

They were caught in a no win situation…

What Makes A Man Tick

The fiancée of the late Viv Graham, Anna Connelly, might have been thought to be privy to all of Viv's little secrets…but she wasn't! Viv was a complex man with complex problems. Somehow, Viv was searching for something within himself, but he was never to find the key to life's problems.

Anna met Viv in 1986 and at that time he did not have a reputation and he was not known on Tyneside. Anna takes up the story, "When I met him in 1986, he didn't have a name and at that time I was still married, but separated. I was out on the town in Newcastle with my sisters and the first thing I noticed about Viv were his lovely teeth.

I knew he was a nice person, but I didn't know who he was. The very first time we met, he came across and asked if he could buy me a drink, he bought us vodkas and we were laughing together. We went back the next night and got more vodka. We kept going for a few weeks, getting drinks off him and then Viv asked me out. My sister-in-law was in the town and one of Viv's friends said to her that I was seeing Viv Graham. I hadn't been seeing Viv at all up to this time because I was married, but my relationship wasn't very good.

My sister-in-law went and told my husband that I was seeing Viv, we had a fight and after about five weeks we split up and I went to stay at my mam's. About three weeks after that, Viv found out and he came to see me and said, 'You're not seeing your husband now so will you go out with me on your own without your family?'

Viv was a gentleman in every way, pulling seats out and opening doors. He was like that with everyone. Someone who was being nice to me made the difference, as I was used to that. I remember Viv walking towards me with a big smile on his face and he said, 'Do you ladies want a drink?' There was about six of us sitting there. He kept looking over all of the time so I knew he wasn't going to come over and just ask the time. I wasn't aware that Viv was having a relationship with anyone else at that time. Although he said he had a few ex-girlfriends with kids to him and that he would always see his kids, but he was a single free man.

At that time he had a girl, Jodie Annie, to Julie Rutherford and had one boy, Dean, to Gillian Lowes. I had been in love before, but not in this way. I'll probably not meet anyone again.

Viv was still close to his children, Viv's parents love their grandchildren and were visited every day by them and Viv called to see them every day. Our relationship didn't interfere with this. It wasn't like a duty for him, he loved his kids. He loved to see them happy. He travelled to see them every day no matter what. At one time Viv started work as a labourer for John Wilkinson and he started travelling up to see his children at night time so he could fit the job in. Viv was working on roofs and that helped supplement his income at that time.

In the beginning, he wasn't really known; the only thing he did was to have a few fights. His name wasn't big then, but as time went on it became bigger. He wasn't a villain, all what he used to do was have a fight.

If you were in the pub and you were a big lad and were being cheeky and the manager said, 'This man is being cheeky here,' then Viv would come across and say, 'Look, will you please leave the bar and stop causing trouble.' He didn't come across and cause you trouble or beat you up.

He would ask you a few times and if you didn't leave he would then hit you and knock you out. He didn't like picking things up and hitting you with it. When he hit them, he used to catch them before they fell and take them outside and wait with them until they came around and sent them on their way by saying, 'Son, don't come back. I've asked you three times and then you wouldn't leave,' and that was Viv. He wasn't a rotter like the West End lot, hitting you with anything, punching you all over and then kicking you down the stairs! Viv wouldn't dream of anything like that. People come for him to sort out the bother, he never ever asked them. People came to the door to ask him to go and sort trouble out in the bars, saying that the police had sent them.

I had a marvellous lifestyle; I bought dresses and things from *Peaches & Cream* (shop in Newcastle City centre dealing in clothing for the elite). Viv would buy me dresses valued at £600 and £700. He would spend £1,000 on a dress and shoes to match.

Whatever I liked he would buy it for me and that pleased him, as long as it made me happy then he was happy. He liked to give things, but he didn't like them if they were short dresses! He would buy me them and then when he got home if he didn't like them he wouldn't speak to you because they would be too revealing and he would say, 'Have you seen how short that dress is?' I would say, 'What did you buy it for then? You made me try it on in the shop!'

Then we would start arguing and then the dress would get ripped up and that was the end of that. My mam would say, 'What have you paid all that money for?' Viv would reply, 'Well, Irene, it's bad enough being in the town watching your own back without lads looking at your lass with short frocks on, it just makes matters worse!' I said to my mother, 'He just wants me to wear polo necks and long skirts.' I didn't want to wear them because I was only in my twenties.

He underestimated himself all of the time and he was a bundle of nerves and his stomach used to turn over! He really underestimated himself and he'd end up sitting on the toilet. 'I'm Viv Graham, don't mess with me!' He was never like that; he didn't have loads of confidence. If he ever lost a bit of weight he would think he was too small. He was never six foot odd tall, yet his father was. Viv was only 5ft 11in tall.

He would be worried if he got involved in a fight with a

gang! Viv never had loads of confidence and he loved to be really big and if he looked in the mirror and he was really big, then he was happy! He was big, but if he lost any weight he didn't like that and felt uncomfortable.

It was because of his name really, but he never used to be that big when he boxed, as his weight was only thirteen stone. He could do the same when he was big as he could do at thirteen stones, he was actually fitter. Then he got into the bodybuilding stuff and he went even bigger! He got involved because a lot of his friends were doing that and eating the tuna and chicken. When he was in the gym it was one against the other, he didn't want to be fat though.

He went to the gym two and three times a day and he did once try steroids by injection, but he took bad with them and he ended up with an abscess on his backside and he needed an operation (this was declared on his insurance application when asked about his health) he was frightened of needles. I said, 'I'm telling your dad on you.'

He used to get in bad tempers, but he never touched the kids or me. He used to pull the doors off, but I wasn't bothered because he used to replace them the next day. The confidence he lacked, the steroids gave him. He couldn't ever get the confidence because he wasn't an aggressive man. He couldn't get in to a bad temper easy. It used to take him a long time to get like that, people used to worry thinking he was getting softer. When he was supposed to do things he couldn't get the aggression there. But with steroids the aggression came straight away, but then that wasn't him.

He knew where the aggression was coming from (steroids) and he decided himself to come off them because his dad said, 'You don't need steroids son, you're a big lad.' Viv was disciplined because of the boxing he started when he was thirteen years old. Boxing training was really well disciplined and he did that right up until he was in his twenties. Most people that ever met him knew that he was a gentleman and very soft hearted. He could easily cry over his nanna's memories. He always had a wreath at Christmas to put on her grave.

Viv used to give me chocolates and flowers as a romantic gift, but he never wrote me any poetry, as he wasn't a good writer...but he could write a bet out no problem.

He used to nip into town and get me makeup and lipstick and buy me nice underwear. He went into that shop called Secrets, regardless of his size and being well known. It never bothered him a little bit and if I ran out of a lipstick then I would say, 'Oh! My makeup!' He'd say, 'Where's it from?' 'Fenwicks!' I replied. Straightaway, he'd run there. If I wanted stockings, he'd ask, 'What colour do you want?' If I wanted lipsticks, he got me ten lipsticks. Viv and his friend, Alan Rooney, who was with him every single day, went for the makeup.

Alan Rooney: Alan was later charged with blackmail because of something he got involved with and it was traced back to Alan because his child had picked the telephone up and said 'Hello?' That's how he got caught in a blackmail plot when he had threatened a publican's husband with Viv because the man had used Viv's name in vain. This other man was using Viv's name, but Alan ended up getting eight years for something stupid like that.

(Author's note: Blackmail is a heinous filthy crime, I should know, having been criminally blackmailed by a well known County Durham based man. All will be revealed in a forthcoming book. But in Alan Rooney's case it would seem that the word 'blackmail' should be changed to 'demanding money with menaces'. If you play with fire then you get burnt, this publican wanted the best of both worlds. He wanted to use the threat of Viv without any expense being involved. Rooney was simply capitalising on that.)

Alan was just out of hospital after that, having had some sort of virus; he was really bad with it! It took over his whole body and you know when you see someone with multiple sclerosis, he was just like that for months and months.

Alan was at our house every day, but Viv had been told when he was in the town that this man had been using Viv's name. (The man that Alan eventually blackmailed.) Alan had no money and said, 'Should I phone him up and say whatever?' Viv said, 'Do what you want.' I think he said, 'I'll burn your house down.' But, he had no intentions of doing it. That man was in the wrong, he knew he had used Viv's name and was taking money off people. He really thought Viv was going to get him because he had done the wrong.

Before Alan had done all this, Viv and I had went to that man once and he had given Viv money for something he had done. From then on he thought he was well in with Viv sort of thing, 'I've give Viv a bit job and paid him some money, me and Viv are like that.'

That's when he started using Viv's name and getting a lot of money out of it for himself. Viv never knew nothing about it, he never seen that man again. The publican was from over the water, Sunderland. He had a pub in Hylton or some place like that.

Alan got eight years for that when really that man was in the wrong. It never happened that way, it just so happened Viv died and then the man wouldn't drop the charges, but if Viv had still been alive he wouldn't have had Alan charged because he knew he was in the wrong.

Even if the man hadn't of paid Alan, Alan wasn't really bothered, he was just testing him. It was a stupid thing, it ended up Viv died and obviously he couldn't go to court on Alan's behalf, but had he of been alive he would have went to court as a witness. By this time Alan knew who the man had been taking money off by using Viv's name.

When Viv lost his driving licence for twelve months (banned from driving) Alan was the one to drive him around. That was another story, Viv went to pick the kids up and this woman stepped straight off the curb and he bumped into her, luckily she wasn't hurt. I went straight to the scene and found her with broken glasses. A couple living opposite had seen it happen and phoned me up and I went straight there. Viv was absolutely devastated! The woman said, 'Son, I'm all right! I'm all right!' She had a pound coin in her hand; she was running for the bus.

Viv gave her £200 to replace the broken glasses, we went to the flower shop and got a big bouquet of flowers for her, found out where she lived and went back to the house with the flowers and gave her another £100. Her husband was there when this took place and she, again, said, 'Son, I'm all right, I've just got a little bit of a headache where the glasses have caught me.'

Within six weeks, she took a private summons out and got him done. As it happened, his car wasn't insured. She thought she would get a lot of money and then she claimed. She said she was getting severe headaches, but when she issued a private summons and the police wanted Viv's documents. He wasn't insured and he lost his licence. She still carried on with the private summons, someone must have told her who Viv was and that he had money. She couldn't do anything about it because Viv died before it reached court.

Viv was genuinely sick with it. He gave her that money and was worried about her regardless of the insurance, as he did not know his insurance had expired. The old lady said she was over the moon with the money, her glasses weren't even worth £200, but she still done that and took him to court. That will show you what type of a person Viv was.

When people asked Viv to do them a favour, he always had respect for the elderly and many a time turned down a job if the person he had to go and see was old. Many a time, though, he didn't really have to do anything. A lot of businessmen came to him. Say, for instance, you had fitted windows to a house and you knew you weren't going to get the money; they would go to Viv for help to get it. Then the money would be there the next day when Viv called to collect it.

Some of the things said about Viv were all lies, saying things like he was a big drugs baron! He never ever dealt in drugs! That was one thing he never ever touched! He never needed to deal in drugs; he made a lot of money from other things. He had bars and nightclubs from Whitley Bay through to Wallsend and Shields Road into the town (Newcastle City centre).

Some weeks he picked up maybe £15,000, that was apart from businessmen and other people knocking at the door. I was there when Viv had to collect £60,000 and he got £30,000 in a carrier bag, he never needed to touch drugs. People just accepted what was put out about him; no one would stand up and defend him when he passed away.

Viv never thought of what he could do with his money, he did at the finish with this house, but before that he wasn't interested, he just liked to spend it, he didn't drink and he didn't smoke…he just liked a bet. Viv could have bought the house outright, he could have bought his car outright, but he got it all on finance. After Viv's death his dad paid for his car every week.

He liked it better that way; getting the house on a mortgage. He didn't have a penny put to one side for emergencies! As quick as it came in, the quicker it went out. He could have had £30,000 in that hand and within an hour he wouldn't have £1 for the electric meter! It never bothered him, he knew if he spent it by the Monday he would have more by the weekend. Tomorrow didn't matter, he lived for the day and I was just the same.

At times it was a competition to see who could win the most money. Every day we were in the bookies, he would say, 'There's your money.' I would put a bet on and say, 'Give me £100 so I can put this bet on.' I would maybe win because I was luckier than he was.

I still put the odd bet on now. I had done that prior to meeting Viv. We bought a greyhound and it cost us a fortune it didn't come anywhere in the races it ran in, but we could watch it in the races and have a night out. We even thought about buying a racehorse, but that's as far as it went.

We had 32 rabbits, two geese, five dogs and 36 chickens and they took a lot of looking after. Viv loved the chickens and collecting the eggs in the morning. Although Viv ate chicken for his meals when he trained, he wouldn't have been able to eat one of these chickens for Sunday dinner. He went shooting with his dad, but he couldn't have shot anything we had just for the sake of eating it. He shot at pheasants in the wild on these shoots, but that was it.

Viv and I didn't lead a boring life, we went to the best of restaurants and everything. Viv didn't like paying his debts although he did pay up in the end. If we got anything on HP it would end up not getting paid, so we used to buy things outright. A television man knocked on the door and Viv wouldn't pay him. When he seen it was Viv he didn't come back. The poll tax man came and he saw Viv and asked who he was and I just said something like, 'He's my brother,' we were all laughing. Viv said, 'You'll get no money from here!' The man said, 'I'm away, me.' He didn't come back.

He loved life and he was up at six o'clock in the morning with the dogs. He was even happier when we got Buster (the dog). There was a big field at the back and he was looking forward to getting up and running because he loved training. He used to make me get up with him and wanted me to run around the field with him! I still had my pyjamas on and used to walk around the field with the dogs.

The neighbours next door used to laugh when he seen me out with him. Viv didn't like me smoking because he didn't, so he limited me to ten cigarettes a day, but I had my secret supply hidden. I used to keep the same packet and top it up. He would say, 'You've only had two tabs today!'

Although Viv went into an environment where there was cigarette smoke, he didn't like me smoking because it was bad for my health. He couldn't stand the smell of the smoke and he used to get bathed and showered two and three times a day. Every time he came back from the gym or from somewhere smelly, he would have a shower. We had someone come in and help out with the cleaning so we didn't have a big pile of ironing building up in the corner.

As for Viv's safety, he confided in me about this and many a time raised his concerns about him or I being shot. He used to say all the time, 'I'll never reach forty because I'm telling you, they'll shoot me.' I thought he was invincible and nothing could happen to him. I just thought that when he said it that they would be too frightened to come and they wouldn't try it.

A gang of masked men came to my house when I lived in Daisy Hill at Wallsend and the windows come in! There were two carloads of them and they had masks on and were carrying guns! Viv didn't hide from anyone and his telephone number was available from the telephone directory.

Andy Winder: We used to go on holiday and our favourite place was Greece. I would see a different Viv. We never ever went where it was lively; sometimes we were the only people on the beach. We would come back, get changed and go for a meal. We did not ever go to Tenerife though, as it was reported that Viv had been there and had a fight with a man called Andy Winder. Winder did timeshare in Tenerife.

(Author's note: Winder was originally from Darlington and it was alleged that he placed a £30,000 hit on Viv if anything ever happened to him. The reason for this allegation was, it was claimed, that he had supposedly come off the worse from a fight the pair had. That fight did not take place though and this story is unfounded and will always remain exactly just that; a story.)

Paddy Leonard: Paddy wanted Viv to come across and do the timeshare. Viv had discussed this with his dad as he always did and his dad said, 'No way!' There are things coming out these last few years that even I didn't know about because I was so high on Valium! In all of that time there are things I am just starting to question now.

When we went on holiday, we went there as a family and we didn't want to come back. We wanted it to last forever and wanted to move away, but we said we'd just stay here for a few years. He loved the country and he wanted to be away, but his work was here and he was becoming more established. Half the time he didn't even have to show his face, he had the likes of Rob Armstrong and them in nightclubs overseeing it for him.

Viv was going to get contracts on the books and do it properly; some jobs could pay £1,000 a week. That was just happening before he died. It was all coming together, he was going to give the town up and leave it at that. He was sick of having to put his face up against it all of the time. People wanted to use Viv's name above their doors.

Higgins Security: They came from Birmingham and asked Viv to visit them there and meet their top bosses. Viv told his dad and he was told not to go there and to make them come here to meet him. They told Viv they didn't want to take over the town because they knew he was Viv Graham.

A lot of the doormen were complaining because they feared Higgins were coming here to Newcastle and taking their jobs and they were saying to Viv, 'You'll have to stop them because they're taking our jobs! You'll have to show them!' They knew all about Viv and he went to see them and they said they had no intentions of taking over the bars. Viv sorted that entire lot out for them.

Viv hated me wearing short skirts and sometimes he went overboard. I remember once when we were out, off he went to the toilet through a crowd of women and he would keep his hands in the air. If he seen anyone touch a woman and they complained, he didn't take kindly to that happening, especially if it was to me.

I remember once when someone was talking to me, Viv went across and said, 'That was my wife!' They didn't do it again. When I first met Viv he was with me constantly, but sometimes there would be one night when he wouldn't be there and the next day I would say, 'Where were you?' He would tell me a pack of lies and say, 'Oh, I was in the casino in the town until seven o'clock this morning, I had my breakfast.' Which was a load of crap!

Viv's best quality was his kindness; if he had a fault then it was being overly generous. People would call, crying to the door, saying they had a gas bill. He would pull the money out and give it to them, but he never got it back from them.

I don't think Viv was trying to overcompensate because he was a non-believer. I was a good Catholic. Viv's funeral was in a Protestant church although he wasn't a believer in God and had no intentions of accepting my faith, so he had no reason to want to prove something.

I believe he started to believe in God more, although his father was a staunch non-believer. I think it was because Viv got on well with Father Conaty and the fact that missionaries from Bosnia started coming to our house when we put them up. It was through me that he started to change his views.

I remember it was the first Holy Communion of one of my daughters' and the table was full of religious gifts, he bought the full whack for all the kids there. Once you met him you never forgot him and I used to say to the Father that he was something special because he was somebody special to me. I couldn't believe how very kind in his ways he was and yet still have this power inside of him. He was very strong, he could lift a five hundred and eighty-pound bench-press, not a problem to him. He gave a lot of help to the local boxing club and had the heating put in and did a lot more, Viv paid for everything.

We had our arguments just like anybody else. Viv would come back from the gym, lie on the settee, have loads of sweets and watch videotapes. That's what he liked the most; he would lock the door and take the phone off the hook.

As for children, I didn't think we needed a child to cement our relationship and Viv didn't because I had my children and he had his children, but then there came a point when he did. We did try, but it just never happened. I went to the doctor and put a pregnancy test in and I was frightened to say the real results after the way he went on. We came out of the surgery and I told him I was pregnant and he jumped for joy and wanted to tell everyone. We rushed back home and he was starting to telephone his mother! I put the receiver down and said, 'I've got something to tell you.' I was frightened after the way he went on. I thought, 'Eh! Why did I say that to him?' I said, 'I was only pretending,' and he went, 'You what!' I said, 'I just pretended to you just to see what you would think.' He was gutted, really gutted and then I realised he really did want a baby.

I was frightened in case I had a one, as he wouldn't love my kids in the same way. We did want a one then, this was about three months before he died, so we did start and try. He loved them and they loved him and they even called him their dad. He spent more time with them than he did with his own kids.

I was from a mixed family and I knew there might be problems, as I had some problems in my family although they weren't problems of a bad nature. Because I had the experience from that I thought that Viv might encounter some problems with that scenario.

Viv said, 'I would treat them exactly the same.' I said, 'Other people's are never the same as your own. Your two come here and I love them, but I don't love them as I love my own.' So I knew if I had ever had a baby then that love would have been a special love, different to the love he would have for them.

This would have caused arguments and I didn't want that because we had a happy relationship. I didn't want that. I didn't want to start fighting. I knew he really did want a baby and we did try. My children said, 'We can have a little baby sister or a baby brother.'

They (Anna's two daughters: Dominique and Georgia) talk about him every day. They've got their pictures in their rooms and they talk about him all the time. They absolutely loved him. She's got her own little book that she (Dominique) makes her own little poems in. The kids put the monkey hanging on the rear view mirror that was in Viv's car and he just left it there.

Sometimes Viv's business and private life overlapped. He would call me and come and get something to eat, then he would go straight back out to the gym and from there on to the bookies. He would come out, go for something to eat and go and get some videos, then, seven o'clock, he would ask us if we wanted anything from the shop. He would watch a video with his bag of sweets, with the phone off the hook and the door locked. If something cropped up, which usually it did, he would take me with him and I would sit in the car waiting. My sister, Mary, and him were very close; she would stand up to anybody, even a man!

Harry Thompson: Just after I had lost Viv, there was further tragedy when my brother-in-law, Harry Thompson, was tragically lost to violence. Mary's husband had gone to sort out someone who had burgled his home and he was stabbed. I couldn't believe it. He died about nine months after Viv. I was just starting to get back on my feet. I couldn't believe it; I just couldn't believe it.

Viv's teeth were his pride and joy Viv was going to have gold fillings in some of them, he liked to look after his teeth. A ship had pulled into the Tyne and the sailors were causing bother. One of them was a championship boxer about 6ft 10in tall. He touched a woman's behind, Viv said, 'Here, you wouldn't do that where you come from so you won't do that here in Newcastle, touching lasses backsides!' So he takes his sunglasses off (sailor) and said, 'Who are you, man?' Viv said, 'Never mind who I am!' He (the sailor) just went bop! Viv's tooth went through his lip. Anyway, Viv banjo's him and the sailor went down. The police were sitting in their car watching it. They said they seen the big coloured man and stood up for Viv, as a lot of the police liked Viv. Viv got away with that one.

Where we used to live was terrible! There was smack and heroin! You could go and knock on any door and get it. When the football club was there, Viv would take about fifty kids on the field and he would say, 'Don't take drugs, get training.' Kids loved him, if they could get into the car with him it made their day. I knew all the hard men you could think of or name and Viv was nothing like that.

Paul Ashton: If Viv hit you, he wouldn't let you fall in case you hit your head on the ground. Viv never took liberties with people, yet they did and they are all still alive? Viv first started in Wheelers nightclub and he had trouble with a Gateshead man called Paul Ashton, now serving 31 years for violence!

Stevie 'The Hammer' Eastman: Viv wouldn't use his power against someone weighing only about eight or nine stones; he would pull his punch back. Viv gave Stevie the Hammer a nasty bash! I was there when it happened. I didn't like fighting and it wasn't as if it was a fight that would last for ages. Viv was as fast as lightening!

If you were a big person, he knew how to punch through the boxing, so if you were a big person he would give a harder punch. He wouldn't punch a man of eight stones the way he punched Stevie the Hammer because it would have punched their face in. After all of that, Stevie did not hold any grudge against Viv. He thought the world of Viv and they still remained friends even though that happened and Viv thought a lot of Stevie.

The press told lies about Viv! Every New Year they try it on, even ten o'clock at night. They phoned me up one day. I had been going to the spiritualist, I didn't know where I was at that time and I felt that I needed it.

(Author's note: The Catholic Church frown upon such practises of necromancy – contacting the dead.)

They tripped me up by pretending to be someone I knew. A woman rung me up and said, 'How are you? Have you had anymore messages from the spiritualist, have you, were you there on Sunday?' There am I blabbing away because I didn't really know who it was. I said, 'Yes, I got a message.' I was telling her the full message and by the end of the conversation I still couldn't work out who it was and I said, 'Who is it anyway?' 'She said she was from the Sunday Sun. That weekend it was plastered all over the newspapers.

Gary Ward: The police called about this Blackpool thing where a lad was charged with murder of a man, Mark White, on Blackpool beach. Viv had never ever been to Blackpool, never ever.

What Makes A Man Tick

(Author's note: Viv had definitely been to Blackpool. Julie Rutherford confirms this when she says: "March or May of 1989 and that was supposed to be a new beginning and we were sitting in a pub called the Manchester Bar.")

It just so happened that month being September and my birthday is the 1st of September, he definitely wasn't there. If Gary Ward was innocent then I wonder where Viv Graham comes into it. I wish that woman had come to me (Gary Ward's mother) I would have said that no way was Viv there. The police said the man was eighteen years old and fighting Viv on the beach. He wouldn't have had a chance with Viv.

Stephen Craven: He could still be innocent, look at Stephen Craven who is in prison over the Studio nightclub murder of Penny Laing. It was supposed to be another man and that man went to London. Viv phoned the man up and told him to come back. He was in the marines or something and the doorman at the Studio nightclub was alleged to have let him out of the side door. Viv had a confrontation with the doorman who supposedly did that and eventually Viv ended up being good friends with Stephen Craven.

Every night I go to bed and I can't sleep very well. I might sleep maybe about two-and-a-half to three hours. I must be in a deep sleep because by the next day I'm fit enough and not worn out. I'm always on the go so that must be all I need. Before Viv died, you couldn't get me out of the bed, I could sleep and sleep and sleep

Viv's views on someone who committed crimes against old people were what you would expect from someone like him. Viv had no proper friends except for those in my family who were really close to him. Since he died, I can say he has no friends. No one has given me any support that could be looked at as anything real.

Robbie Warton: He was a good true friend to the children.

Rob Bell: He has helped, they were very good to Viv's family, but the rest of them just used him. Rob Bell nearly died when he was attacked in Newcastle on a night out in the

Bigg Market, it was because of an argument and words were said, but I couldn't swear on this, I wouldn't dare, but Rob might have hit one of them.

They went to Santino's restaurant; it was a night out on the spur of the moment. Some men walked in with the gun towards where Viv and Rob were sitting. Viv said, 'Put that gun away before I shove it up your arse.' Viv grabbed the gun and then they went outside. After a fight, it ended up, allegedly, that Viv broke the jaw of one of Rob's attackers, as Rob lay there nearly bleeding to death after being stabbed in the heart by one of the men.

Stuart Watson: It was said that Viv was put into prison for a savage attack on Stuart Watson. Why didn't the newspapers say that the man Viv attacked was eighteen-and-a-half-stones? Eventually, Viv and Stuart became friends because after Viv got out of prison things were said and the air needed clearing so Viv went to see Stuart and the matter was settled without the use of violence. Viv was invited to parties that Stuart held so that proves Viv wasn't a thug as the newspapers portrayed him.

Many Burgo: Viv's boxing career led to an involvement with a fellow heavyweight amateur boxer, Manny Burgo, from South Shields. The boxing selectors choose Manny over and above Viv to go and box for the championships. Viv wasn't very happy at this and Manny said, 'Viv, it wasn't my fault.' This is what made Viv throw the towel in, as he knew he was a better boxer than Manny, but Manny was chosen because he looked a better boxer. People say it was because of a frozen shoulder that Viv stopped, but that was the real reason. He went back to boxing after that, though, for a while.

Tim Healy: Viv didn't need to live up to people; he liked to be on his own. We were out in Julie's nightclub one night when Viv was involved in a fight and there were loads of them. Viv was fighting with these men and everybody that knew Viv had moved away from him over to the other side, but Tim Healy hadn't! He come up to Viv to pass by and was clipped, but Viv hadn't realised it was Tim Healy and it wasn't until afterwards that they said, 'You've hit Tim Healy!' Viv thought that he was going to get the police involved. There was a joke that Pat Roach would be coming in to get Viv. Roach was a real life professional wrestler that played a part in Auf Weidersehn Pet.

Viv's hero was his dad and his favourite film was Zulu. There was only one man Viv looked up to and that was his dad. I feel that I could help anyone that ever suffered the loss of a loved one. After the loss of Harry, my brother-in-law, I became stronger again.

Viv was a real professional, he looked after you, but as for himself, he only lived for the day. He didn't put anything to one side for a rainy day. If he got older and couldn't do that profession anymore then he might have thought about it.

We did once try to save; we opened a bank account for a mortgage. He gave me £200 to put in to the bank and I asked for a balance, which was given to me as £2.82. I said, 'You had better check it, as that's not right!' The clerk said, 'Well, how much?' I replied, 'There's a lot of money in, you'd better check it?' So she checked it all and said, 'There's definitely only £2.82 left in the account.' I said, 'Well you'd better get the manager because there's definitely more. I know what I put in!' When all came to all, Viv had been going in and signing a piece of paper and getting the money out for the bookies. Another woman come and said, 'Your Viv's been coming in and signing the piece of paper and drawing out every week.' I wasn't bothered, I went back to the bookies and pulled him, he was full of himself, laughing! He knew when I went in what he had done. I said, 'You're joking, there's me going in and them saying there's only £2.82, well that's me finished.' So I let that one go and I never ever tried to save again. The bankbook is still upstairs with £2.82 in.

My brother, my sister and her husband loaned me the £12,000 as a deposit on this house. We didn't ever get to pay the mortgage, as Viv died. There was an insurance policy that covered it, but it wasn't paid out because it was in probate because Gillian Lowes is contesting it. (Viv's former girlfriend.)

(Author's note: Since then, the insurance payout has been settled and all have received some sort of payment.)

The picture that the press keep using in the newspapers of me wearing that revealing dress was actually stolen. The press came in and wanted to look at photographs and stole that particular photograph. I went to see the police about it and asked for that picture back that was stolen and it's the one that the press continually use without my permission.

John Merry: The police did get the photo back for me. Viv hated it because of that revealing little yellow dress I was wearing. I was promised some money from a hack called John Merry. I said, 'I don't want money, I want the truth!' Merry said, 'No! I'll give you some money.' I said, 'Well if you do then it will go in the reward fund in the bank. I'll put it in there or if nothing happens I'll give it to charity.' He turned his pocket out and said, 'Look, all that I've got is £43. I promise I'll send some more. Promise me you'll not tell any other reporters about this story so as to give me a chance to get it in the papers.' His story appeared in a Sunday newspaper under a headline indicating that Viv headed a £2m Drug Empire and protection racket! So from then on I just haven't bothered with journalists. I wouldn't entertain them at all from now on.

Viv wasn't a gangster as such. The gangsters we know are underground London types where they put people into cement bridges and that sort of thing. He wasn't that type of man, he was a boxer and he could handle himself. The people that knew him loved him, he was an absolute gentleman. The people that hadn't really heard about him thought that he only did nasty things, they just thought, 'Ugh! Viv Graham, he's a rotter!' But, if they really knew him they would have felt completely different.

I had friends that if you said the wrong word to they would run and were terrified of trouble. One of them said she was nervous about going out with us with Viv in our company. When she knew Viv was coming out with us she felt really nervous, but when she did come out with us she couldn't believe how gentlemanly he was. He jumped up, got her hand and gave her a chair and to this day she says, 'What a lovely gentleman he was.' My own mother got the same talk from people, 'He's big, he's trouble and this,' but, she said, 'He was nothing like that.' And she went on to say, 'I met him and knew the difference.'

People knew what he was capable of and he didn't use a weapon. They knew he would come face to face with them and what they didn't know was that he would always give them a chance. He wouldn't just run, he would say to them, 'Look don't do that, don't be like…' and if he got another phone call about them then they were in bother, but he would let them walk away. That's why they kept coming back because they knew really at the bottom of him he was… She (as Anna nods in her mother's direction) knew him to knock a kid out and then give him money after he'd done it.

Brian Durant: One Saturday afternoon we were going for a meal and we bumped into a man Viv knew, he was called Durant. We were out on a Saturday afternoon shopping and going for a meal when Durant stopped us and took his coat off and said to Viv, 'I can't work anywhere, you stopped me from working, I've got a mortgage!' Viv said, 'Me? Not me! I wouldn't stop you working anywhere.' Durant then said, 'I've had enough,' Viv said to the man's wife, 'Tell your man to put his coat back on.' Viv was on parole, he'd just got out of jail and he didn't want to have a fight and he wouldn't. They had a scuffle, the lad fell off the kerb and Viv picked him up and gave him £50 and said, 'I'll give you a job anytime'. It was Rob Armstrong whom he had a fight with, not Viv, but the rumour was he wouldn't let Durant work on any of the doors in the town.

Rob Armstrong: A fight between Durant and Rob Armstrong some time, months earlier, in Madison's night-club had resulted in some damage being caused to this man's eye. Viv was being blamed for it, but it wasn't him who did it.

John Jobie: Then there was John Jobie from Gateshead. He had started carrying a lot of tales and he came into Julie's nightclub with his wife. Viv went up to him and he said to Viv, 'It was a load of lies'. He said to Viv, 'I'll go with you to their doors and prove they are lying.'

Viv said to me, 'Anna, what do you think, do you think it's rumours?' I replied, 'They will be rumours because people like to start trouble, you know what people are like.' I used to believe them, but the rumour was that John Jobie wanted Viv seeing to. Viv didn't believe it and I didn't believe it either. That's how trouble started, but this ended up in a friendly manner and Viv was still friends with John Jobie.

Ray Hewitson: Dodgy Ray was one of Viv's closest friends, but they fell out.

Terry Scott: He was a friend of Viv's, but I wouldn't say he was one of his best friends.

Sayers': I know by when he died that people who I never knew wrote to me saying that they felt safe when Viv was around and that people felt safe when Viv was watching the bars and clubs. Some of the TV documentaries shown made Viv seem like that doorman who glassed that woman in Manchester. That was horrible, it made people think Viv was like that.

The stories about Viv weren't balanced, especially when it showed Viv setting about that club doorman. The reason for the attack was that this man had allegedly attacked two ten stone lads and smashed their jaws, as far as I was told when we came back off holiday.

(Author's note: Stuart Watson was attacked in a totally unprovoked attack designed by people who wanted to oust Watson from his job of stopping them entering certain nightspots in Newcastle.)

At the same time the Sayers' went to Hobo's and as far as I knew they had a falling out with Stuart Watson. They come up to Viv because at that time they were friendly with Viv and they said that the doorman wouldn't let them in there. 'Come down with us Viv?' Viv didn't have a clue that Watson was in there (Hobo's) or that it was Stuart Watson on the door.

Viv had been looking for Watson, as the manager had been in and said that Watson had been in and broke one of their jaws and that was the message Viv had been given from the manager of a nightclub.

That night, the Sayers' went to Hobo's nightclub, as far as I know they must have had this falling out at that time. Viv was portrayed as being a horrible man savaging that man. You tell the story though of a man who was eighteen and a half stone and little men who were only ten stone and that tells a different story to the one reported on TV and in the press. Viv was standing up for the little man, but in doing so he was made out to be the bully, which was not so. (Author's note: Sadly, Viv was the bully supported by numerous other men who were armed with knives, etc.)

Viv and the Sayers' fell out when he was in jail and they didn't make it up, he also fell out with Rob Armstrong, but they made it up, although they weren't as close.

Finally, I would like to say that contrary to an article that appeared in the local press saying that Viv was a police informant. A well-known villain said that Viv was supposed to be a grass. Viv was never a grass and if he was, why won't they stand up? It's easy to say these things because he's not here! Why can't they stand up and say their name if they say he was a grass and tell me what was his name and get the police to come forward to say what Viv was supposed to have grassed to them about?

I don't believe that person exists because it's just too convenient for the comment to target someone who isn't here to defend him or herself. The newspapers are quick to print this sort of thing, but not so quick to admit they used a stolen photograph without my permission."

Viv Graham & Lee Duffy's Parallel Lives

A poem written by Dominique, one of Anna's daughters, is included below.

To My Dad, Viv

What is goodbye? Just a word that makes us cry;
When a soul-like ship pulls from the shore.

In a place where I've been just last night in a dream;
Each saying, "Don't cry for me for I am waiting for you."

In this world of summer's blue the land of eternity;
When I asked, "Can I stay?" they led me away saying,
"It's not your time; there are songs you must sing and plant seeds in the spring.

Lots of Love
Viv

Dominique

The teenage years

Whose a pretty boy - Viv in fancy dress

Tim Healey - Man about 'toon'

" The Godfather "

Viv the falconer

The one that got away

Viv with his secret lover
Gillian Lowes

John Davison with Sunderland's
Billy Hardy

Denny Haig, Harry Thompson and Viv

Witness Statement

(CJ Act 1967, s.9 MC Act 1980, s.102, MC Rules 1981, r.70)

Form MG 11

Statement of ...... Keith FELTON

Age if under 21 O'21 ... (if over 21 insert 'over 21'). Occupation DETECTIVE CHIEF INSP

This statement (consisting of 1 pages each signed by me) is true to the best of my knowledge and belief and I make it knowing that, if it is tendered in evidence, I shall be liable to prosecution if I have wilfully stated in it anything which I know to be false or do not believe to be true.

Dated the 20 day of OCTOBER 19 95.

Signature ...... K Felton

I am a Detective Chief Inspector with the Northumbria Police currently stationed at Wallsend as Crime Manager.

Throughout 1992 I was a Detective Inspector attached to the Northumbria Police Drug Squad.

In September of 1992 I was contacted by Detective Sergeant Sam SMITH of South Shields C.I.D. in relation to drug related information unto the activities of the CONROY family. As a result I was introduced by Sgt SMITH to David GLOVER at South Shields Police Station.

Subsequent to this meeting David GLOVER was registered by me as a police informant under the pseudonym "Adrian SCOTT".

On 21ST September 1992 in agreement with "Adrian SCOTT" I obtained authority for this informant to participate in an operation in which controlled drugs where to be delivered to an address on Tyneside. The operation was codenamed "CHESTNUT MARE".

K Felton

Signature ...... K Felton   Signature witnessed by ......

August 1993

The text submitted to the court on behalf of David Glover Jnr shows his supergrass status

The 'Hut' in Highfield where Viv used to train - place of torture where even the SAS would run from

Wheelers nightclub, Vivs learning ground - now demolished to make way for Gateshead Quays development

Brian Cockerill was on the other end of Lee Duffys' fist to no avail. Duffy said weeks later: "Who in their right mind would want to fight someone the size of Brian."

Harry Marsden, a resilient old school member of the underworld. Now reformed and running the Harry Marsden amateur boxing club. Was threatened by Harry Perry's henchmen to be thrown from the Tyne Bridge back in the 70s. Harry has won many a battle, but his biggest battle was to overcome his fight against the big 'C'.

Paul Massey (some say Manchester's godfather) helped save Sunderland from an underworld takeover

Steve 'The Hammer' Eastland

Robocop Ray Mallon questioned drugs dealer who ordered hit on Duffy

Ernie Bewick could be considered to bo Sunderland's Rocky Marciano, but he would refute this because he is an understated man. He is a popular figure amongst those who have needed his services for pub and club security throughout Sunderland

Gary Ward convicted on
dubious evidence of the
Blackpool Beach Murder
of Mark White

Joe Hunt part of the rave
scene security network in
the early 90s

David Glover Jnr made a statement naming the killers of Viv,
albeit a statement of invention to lessen the severirty of his
own prison sentence

Tommy Harrison, centre left, Lee Duffy, centre right, and
far right, Lee Harrison

Stephen & Michael Sayers May 1999
HM Prison Frankland

Viv was becoming, as some say, too big for his boots and was starting a road to bullying people he felt able to and demanded £15,000 from fellow club doorman Stu Watson

Stuart Watson was always the threat to Viv's macho image. When Viv failed to defeat Watson he always felt there was unfinished business - Watson never flickered and stood his ground

The, some say, pyschopathic
Duffy

The loving father Duffy

The relaxed Duffy (right)

A taste of what was to come in terms of security at the £20m
Freddie Knights murder trial

Richard Haswell, solicitor to John Henry Sayers, on the steps
of Leeds Crown Court, with his back to us is John Henry Snr,
and just visible is the silver silk Jonathan Goldberg QC.
Armed police far right

John Henry - three steps to happiness

Stephen & John Sayers pleased to see the end of the
Freddie Knights murder trial where John was acquitted

A happy crowd of supporters and relations of the two men
acquitted of the Freddie Knights murder

The Victim

R.I.P
Freddie Knights
Murdered 20th September 2000

The alleged Gunman

Dale Miller

Manslaughter 16 years

Lee Watson
Supergrass
Manslaughter
11 years

The Getaway driver

Eddie Stewart

Manslaughter 13 years

Mickey Dixon was, unbelievably, found guilty of conspiracy to cause grievous bodily harm... 9 years. He was the saddest sight to see!! Unwittingly he used a mobile phone he had bought and eventually given back to one of the other co-defendant, he also stole a car! Hope he wins his appeal!

Michael Dixon

In Ever Loving Memory Of
LEE PAUL DUFFY
DIED 25th AUGUST 1991
AGED
A CHERISHED SON A BELOVED
BROTHER, AND DADDY
AND A FRIEND.

Lee 'The Duffer' Duffy was killed in a violent manner. "He who lives by the sword dies by the sword." This was one of Duffy's Sayings and as if though predicting his own demise this is how his life ended. Duffy and Viv never got to meet in that fight that was arranged for them. Maybe fate kept them apart.

Did the killers of Paul Logan continue their carnival of death by killing Viv some seven days later, some police officers seem to think so.

Viv and Duffy are united in death yet it was life that kept them apart. Two Legends the likes of which may never be seen again, the power vacuums being too big for any one person to fill.

IN LOVING MEMORY OF
A DEAR SON AND BROTHER
VIV GRAHAM
DIED 31st DEC. 1993
AGED 34 YEARS.
LOVED AND REMEMBERED BY SONS
DEAN AND VIV

SIMPLY THE BEST.

Harem Nights & Fights

Viv had a plentiful and abundant love life. Three women, and more besides, were involved in Viv's tangled love life. Right to the very end they were involved in a bitter fight to gain the proceeds of insurance payouts. Julie Rutherford, Gillian Lowes and Anna Connelly made up the three women in Viv's harem.

There was no other woman in Viv's life, just other women! Viv used to call Gillian, 'Little Lowesy'. When they were at school they had pet names for each other. Viv used to call at Gillian's home and he used to complain of terrible headaches and that was when he went there directly from Anna's. Gillian put these headaches down to the pressure and not to the boxing some people thought it to be caused by.

Gillian said it was the job that Viv was doing that was the cause of the stress, however, how did Gillian know what job Viv was doing when she said that she did not really know what he was up to? For a woman who was in the dark over what he did, she certainly knew plenty about what he got up to. She went on to say that everybody wanted looking after by him and it really got out of hand and how, in the end, he could not cope! "In the last year of his life," Gillian said, "...he was receiving lots of threats and he was really stressed out."

She went on to say that Viv did take these threats seriously and she assumes for some reason that someone had rung Viv up from London to say they were coming up. Viv did, though, confide in Gillian about this threat he received from London and he said that she had to stop taking the pill if he did receive such a threat. Here it is difficult to tell if this was something Viv had invented just to get Gillian off the pill, as he wanted her to have his baby. Obviously he liked it if his women were pregnant, as it made them unattractive to other men. Maybe that was it, all of the outward machismo had made him feel emotionally stunted within, and whom could he trust? Maybe people had made him empty promises at some point in his formative years?

But all the headaches may have just been a ploy to get Gillian to come off the pill so he could get her pregnant! Viv asked her to come off the pill, and that to Gillian meant he did receive a certain threat he was waiting for, but Gillian told him he had "no chance" of her coming off the pill for him.

If Viv really loved his women so much then why did he practice every male trick in the book to ditch Gillian when he was invited abroad? With regard to holidays spent together, there was a time when Viv and Gillian had planned to go on a holiday to Cyprus when Viv was nominated as a friend's best man. Viv and Gillian were invited out there where the man had spent time whilst in the army. Viv told Gillian that he did not like going abroad, so that plan was scrapped.

To make up for this, Gillian booked a holiday on her own to Corfu. Viv found out about it and he tried dissuading her from going and he ended up taking her to the bus station so she could get to the airport. Was this to make sure she was going on her own? A few weeks later, and without Gillian, Viv went off on a holiday abroad!

A place that Viv seemed to enjoy taking his conquests to was Blackpool, he took Gillian and another couple. As soon as they arrived there, Viv took off to the bookies with the other man in tow. So desperate was Viv to get away to the bookies that he did not even stay to help with the suitcases out of the car boot!

The woman they were with, out of the other couple, whispered to Gillian that Viv had won a lot of money. Viv denied he had won any money at all, but Gillian went on to say that she patted his pockets down looking for the money and then the next day she found it hidden (about £500) in a cushion, she went mad at Viv! If Viv had thought more of his women he would have flashed his cash, surely? This indicates that Gillian was only concerned about where the money was and she eventually found it, as she did not believe Viv when he said he had not won any money.

Why did Viv withhold this information from her? Obviously he was concerned at her finding out, concerned enough to hide it away from her.

This goes against what Gillian had earlier said about Viv telling her everything. If that was the case then why did he not tell her about this big win and the money? The difference between Viv and Gillian, which she admits, is that he did not value money? (Why did he hide the money from her then?)

At the time Gillian was having Viv's first child he was seeing Julie Rutherford in 1985. Gillian did not want to become pregnant, but she had come off the pill because she no longer needed to take it with Viv and her being finished. But although they were not together they started having sex again. The obvious result was that Gillian had a baby, Dean.

Viv said to Gillian that he would not live with her, but when it was all over he would come home. What though was he waiting for to be over? Gillian did not expand on this and for her to say this she obviously had an idea of what it was that Viv was waiting for to be all over.

Viv confessed to Gillian that he did not love Anna the way he loved her and that she would always be his childhood sweetheart. It was recalled by Gillian that Viv came back from one of his holidays, "It was about six o'clock in the morning when he called with a suitcase with three bottles of perfume in it. He said that one bottle was for his mother, but his mother did not ever get it so it was obvious he had bought each one of his three lovers the same bottle of perfume home from the holiday!" A marriage was proposed to Gillian in this early morning visit and she wrote it down on some paper, but it was not to be and Gillian was kept hanging on, as were the others.

Viv went off with Julie while he was still seeing Gillian

and she was gutted at the loss of Viv to another woman. Obviously Gillian must have felt second best to Julie as Julie must have felt second best to Anna when Viv moved on to her, leaving Gillian third best. Julie was all over Viv like a rash in Finnigan's bar. Gillian noticed this and became very jealous.

Viv was promptly thrown out along with his eight carrier bags of belongings. Viv only stayed at Gillian's a few nights of the week, as he was still living with his parents at that time.

Anna had commented on the fact that she used to send clothes to Gillian? "Well, looking at Anna's taste with that horrible yellow dress, what does she look like in that," said Gillian to this claim.

Given that Anna emphatically insisted that Viv had never been to Blackpool it seems odd that Gillian admits to being there with Viv, as does Julie? The Gary Ward Blackpool Beach Murder is considered when Julie is asked if Viv ever took her to Blackpool? "Yeah, it was before he went to prison in about the March or May of 1989 and that was supposed to be a new beginning and we were sitting in a pub called the Manchester bar.

He had said, 'Whatever happens in the future doesn't count, doesn't matter.' I said, 'What are you talking about?' Because I had a few halves and he didn't drink and I asked, 'What are you talking about?' He again said, 'Whatever happens in the future doesn't count, this is a new beginning from today,' and he would go on like that. I was going, 'Yeah, yeah, yeah, right.' Little did I know at that time that he had been with Gill and obviously she was pregnant and he didn't have the bottle to tell me.

I didn't have a clue and then I think we fell out in the September for a while and he was going away on holiday. He said he was going away on business and we ended up having a big huge fight and he went.

My friend was there and she had seen it all. He was on the phone to her from the airport and whinging on and then he was ringing me saying that he had made a mistake and this and the other and he came back. It was just before my birthday, in the September, he was sitting in front of the house, looking up; I was in a different house then. I looked out and thought, 'What's the matter with him?'

Because he used to come up and confess, I didn't want to hear things. He had come to confess; he said he had actually been away with Anna. I went off it, but that was another time. It took him about two hours to tell me it all. I said, 'Just tell me!' He said, 'No, because you'll leave me, tell me you wont leave me?' He wanted me to swear on my bairn's life that I wouldn't leave him. I said, 'Come on, you obviously have something to tell me?' He said, 'You've already just said her name!' I had just said, 'Anna,' and he went, 'Yeah.' I flipped!

Then a couple of days later, it was my birthday and it was crawly, crawly time. I went out on my birthday and he was locked up the same night, on September the 29th. He was actually locked up after twelve that night because we had been out; he dropped me off, went to work and was locked up from there.

Then in December, he hit me with the news that 'Gill had a baby.' Prison visits are about twenty minutes, half an hour or something. I think I made a lot of enemies at that particular time. People would come on the visit with me and I didn't want them on the visit because I needed to know what, where, who, why, how and everything. I think I was nasty to one or two people and after that I stopped going. I said, 'That was it!' I wasn't getting anywhere, I phoned Rob Armstrong's wife and I said, 'Will you tell Viv I won't be back, we're finished,' and she went, 'OK.'

I literally moved house and everything, but then he started to phone. When I went back he had said that Anna had been visiting and he told her that he wanted me to come back in to see him. By this time it was about March. I had stopped going for weeks and weeks, I used to go about four and five times a week. I know his dad used to go on a

Thursday and I would go most other times."

Looking at what Julie says, it is quite clear that Viv was replacing the loss of Anna on the prison visits with Julie as a reserve, as Anna said she had walked out on a visit, leaving Viv with the engagement ring. Viv threatened to smash the prison down! Obviously Viv had a rethink and convinced Julie enough to come back in.

Anna says of Viv's second child to Julie, "Viv always believed that this man was the father of the child to Julie because he had assumed that his associate who he used to train with had accepted responsibility for the child that Viv had denied was his. Viv never seen his daughter (his first child to Julie), but I always gave Alan Rooney money and presents to take up for her.'

Julie: "Well I've got a twelve year old daughter who can be asked if she ever seen her dad, of course she seen her dad. If Anna knew Viv then how could she possibly be certain of what she says? Alan Rooney bringing me presents and money for my daughter from Anna is not true."

Anna: "I always sent Julie things, even Gillian Lowes, whether it was Mother's Day or even Christmas Day. Whoever you get to speak to you will tell you, if you ever speak to Rob Armstrong he'll tell you."

Julie: "Tell you what? Well I don't know where she was sending these things to, but she wasn't sending them here. Do you think I would accept presents and gifts from Viv's girlfriend? No thank you, I don't think so!"

Sheer coincidence meant that both Julie and Gillian were attending a solicitor's appointment in connection with the estate of Viv; they briefly spoke with each other. Julie could not sit comfortably with some things that she heard Gillian relate to her and she needed to put her side of the story.

Anna Connelly stated that for Julie to become pregnant by Viv she would have had to have had sex with him on a prison visit, for that to be his child (Julie's second child to Viv), whilst he was serving his three years for his part in the assault on fellow club doorman Stuart Watson. Julie said, "It's true," she did have sex with Viv whilst on a prison visit and conceived their second child, Callum!

Anna claimed, in a seething allegation, that Viv knew Julie was seeing someone else, "…it wasn't a thing that bothered me, I said to him 'You did have sex with her and it could be.' (Meaning Viv's child.) Julie retorted to this allegation by Anna saying, "She's lying on that! I had never to go out, never mind seeing any other man."

Anna: "It wasn't a thing that bothered me because I hadn't been visiting him and he said, 'Nah!' For some reason he didn't think it was his child, he knew Julie was seeing another lad, Viv used to say to her 'You want to get your maintenance paid for that bairn.' Viv felt the real father was a man he used to train with in a gym who gave Julie a lift to prison to see him. Viv fell out with that man and went to train in another gym."

Julie: "Rubbish, the man was Viv's very good friend. There used to be two guys, one used to take me up to see Viv, but he used to aggravate things because Viv was very, very jealous and he used to say stupid things to wind him up. Anything would wind Viv up, 'I saw her knickers when she was getting into the car,' and that was it! So Viv had said, 'I don't want him to bring you in anymore,' because he was a wind-up and other reasons.

Viv had this other man bring me in, as he had Viv's car at times. I know that Viv had been told that the car had been seen outside of my door at six o'clock in the morning, which was a load of rubbish as this man was petrified of Viv. The man that Viv's friend had said was at my house whilst Viv was in prison wouldn't even look at me from across the road. Who in their right mind would? Who would do it? Would I do it? Be stupid enough to get pregnant by somebody else and face the wrath? No! I don't think so, that's silly," says Julie, as her voice dries up with emotion.

Julie mentioned facing the 'wrath' so it was put to her that Viv was assumed to be a gentleman and if it was the case… "I would have emigrated, I wouldn't have done it." It is again put to Julie that surely Viv would not have been as nasty with her as she was suggesting he could be, especially if he thought she was pregnant to someone else? "I think it would be a different kettle of fish if I had of told him that I was going with somebody behind his back! Viv was a very, very jealous and possessive man. I don't think he would have took it lightly, I don't think so.

I didn't understand why he wasn't at Viv's funeral? Somebody had said they had a fall out, why did they fall out? I've never seen this man from visiting prison and I still don't know why they fell out.

When Viv said, 'You want to get your maintenance paid for that bairn.' He would say that! In a joking manner." What if someone else had said that, would Viv have accepted that as a joke then? "If somebody had went in and told Viv that I was going with somebody else…" Julie has difficulty accepting this scenario and says, "No, no, it's too stupid for words, nah!"

When Gillian Lowes had been engaged to Viv, everything was fine until she discovered he was seeing Julie Rutherford and she then gave Viv his engagement ring back. This scenario is uncannily like the one in which his last fiancée, Anna Connelly, allegedly gave him his engagement ring back on a prison visit after she discovered Viv was seeing Gillian behind her back and that he was the father of her latest child.

This so much incensed Anna that she walked out of the visit and did not go back, in fact it was Viv who went cap in hand, so to speak, back to Anna to beg her forgiveness and dedicate himself to being loyal to her (once more).

Anna says of this, "Eventually I caught him out when he went to jail and one of the other two, Gillian Lowes, was pregnant. By this time we had just got engaged and just come back from our holiday. I had found out when she (Gillian) had come to jail to visit and someone I knew had seen her on that visit and they told me she was pregnant.

I pulled Viv and said that Gillian was pregnant and Viv told me that she had got herself a man. He still wouldn't say it was he until I found out. I went to the jail and gave him the engagement ring back and I told him, 'That was it!' He pleaded with me to listen, 'Please listen to me! I'll tell you the story!' I said, 'No way.' He said, 'You walk out of this jail and I'll smash this jail up!!' I said, 'You best smash this jail up because I'm away!' And I went. I got a letter sent from his mam to say that he had been full of drink that night (the cause of Gillian Lowes becoming pregnant).

(Author's note: Anna says she gave Viv the engagement ring back, yet Anna says they got engaged when Viv came out of prison on Mother's Day. Maybe they became re-engaged? See further on!)

I never went to the jail to visit him, but Gillian Lowes and Julie Rutherford had been to visit him. Julie already had one child to Viv and she claimed a second to be his, which meant she had to have had sex with him on a visit for that to be his child. Viv loved his children and I think that if he thought that had been one of his children he would have accepted it as his, but for some reason he wouldn't have that. I said to him, 'But you did have sex with her and it could be?'

After he come out of the jail he came to me and said, 'Will you come back to me?' He had sent me letters and cards and that. I said to Viv that he was a single man and he could do whatever he wanted and to go with Gillian or to go with Julie and whomever he wanted, but he didn't want this, he wanted me.

We were going to get married and we got engaged on Mother's Day. I said, if he came back that would have to be the finish with Julie and Gillian and he couldn't have the one night away here and there because that's not what I wanted neither. I wanted a proper relationship. He loved my children and they loved him."

Right up until the day Viv died he was sneaking off into the arms of Gillian Lowes. Gillian said that Viv did not keep anything from her and obviously this then meant that while she and Viv were having their secret meetings continuously right up until the day he died that she knew of Anna's position in all of this.

At the time of Viv's spell in prison, Gillian and his family were all friendly way back then and acted like a family by visiting him as a group. Julie, though, stopped visiting and so had Anna, which just left Gillian to receive Viv's attentions! Gillian is recalled to have laughed at the memory of her being the only woman out of the three that had visited Viv who was left.

During Viv's imprisonment she had given birth to young Viv and a number of people connected to Viv had called at the hospital to see the newborn baby. A man close to Viv at that time, 'Dodgy' Ray, took some photographs into prison so as Viv could see his newborn son.

Gillian knew of Anna Connelly and Julie Rutherford's existence, yet she still continued seeing Viv intimately! Anna had thought that Viv was only calling to see the children when in fact he was sneaking to see Gillian! Both Anna and Julie did not know that Viv was still seeing Gillian behind both of their backs!

Gillian asked Viv why he did not want to live with her and the children. Viv put her off by telling her to wait until everything was finished. He used the excuse that the children or her could get hurt, but in reality he was living in Newcastle with Anna and her two children, so that argument goes out of the window as there was more chance of something happening in Newcastle than in a little Village with only one main road leading into it. It sounds like Viv was stringing Gillian along in his classic *keep them hanging on and pregnant* approach.

When it was put to Julie that Viv begged to be taken back by Anna she says, "I've heard it all before. I've heard the same lines when I was pregnant and Viv liked getting you pregnant, but he didn't like having the responsibility of the pregnancy, certainly not. I threw him out actually when he went back to Anna." Julie repeats this whilst exhaling and this gives her a voice a husky quiet sound, "I threw him out right.

We had a fight because my house was nearly burgled and it was because he was late, so of course I went off in a tantrum and ended up falling out. He came back the next day and he got the alarm fitted and then obviously he went back over to Anna's and came back weeks later, but then I wasn't interested, but it was all right because I was safely pregnant and you were safe for nine months. Nobody is going to fancy you in nine months."

Did Viv feel that after the pregnancy he could return to Julie? "He came back, yeah. You are his possession, YOU ARE HIS POSSESSION, you're right! That's exactly what you are, until he says different. He didn't want to lose anybody, he didn't want to lose Anna and he didn't want to lose Gillian and he didn't want to lose me!"

Viv was reasonably honest with Gillian, but how honest was he with Julie? "He wouldn't have dared! He was obviously open with Gill, but not with me, no! Obviously I knew that he was living with Anna. He used to come and confess, but that was after I had Callum.

He was Anna's, because she could have him as far as I was concerned, but it doesn't stop you loving him. And I loved him and I still love the man, but I hated him at the same time. I knew for a fact that he was living with Anna then, but it didn't stop him from coming here."

So Viv had not ever made a decision whereby he said, 'I'm going to live with Anna'? Julie: "Not likely! He had every excuse in the book." It was explained that Anna said Viv had no time at all to be able to have these trysts with you or Gillian? Julie: "If she could keep an eye on him then she's a better woman then I am."

As far as Anna was concerned Viv did not have the time for such flings, as he was always on the mobile telephone speaking to her. He would be back from wherever within a short time and he would bring Anna her cigarettes in because he did not like her going to the shop for them. Julie: "I wasn't allowed to go to the ice cream van." Julie says this with the tones of someone being told off for something they hadn't quite done wrong.

Was Viv frightened that Julie would run off with another man? "I don't know, I just know he knew I wouldn't do it. Viv was dead for some time before I considered going out again. He was definitely insecure within.

There was one night I went out and he was here eight o'clock in the morning! My female friend and I had been out and we were lying in bed laughing and carrying on when he opened the door. He was just standing there because he knew I had been out the night before, which was when he was with Anna. Anna was, like, saying, 'He's my sole property.' Anna is silly because she knows that's not true. IT'S NOT TRUE!

There was a mutual friend of ours and he used to phone every day even when Viv and I weren't speaking. He phoned her every single day. It came to the stage where I stopped going to her house until after he died because she told him everything, what I had on, where I was going and everything."

Viv's affair with Julie resulted in two children. Gillian said that DNA tests were being carried to ensure the second child Viv had with Julie was his and that Viv's parents were not co-operating with this as Julie's solicitor had contacted Viv's parents' solicitor. Gillian gave the history behind Jodie Annie's name; Viv's child to Julie, the name is that of Viv's grandmother.

(Author's note: Since this wrangle over DNA tests it has been accepted that Viv is the father of Julie's two children.)

Gillian went on about how she had babysat Jodie Annie and that she was all right but she was pleased to carry that out only occasionally.

Queen of the Castle seems to be where Viv put all the women in his life and if the worse came to the worse he put them in the tower, metaphorically speaking that is. By making them pregnant he made them less attractive to other men and thus he could devote his time to others in his life.

Gillian felt on cloud nine by knowing all of his intimate

secrets that none of the other two women knew and obviously this made Viv more attractive to her in the fact that their relationship was clandestine.

Viv was asked not to lie to Gillian and his favourite saying to Gillian that most of the other women fell for was that he felt relaxed in their company and that their home was like a sanctuary, but that sanctuary only lasted for a short while! Viv's watch was his master and time made him hurry to his next appointment. He would say, 'I've got to fly now, bye.'

Gillian accepted that she was one of Viv's harem and she went along with all what he demanded of her. Gillian went on to cover the fact that Viv had hurried off more quickly for the bookies than anything else, but he always telephoned her and he was never off the phone, calling at all times of the day and night. (Obviously checking on her whereabouts?)

As for Gillian going out, she would disappear and then return to find Viv had been on the telephone demanding to know where she had been and why she was not back home by eleven!

Viv would be at Anna or Julie's home and it would not be wise for Gillian to call him, as it would cause problems. Gillian had somehow turned from being a childhood sweetheart, in which Viv acquired her because of a £5 bet with a fellow pupil that he would kiss her, to her now being the other woman in his life.

Somehow, though, Gillian was not going to lose her grip on Viv and it would have been easy for her to let him go and make of her life what she could, but it did not turn out that way. She wanted him regardless of his lifestyle and his commitment to other women in his life. Somehow Gillian had changed from being Viv's first choice to being second best.

Gillian Lowes

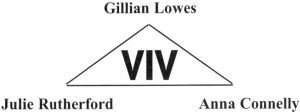

Julie Rutherford   **Anna Connelly**

Viv Graham & Lee Duffy's Parallel Lives

Anna's Connelly had claimed that Viv had not made any allowance for Julie's children when he died because he had assumed that his associate, who he used to train with, had accepted responsibility for the child that Viv denied was his. Julie: "Load of rubbish, load of rubbish, that's maybe what he told her." Why then was Viv in a state of denial about this child? Julie: "He just told you what you wanted to hear, he was the same with me. I'm not saying it's the coward's way out; he just didn't answer you, he just didn't like to hurt your feelings. If that got him away with it then he would say it. If Viv had of admitted that he was the father of our second child then Anna would have had a fit, wouldn't she? That's probably what he thought anyway."

Was Julie and Viv's relationship over with after she had Callum? "Well, it was over for that time, but it was on and off all the time. That would be it for a couple of weeks then he came back in about the March and I was getting ready to go out and I didn't really see him much after that, but I used to keep in contact with him and he would call occasionally.

He had paid for me to go on holiday, Primrose Valley, the four of us (Julie and her three children) in a caravan. I have an older son and two little ones and I went off with my cousin and I never heard from him until the Christmas. Viv had sent the money for us in 1993. He phoned me from hospital (abscess occurrence), I had never been on holiday with the little ones, he asked where I was going? 'Caravan.' 'Yeah, that's OK.' So he sent me some money over via taxi. When I come back that was it, I never rang him, if he wanted me then he knew where I was.

Then he sent Robbie Warton at Christmas. He was gone in December; I had not been seen going out with him in the last two years of his life as he said, 'It was too dangerous, you wouldn't believe the lifestyle I've got now, Julie?'

He came here and it seemed he had the world on his shoulders. He knew it was his sanctuary and he knew he was safe." It is mentioned that Gillian was told the same thing from Viv that he was feared for her safety, yet Viv was living

132

just about in the heart of Newcastle with Anna!

If he felt threatened then what made him stay in such a place that made him more vulnerable with his fiancée and her two children? He had warned Gillian and Julie of the dangers that his life now carried, therefore it did not make sense that he should want to stay living somewhere that would cause harm to those he loved. Conjecture in this matter throws up a few answers, one might be that he used this point as an excuse to keep Julie and Gillian hanging on a thread for whenever he wanted them, thus he could have his cake and eat it, so to speak.

Julie quotes directly from one of the many letters that Viv wrote to her whilst he was serving his three-year prison sentence. He said the only way he would get out of it was if he was shot. "But it might just have been an excuse," says Julie, "...as the man was full of excuses. The last two years of his life were totally different to the time we spent together, totally different.

The exact words Viv wrote down are: *The job I do, you don't know when the fuck you could be killed...Julie, from what you've heard today you will see I live a dangerous life the only way I can get beat is by getting shot.* That was letter number 134 written on 11th June 1990. This is what he wrote when he was in prison, but his life was different when he left prison. The last two years I don't know what happened?

Yes, I know people used him, they always did though, he was too nice. Viv's father said they used Viv as a moneybox, that's exactly what they have done."

Did any of Viv's supposed friends ever give Julie any support? "Oh yes, they've asked, 'How are you?' 'Fine.' I made a lot of enemies when Viv was in prison, they used to think things. This friend of Viv's has a lot to answer for as far as I'm concerned. He used to say to Viv, 'She's working herself again!' I used to get letters from Viv and he would say, 'I don't want anybody but you to come in,' that included his friends. He would say, 'I love my friends, but

I'll see them when I get out.' That is the way Viv was, his friend would say, 'It's her!' And so, I was the villain of the peace."

Was this man's friendship with Viv under threat? Julie: "Definitely. I was the scarlet woman by the sounds of it. I think he did the same to Viv's dad. Viv had said that I couldn't put right the damage caused where his dad was concerned. I would say, 'What are you talking about?' I don't know what he said. I hadn't ever spoken with Viv's dad. I was a threat to this man. He wanted to be the closest to Viv."

Somehow this man and Viv had a falling out? Julie: "Well exactly, I had said that to Viv's dad at the funeral. I said, 'Wouldn't you have thought that after what he had done to you that you would realise the things he had said about me were lies?' He would Say, 'I know, I know.'

My one and only concern is my son and what people have said about him. Viv just wasn't the same guy. He used to always be happy go lucky and couldn't give a monkey's. He didn't and wouldn't involve me in his private life. I didn't open the door to the press I was just put down as Viv's secret love and I just let them get on with it. They had my name down as 'Coffell' in the papers. I let them get on with it, I couldn't care a less what they said, I wasn't reacting so I thought, 'dead end.' Anna had made me react to this because of what she had said about my children."

Anna alleged that Alan Rooney brought presents from Anna because he had at that time lived nearby to Julie. Julie: "He brought the little one's car, a 'Noddy' car and he fixed it up. It was his birthday or something; Robbie Warton brought a big tractor and a couple of buggies, it was when Viv was banned from driving. Viv would phone and say he was sending them over; they never came when he didn't tell them to. Viv did not like me to have money; he thought if I had money I would go out. If we weren't speaking then he would not give me money.

When I first met Viv it was in Finnigan's bar, at Felling,

in Gateshead. Viv actually nipped my derrière; he wasn't as suave as people would believe. He wore a pair of crimpelene trousers and a flyaway collar shirt, but he had the charm and he had the smile. Apart from that fact he had a lovely bum, he nipped mine so I had a little bit more to drink and then I nipped his. Apparently he was with his girlfriend, Gill, and she had seen it and it had caused an argument, that's what I remember from it and from then on that was it. We were an item for years and years as far as I was concerned until he was murdered."

Anna Connelly says, "Viv was an organised and neat person he would even get the vacuum cleaner out. He wasn't a very good cook though, but he could do egg and chips. If I wasn't very well and he made a meal it was egg & chips. If we went to his mam's she always had a dinner on the go, one for each of us, she knew I wasn't a very good cook.

Viv could be timed he would take my children to their school and then he would leave time so that his children would be in the playground at their school in Rowlands Gill for, say, eleven o'clock. He would visit his children in the school playground for five minutes and then go straight to his mam's. (So she thought!) I could time him. Because after he had died it was suggested that he had been seeing Gillian behind my back. I don't know where he got the time from because he was never off the phone to me, ringing me from his mobile telephone soon as he got to his mother's. If I needed cigarettes he would say, 'I'll be there in ten minutes. I'll get you them.'

I couldn't go to the shops. I couldn't go and visit friends, they had to come and visit me. That was the only bad thing about him, the jealousy. That wouldn't have happened if we didn't go out and had stayed in. Sometimes I would think, 'Instead of going out, just stay in.'

I don't mean every time when we went out, it just depended on what I wore. I dropped the short things and went into long dresses after that. I could never go out with the girls and because of that he couldn't go out with the boys either.

If he said, 'Can I go out with the lads?' I would say, 'All right, but can I go out with my sisters?' He would say, 'No!' I would say, 'Well, you're not going then.' He was over the moon and would then say to them, 'She'll not let me go out.' He wouldn't let me go so I wouldn't let him go. His friends would twist their faces. People used to say, 'Wherever you see Viv you see Anna, he never leaves Anna, the two of them are constantly together.' If I went to the toilet he would wait outside the toilet door, everybody knew that. People used to say, 'He's outside the toilets? Oh, Anna must be at the toilet.' If I was in any longer than five minutes he used to open the door and shout, 'Anna! What are you doing, who are you talking to?' He didn't like that! He used to say, 'What were you talking about?' I would say, 'What do you think I'm going to do? You know how much I love you, I'm never ever going to leave you, we're so, so, happy. So why is it that you act like that?'

I used to think that because maybe he had been sly with me by going with them (Gillian Lowes, Julie Rutherford and others) and telling me lies and then when he was sent to jail and came out he knew I had never ever been with anyone. I've never been with anyone since the day he died or ever lived with anybody, so he knew what type of person I was. So I thought, 'Maybe he thinks I'm going to do back to him what he did to me and this is his insecurity with me.'

He said to me, when I gave him the ring back on the prison visit, 'You'll love somebody else.' I said, 'That's one thing I'm not going to do, go with somebody just to pay you back for what you've done to me. That's just not my style.' I wouldn't do that, get a man and think, 'Well, he'll be sick for what he's done to me.' So he knew I wouldn't do that. I think he had this insecurity where he thought I would like to do back to him what he did to me, that's what I thought anyway.

Julie Rutherford, among others, has also contested Viv's

estate. Viv hadn't bothered making any allowance about Julie because he had assumed that his associate who he used to train with had accepted responsibility for the child Viv denied was his. Viv always believed that this man was the father of a child to Julie because he gave her lifts to prison to visit Viv.

It was sad, because Viv never seen his daughter, but I always gave Alan Rooney money and presents to take up for her. (Alan lived nearby to Julie.) Even Gillian Lowes, whether it was Mothers Day or even Christmas. I used to pick the kids clothes and send them to them and pretend they were from their mothers' for their birthdays.

(Author's note: Any doubts as to the paternity of Viv relating to Jodie Annie and Callum Vivien, the children of Julie Rutherford, have been settled. Viv Graham is their father and all claims to the contrary have been quashed.)

Dead Money

When Viv passed away, all seemed done and dusted when it came to his insurance polices paying out to the bereaved family... We all know what insurance companies are like, they bury your money and sit on it and when it comes to paying it back out they have every excuse under the sun! In the case of Lee Duffy, he did not even have the most basic of insurance cover, yet Viv had more foresight and relied on his 'canny' instincts by securing a total of £150,000 worth of cover.

But if money grabbing insurance companies are bad enough then it was an even worse scene when it came to the fight that was on to lever the money out of the insurance companies in question! Viv's death, the insurance company said, was "self-inflicted."

Viv's father, Jack said, "If the insurance pays this other money out then how can they not pay me out. If the insurance company says something's not right then nobody should get paid out, although I don't begrudge the grandbairns their money. They should either pay everything or nowt out."

"The next legal friends have applied for a grant for the children, but Anna has not had anything" says Viv's mother, Hazel. She finishes off by saying, "I mean, he lived there." The situation must be terrible for Jack and Hazel being in the middle of it all while those around them are fighting for the money. It is not a case of the state helping Jack and Hazel fight for their rightful share. They have paid out considerable legal fees that they can little afford.

Jack: "They took his bloody money and the lads that made it all out who signed the forms and all that, they were the people that gave him the thing and everything. They signed forms to say they knew everything he was doing. He's got payslips and tax forms to say he was working. I'm just sorry for the situation, the way it has went, because if Viv had said, 'Mind, that house is for the two bairns,' then I would have said so, but he didn't say that. I would not betray the trust of my son and what he wanted.

He said she (Anna) had to have the house and the two bairns had to have the money. I know he didn't make a will, but it's what he said. That's what my son wanted and that's what my son will get, if I get my way. Viv was like a father to Anna's two bairns."

Hazel has a copy of the paperwork that Viv signed and annotated for the insurance side of things. The insurance policy, that Viv wished his mother and father to receive a payout from should anything happen to him, was valued at £60,000. Viv had signed a hand written authorisation on the insurance proposal form: *Along with parents I would like to share out along with my two children.*

It meant that this particular policy was to be shared between his two sons to Gillian and his parents. That could mean a number of things: 50/50, half to each pair or 1/3 to each of his sons and the third share going to his parents. Statements were supplied from: Rob Armstrong, Joe Blackey and two others. The three who worked for the company have all since left.

Viv had signed the following statement for this particular insurance policy in question: *I would like my children to have a good start in life and I would also like to have my money instead of wasting it. I would like to leave £20,000 to my parents and £40,000 for my children.*

The insurance company in question, Providence Capitol (formerly Old Mutual), immediately withdrew insurance cover for one of those who made a statement against them – Rob Armstrong. This was covered in more detail whereby a letter was sent to the insurance company concerned with the permission of the Graham's and a meeting with Tim Gray of Sinton and Co Solicitors representing the interests of the

Graham's allowed media representation on this matter.

There are other outstanding payouts on other policies that are part of the legal argument. Jack: "All these doormen in the town, any town, that means any of them getting murdered, then all of their insurance policies would be void." Hazel: "They have paid two small ones out as far as I know. Anna paid her mortgage for months and months and it is a good job she had a big family. The house was full every night. We still have a talk on the phone (Anna)."

Anna Connelly: "Gillian Lowes contested it, she had checked out to see that my name wasn't on the mortgage. The reason for that was because of our lifestyles and that Viv had got a letter from the solicitor asking us to come in and get it signed because the people who owned the house wanted it signed over.

I kept the letters and even the solicitor was sick of writing letters and at that time Viv didn't have his driving licence and that was when Alan Rooney was driving for him. I said, 'Go to the solicitors, and get this signed, with Alan.' He said, 'It had better be the two of us, both our names?' I said, 'No, just put your name, as long as it's signed.'

That is honestly and truly the way it was, I didn't think for one minute if he had left me for somebody else that I would not have still had this home. I knew what type of person he was, he wouldn't have went, 'That house is mine, you get out with your two kids.' That wasn't Viv. I didn't think at that time, 'Oh! I better get my name on it before Viv dies or something happens,' so when she (Gillian) contested it, I just couldn't believe it.

She wanted my house, so what she decided to do was pal up with Julie Rutherford because she must have thought, 'If there's two of us up against her we'll definitely get it off her.' It didn't matter if there was fifty of them against me, they both hated each other and they made friends, got the same solicitor to fight me, but since then I don't know if they are still friends, I think they fell out. She knew how kind I was to her and she knew Viv was here. She knew Viv would have

140

wanted me to have our family home."

Julie: "I didn't hate Gillian as Anna claims. I don't hate anybody, I didn't know the woman. Gillian might have hated me, I mean fair enough, but I DON'T HATE PEOPLE. Then again Viv told me that they hated each other (Anna and Gillian) and that she (Anna) hated me and obviously she has because she's given me all this grief."

Anna had said that Julie and Gillian had decided to pal up with each other. Julie: "We didn't do anything of the kind." She (Anna) could not believe it when 'Julie and Anna contested' and wanted her house.

Julie: "Robbie Warton came knocking on my door a few months after it, maybe weeks, because there was no talk of any solicitors, no talk at all and he had said, 'I've been told to tell you that you have to get a solicitor.' I said 'For what?' He replied, 'Because Gill is trying to take everything including the house.' I had no contact with Gill at that time and I didn't really know what was going on and he had said, 'Just get a solicitor!'

Also, believe it or not, from a very strange source, which I was told came from an area west of Gateshead. I didn't believe the man because I thought, 'This is him giving me advice and pretending it's come from up there.' The advice was to get a solicitor and this was within a matter of weeks from my first being told.

So I said, 'Right! What the hell's going on.' So I got my friend and I asked her to ring Gill and ask her if she'd got a solicitor and she had said to this woman, 'No I haven't.' So my family had said something's going on so 'go anyway' (to a solicitor). And here I discovered that some lies had been told whereby Gillian had said she did not have a solicitor.

When I went to a solicitor they said that she (Gillian) did have (a solicitor). So I thought, 'Well what's she lying for?' And then the funeral actually came around and they came and introduced themselves they were very nice to Jodie. They took Jodie to the grave, they took her forward and I was with my family at the back of the church in the seats and I was actually talking to Gillian's dad and I said to Gillian, 'You told me you didn't have a solicitor?' She went, 'Well I didn't know where you were coming from. I didn't know how to react to you because we had not ever spoken before.' That was the first time I was introduced to her, she came up and introduced herself."

Jodie Annie has met her grandparents; did she stay with them from time to time? "Yes, she had been to see them through the day but she had not stayed with them overnight." Obviously then, it was put to Julie, the grandparents accepted Jodie Annie as their granddaughter? "They also said this is my grandson,' because his mam (Viv's mam) on the day of the funeral went, 'I know. I know it's our Viv's, Callum Vivian Graham is his name.' What can you say to that?"

Julie is asked if it is right that property should be fought over? "If Anna wants a house then why doesn't she buy a house the same as what Gillian and I would have to do, it's his children we have to think about. Her children have got their father, our children haven't!"

Julie feels that her children should be compensated for the loss of their father and who is to argue with that. That is Julie's belief and it does not contradict any loving mother's feelings.

Anna expresses that neither Gillian nor Julie has had to put up with their windows being put in or that neither of them challenged Viv's killers and all the staring in the street and the fighting.

Julie: "I wonder why?" Anna says, "Why haven't they come across then and got Karen Young? They want the money..." Julie: "Sorry, who?"

It was explained that Karen Young was arrested on suspicion for having some involvement in the murder of Viv, but later she was exonerated from being involved. Julie: "The reason I..." Julie changes tack mid sentence, "...as far as I was concerned I was out of it and I hadn't spoken to Viv for three months."

Anna Connelly went on, "His mam and dad thought the

Dead Money

world of Gillian Lowes, they liked Gillian and had no reason
not to like her, even the dad (Viv's) couldn't believe it and he
said, 'Gillian, that was Anna's.' It was talked about at his
parents and with his brother and sister and Viv even said,
'...and David's (Anna's brother-in-law) lending me the
£12,000.'

His father knew he wasn't a saver, but when David said,
'I can lend you the money,' this thing that I told you that was
all going ahead. That was David's tax man money and he
had the money put away and David said, 'Viv, I'll lend you
this money, I'll lend you the deposit and you can pay it back
within six months because it's the tax man's money.' Viv
was getting £1,000 a week of this man with a bar in
Gateshead, he said, 'I'll just leave that for a few weeks until
it mounts up and I'll give you that money back in twelve
weeks.'

It wasn't written down on paper. He didn't know the
score over that, he wasn't going to say, 'I hope nothing happens!' I mean Viv's diamond ring was worth five grand, but
Viv had spent the money and David said, 'Here, I'll lend you
the money.' Viv did a job and maybe got ten and he gave
David the five grand straight back.

David did a lot of things like that but, Viv always told his
mother and father when he went up he said to his father, 'Oh,
I've got this diamond ring David's loaned me the money for
it and I'll pay it back next week.'

He was making more money by this time so he wanted
nice things, the dad and the mam knew that David had loaned
him £12,000. Lately it has been alleged that Gillian Lowes
said, 'There's no way David lent him (Viv) £12,000,' and she
wants to see it on paper. Why would she want to live in my
house that Viv and I lived in? So David's been to his
solicitor and had to pay £700 out of his money to get this
going and David's solicitor said, 'What's the proof?' David
didn't even have the money in the bank to prove he got it out
and David Says to his solicitor, 'Here, I'm not a liar, I'm not
gaining anything by saying I lent him that £12,000. I didn't

even want it back.'

David didn't want twelve grand off me, but when they (Gillian and Julie) started being horrible it was then that David said, 'What about the twelve grand? I want that back.' There was a bit of friction in the family, but all what Viv's dad ever wanted to do was to have Viv's wishes carried out. He said, 'My son said that house was for Anna and the insurance money was for the grandchildren so because he's not here I'm not going to change his wishes.'

He only wanted to stand by Viv's wishes he never went on my side and never went against anybody. He never went against his grandchildren for me or for them; he only wanted to do what his son's wishes were and what Viv had told him.

At the end of the day they want the money and they want this house. What about all the grief my family has suffered? What about my windows being blasted in with a gun and my two children? Have their families suffered? Their windows have never been blasted in with their children in the house. I've had to put up with it all and them coming to the door and all the staring and them fighting with my brothers, none of their brothers have suffered this or any of their sisters.

Why haven't they come across then and got Karen Young? They want the money, Gillian Lowes and Julie Rutherford; I confronted Karen Young and bided my time. They don't want to live here because they aren't from here, they want it up for sale and they want the eighty-five grand. The last time I saw Julie was when Viv got buried, her maiden name was Rutherford, then she was Coffel and I think she has another name now.

What happened was Julie Rutherford never knew about any type of insurance, but I didn't think it was fair because at the end of the day I didn't know if the second one was his? The girl was though and I thought, 'Well really she should get something because she was Viv's daughter and so was treat the same way as the two sons.' So I, Anna, dozy me, goes to my solicitor and said that I would get a loan for £40,000 as my house was paid for as it was worth £80,000.

Dead Money

Julie Rutherford knew and joined up with Gillian Lowes and they didn't even want that offer; they wanted the house!

There are solicitors and three barristers involved, the costs are all whittling away the insurance money, if it ever gets paid out?"

Like the King on a chessboard not being able to meet the other King face to face, a confrontation was to happen and all three of Viv's lovers were to meet at the funeral of the man they all professed to love. Julie met Gillian, as Gillian walked up to her and introduced herself. Julie was quick to raise the fact that Gillian had lied about getting the services of a solicitor to fight for the estate of Viv.

Anna and Gillian did not speak at the funeral, but both instinctively knew who the other one was. Gillian was asked if she thought everyone who was involved in the fight to get at Viv's insurance money would abide by what the court decided and her reply was, "Yes." But, if it did not go her way would she say 'No!'

Of course, as Gillian said, she is not losing anything as the fight can go on until the oldest child is eighteen, in another five years time. Since She has two parts of the jig-saw in the children, that are not being disputed as Viv's children, she stands to gain quite a bit and her father as legal next friend will have some say in the use of that money when it gets shared out. That is if there is any money left to share out.

This whole situation boils down to money and property. Julie says about Viv's lack of leaving a will, "Believe me, Viv used to do silly things to spite us and this was probably one of them."

Miss Lowes' father, John, was nominated as the legal 'next friend' of the child beneficiaries of the estate. This legal jargon simplified meant that Miss Lowes' father is the person fighting to get the money out of Viv's estate for the children of his daughter. Usually it is the mother who is nominated to this role if the father is dead, as in this case.

Mr and Mrs Graham did not have a very good relationship with Miss Lowes, as she has fought tooth and nail over the money locked away in insurance policies worth in excess of £150,000 plus the house that Anna Connelly is still living in with an estimated value of over £90,000, which gives a total of nearly £1/4million.

The gloves were off in this mammoth fight by the Lowes family to grab some of this wealth. Viv's father had said what Viv's wishes were and Miss Lowes went against this and brought in a legal team. Now both Gillian and her father are chipping away at the base of the money tree.

Miss Anna Connelly raised her concerns in the matter of her home being repossessed from her and her children who Viv accepted as his own and the children equally accepted Viv as their father. Miss Lowes made it known of her anger that Miss Connelly's children would have a roof over their head when in fact her children had to live in a council house.

What Miss Lowes has forgotten is that Viv's wishes were that her children should get a share of his insurance policy while Anna would get to keep his house for her and the children. That has been ignored here and the whole lot looks to have been thrown in to a pot where winner takes all in this real life game of roulette where everything at stake is gambled on one turn of the wheel of life. Gillian, along with her father will be happy with the outcome as long as the ball lands on her number and they scoop the loot.

A friend of Gillian Lowes, Tracy Paxton, offered her support to Gillian by saying, "They are Viv's children and should be provided for, Gillian is going to get nothing out of this. If they (the court) said tomorrow, 'Right, Dean Graham and Viv Jnr Graham get £100,000,' it's not going to help her. It's going to help them when they are older and they will benefit from it, not Gillian.

They should come first to be provided for, you've got Gillian and her family, you've got Julie and her family and you've got Anna and her family. The outcome was that Anna should get the house because Anna has had no money for her children, but Viv's own children, both his two children here and his other two to Julie, they are in council houses except

146

for Anna. The council provide these houses, they haven't been bought."

Gillian finalised what Tracy said by saying it was all right for Anna living in that house, but the fight was not over the house, as it was the newspapers that stirred it all up when they wrote about Anna's children having a home, but Viv's children not having a roof over their heads.

Gillian is placing a lot of faith in the judge who decides which family gets what. She tries to hide her feelings of disappointment that Anna is still in her home and she says that the fight is not over the home Anna and her children are living in right now.

Tracy goes on, "Anna has to claim the house and the money is to be split between Anna, Dean & Viv and Jodie Annie & Callum. Fair do's, if that's the judge's word then that's it, it's over, it's finished, but it's just a case of their solicitors working for them to get what they are entitled to, that's all it comes down to. To me there won't be any bitter feelings, none whatsoever." Tracy says this with a great big omission from her statement about who should get what on the other side of things.

It is obvious that she has lost sight of whom the money was actually to go to based on Viv's wishes. Viv's parents were in Viv's wishes; the children were in Viv's wishes for the money side of things and Anna having possession of the house was in Viv's wishes. Viv's father, Jack (Eric), has confirmed this.

There was not ever any mention of Anna being awarded any money nor is Anna interested in that side of things. That is the side of things that Tracy has lost touch with. Provision was made for Gillian's children, yet she is fighting for more and going against Viv's wishes.

The insurance policy valued at £150,000. Tracy, "Yes, yes, that's the house one." It seems that Tracy is in possession of quite a bit of knowledge about these affairs.

Gillian denied ever hearing of an offer that Anna had passed to her solicitor about the property.

Viv Graham & Lee Duffy's Parallel Lives

(Author's note: Since all of this within has been written, the insurance monies have been awarded and the estate of the late Viv Graham has been settled.)

Son, There's Always Someone Harder

Surely the other woman in a man's life can reveal more of his inner secrets than anyone else. Viv, though, was a hard man to read, he had so many little secrets about him that it would have taken a poker player to really read what was in his mind. Maybe Gillian Lowes, one of Viv's permanent three lovers, can reveal some of his inner secrets.

On the way back from Blackpool Viv spotted a jewellery shop where he picked a ring for Gillian. Gillian said she had previously been engaged to Viv and felt uncomfortable about which finger to put this ring on. Viv's comments were that he wanted them to become engaged again and to marry, but Gillian felt uncomfortable at this thought. She felt it was fine being his girlfriend and enjoying the odd holiday and so on but, that was as far as she wanted to take it.

Gillian explained how Dean, Viv's oldest son, had absolutely idolised his father, but when Viv was murdered he had to undergo private counselling sessions to come to terms with this terrible trauma that still continues to this day. As much as Dean idolised his father the same could be said of Viv idolising his father, Jack. Viv listened to advice and counsel from him. Gillian went on to tell of the struggle Viv had within himself in trying to get out of what he was doing, but he didn't know how and he wanted somebody to help him achieve this. Viv would often say, 'I wish someone could help.' Gillian told Viv to pack it all in, but he just could not find a way to get off the tiger's back! Remember, 'He who rides the tiger cannot dismount.'

A close friend of Gillian's, Tracy Paxton, says, "The day Viv died I think his father died and he's got to walk around with that for the rest of his life, they had a very strong bond."

Gillian relates how Viv would come back to the little community villages of Rowlands Gill and Highfield and have the odd drink in the local bars. People just accepted that he was Viv, one of the locals. But when Viv was back in Newcastle he was looked upon with awe. There seems to be a big difference in how Viv revelled in his newfound status in Newcastle compared to how he would use it if bumping into someone in the local bars of his home village. He liked that and he could be himself.

Fishing books were a fondness that Viv loved to read. He was a typical countryman who was at one with nature. A book about ferreting was passed on to Dean by Viv's father. Viv did not have the time to carry out his hobby of fishing because of his other commitments.

Tracy: "Do you think the type of person they made him out to be in the papers was an impossibility for the life that Viv was supposed to lead and still travel here to see Gillian seven days a week? To me that wouldn't even come into his lifestyle if that's the type of man he was supposed to be."

Gillian is rather coy when it is put to her if she has been asked out since the passing away of Viv, she does not really answer that with a 'yes' or 'no', just a 'not really.' The activities of Viv's children in the sporting sense are coming on fine and Dean is pursuing a number of sports including rugby, football and swimming.

Gillian says that Dean wants to be a policeman and he does not want to be a troublemaker. Tracy: "He wants a career, doesn't he. He doesn't want to follow his father's footsteps that way by going into boxing, he wants to branch out and make his own decisions. He's sticking in at school to try and do that as well."

Viv's involvement with Billy Robinson of Gateshead was said by Gillian to have started after Viv became a doorman at the Hedgefield in Ryton village when a friend phoned him to ask for his help because there was a bit of trouble in a pub at Gateshead. The trouble was not involving Billy Robinson or Paddy Leonard, but later on the two of them walked in to a

Son, There's Always Someone Harder

bar called Wheelers. Billy Robinson and Paddy Leonard walked in.

Gillian was sitting beside Viv and he sort of writhed a little bit, but he did not let that show to them and he stood his ground. From then on Viv and Billy got on like a house on fire.

Gillian blames the couple from the small village nearby of Burnopfield for sending Viv there and ultimately being responsible for his involvement in the club and pub scene that was to lead to his eventual death.

Viv's temperament was questioned and Gillian said that Viv was not easy to get angry and he had to be pushed to the limit before anything happened and he was really soft. Viv was heartbroken when Gillian kicked him out and he would not stop going back to her.

Part of Viv's stress, Gillian said, was caused by the fact that he had to be everywhere at once and there was just not enough hours in the day. He just wanted to keep everyone happy. Viv used to call in for a sandwich during the day when the boys were at school and then call to see them during their break time.

People from different parts, who were bigger and harder than Viv, wanted to have a go at him, but he did not want that. Viv was seen as a target for people who wanted to set up a fight between him and their man.

In fact one of the people lined up for Viv to fight was claimed to be Lenny McLean (*The Guv'nor*) from London, but Viv wanted to see him fight before he would take up the challenge. It is rumoured that Viv's father, Jackie, watched a video of McLean fighting and sternly warned Viv to steer clear of McLean.

It was also alleged that a man called Andy Winder from Darlington, who had moved on to time-share scams in Tenerife, had a fight with Viv. This was denied by Gillian, but she did say that later on it started to get really heavy for Viv and he did not know how to get out of it.

Gillian says that she and Rob Armstrong are close and he

calls to see how the children are doing. A story is told about how Rob went to see Viv after they had fallen out and he called at the house Viv had just bought when it was being done out. They had a heart to heart, but Gillian did not go into detail and she said Rob would explain it all. The reason for this fallout is thought to have been in connection with the Stuart Watson situation mentioned in a previous chapter. Viv and Rob had a fallout over certain matters…they healed their rift, but the friendship was never to be as strong as it had been.

One thing to come out of this is the strength of the bond that Viv had with his sons, Dean and Viv Jnr. Dean, in particular being the oldest, suffered the loss of his father the most. Viv used to tell Dean, as he sat him on his knee in the school playground, that there was always someone who was harder, bigger, stronger and faster than you and violence was not the answer.

The Grasshopper And The Squirrel

Eric and Hazel Graham are the parents of Viv. Eric prefers to be called Jack and from now on that is how he will be referred to. Asking to interview the parents of Viv was not an easy thing to do. Journalists had pursued them in the midst of their grief at all hours. There had been a big bust up as a direct consequence of the 'Cook Report', I was, after all, only another one of those investigative journalists to request a comment, who was I after all; there was no cut and dried way to get through the red tape. Promises would not get me anywhere, not that many people had kept their promises to the Graham Family. To talk to the parents of Viv would be a great honour.

It might sound like this chapter is dedicated to Viv. That is not the case, it is a dedication to the two people who brought their little baby into this world with all the hopes that nearly all parents have for their children. Everyone's little Johnny is going to play football for England, learn to play the piano, become a great painter and anything else they thought he was good at.

Viv's parents got to see their little Viv become big Viv. On the achievement side of things he made his parents proud, not just because of the boxing medals and cups he won or the football talent he possessed as a schoolboy, but because of his kind and gentle nature! If any parent can bring their child up with a kind and gentle nature then they have achieved something far more in excess of winning a World Cup winner's medal.

Jack and Hazel Graham achieved the success of being able to instil something into Viv that not many people could learn in two life times; manners. The old fashioned way of bringing up their son, Viv, and their other children has shown that the old qualities have not completely died out. Modern living, fast talking, fast food, while-U-wait services, processed in one hour, 24 hour supermarkets, all day drinking, 0906 premium rate numbers, express services, next day delivery, take now pay tomorrow, therapy sessions, pay to view channels and the like have, to some extent, killed off what was left of traditional upbringing.

Smaller communities can still impress the rest of us by showing the true grit style spirit. Viv would see his parents just about every day and who can blame him, when you read this chapter it will give a different perspective to how Viv is seen.

Surrounded by fields, Rowlands Gill could have been any rural area of England. There was one difference here though, and that was there was no snotty atmosphere of plastic card dwellers or curtain twitchers. This was a down to earth rural village council estate where just about everyone knows everyone; a working class 'Emmerdale.'

The initial atmosphere was strained, Karen, Viv's sister and her husband Martin were present in the living room, which was lit by a low wattage table lamp. Mrs Graham escorted us in, but there was one noticeable absentee, conspicuous by his absence, Viv's father. Jack Graham had not spoken with anyone about his son's death and sure as hell he did not want to talk to another interested party.

"Why do you want to ask these questions?" Mrs Graham asked as she was shown a question list of considerable size. It seemed they thought I was having an inquisition in to the secret background of Viv. I stated my case, I had been asked to write the story of it all, some two years after Viv's death, by an interested party, but at that time I felt it was too soon after Viv's death to delve into his past and to ask the questions I would be asking now.

As I was talking to Mrs Graham I heard ominous creaking's of the floorboards coming from an upstairs room. I had heard the floorboards creaking for the past few minutes and I could tell someone was walking around. That someone, of course, was Mr Graham. Jack Graham did not come down and I progressed with my point of view, when I heard the stairs creek, someone was coming down. Everybody just stopped talking and all eyes in the room were fixed on the living room door!

The silence within the room had created an expectancy that something was about to happen. Like when the camera zooms in on the bomb and holds for a few seconds, everyone expects it to blow up, but the bomb does not blow up and the suspense increases! It was as though everything had slowed down and things were moving in slow motion.

We were all sitting in this dimly lit room, the door opened and my pupils had dilated!! All what I could see was a magnified silhouette that seemed to fill the whole doorframe!

It was the eyes that I noticed at first, dark and powerful, a nod and a wink and you were shifted out of the way sort of thing. The light just caught the shaven head of Mr Graham. The darkness that came from behind him exaggerated every-thing, making it seem that he was looming larger than life.

What was I to do? I stood up and walked across with my hand gestured out in the handshake position. "How do you do, Mr Graham, sir, pleased to meet you?" The hand that met mine seemed to be twice as big as my own size eleven hand.

The ice was broken and the best interviewee I have interviewed throughout all of this took centre stage. Jack is a natural orator, but Hazel keeps him supported throughout the interview, which is an exclusive, as he has not spoken to anyone at length over this matter and I can understand why. Jack is a man's man and, although he has seen better years, he still has an aura of power, immense physical power! Even though he has suffered some illness, he is still a man to be reckoned with by virtue of his worldly-wise wisdom.

David Lancaster, Fish Tams & Sayers brothers: Jack is prompted into talking about the Hobo's incident where Viv was convicted of a vicious unprovoked assault. "Our Viv was at the court case, there was the two Sayers', Davie

Lancaster, Fish Tams and there was a sixth lad and they were looking for him. He was going into Durham jail every week visiting them. I don't know if somebody must have tumbled, but it was weeks after because they chased him, busies in their cars and they caught him outside of Durham. The QC for the prosecution, Williamson, and you know in a court when they keep having little recesses, he was standing there and his words were, 'I don't know what the effing (fucking) hell I'm wasting my time here for? A fight between two bloody doorman.' They were his exact words.

The busies had got the lot and fetched it in as an affray. If you seen the tape, from them going through the door to them coming out, it was only minutes. Three minutes, it took three minutes. Now then, there were two busies in Hobo's and they were on surveillance for drugs. They were from Tadcaster, they were Yorkshire busies; they weren't from here.

Stuart Watson: The policeman said he had never seen a fight like it in his ten years on the police force. He said that our Viv started on Stuey Watson, moved off, two attacked him kicking and punching, they come off and the other three went in kicking and punching.

So that's six blokes kicking and punching one man and if you look at the video, Stuey Watson comes out and he's hardly got a mark on him. How they can tell me…I mean six old pensioners should have put him in hospital. You've got six blokes kicking hell out of him. They said to the busy, 'Why didn't you show your warrant card?' They said, 'We were on surveillance.' They were asked, 'What would happen if a lass was getting raped, would you have just sat back and watched it, like?' Viv got three years for it in the end.

John Merry: There's another thing about your stinking journalists, John Merry. Sitting in Anna's on the Thursday night and the reason he was there, he said he was going to try and get a story together to see if he could sell it to the papers to put the money into the reward fund. He even threw £43 on the table, he said, 'Here, that's all I've got on me. Now listen, please don't approach the press and if you're approached by the press don't say a word because I'm going to get the best deal I can here.' On the Sunday morning, in the Sunday Sun, **£2m Drug Baron**, that was it. There was a photo that was stolen, the one where Anna is wearing that yellow dress the one that was in the papers, it's always in.

The thing is there's been that much written and said about Viv Graham, whatever happens to whoever or a friend of Viv Graham it's in the papers. I think the photos have stopped now because Dr Dawson got on about it. It's been four years, why can't the papers leave Viv alone."

To signify how the newspapers had got it wrong Jack says, "And I had to pay his car off. Me, like a silly bugger, had to go and put my name down." Jack says it is not so as to go against his son, but to show how that if his son, as was claimed, was making so much money from his alleged drug empire then why was he having to guarantee his son's car and now he had to take over the payments.

Hazel interjects, "The bailiffs came here twice to take furniture out for this car money owed. He said, 'There isn't sufficient in here to cover it so I'll just tell them you haven't got nothing.' He was brilliant."

In a way, Hazel was right, what could the bailiff have taken to cover the £000s that was still owed on Viv's Ford Sierra Cosworth? After all, this was a humble home, clean and comfortable with all the items needed to make life bearable, but with nothing that could repay such a debt. Any bailiff taking items out of Jack and Hazel's home would have to have a heart of stone.

It is asked what of Viv's friends, could they have helped out? Jack says, with a certain amount of anger in his voice that sums up his feelings about those who were the supposed friends of Viv, "I'll tell you, and you can put this in the bloody book as well, they weren't friends they were hangers on; he was a moneybox for them." Jack says this with conviction in his voice and is so sincere about what he says that this book and the writings within it cannot relay the sadness of the situation. You would have to hear the sincerity in Jack's voice to know what he says comes from his heart.

Jack continues with the same frame of mind when he says, with sadness in his voice, "And he was a minder for them! That's what he was." Jack is speaking for a lot of people when he says this, "When they were with Viv Graham they were ten foot tall! 'Oh, I know Viv Graham, good friend of mine,' so people would back off."

What Jack says is so important here because he says in a few words what others would be fearful of saying. I am pleased that Jack had the courage, which surely it took, to come down those stairs.

Jack strikes me as the type of person who would give you his last, the typical Geordie man from the past, hands as big as shovels and shoulders broad enough to carry the world on. Nothing could ever beat such a man, that was until his son was murdered in cold blood with the best part of his life ahead of him, how could any man bear such a loss, no matter how wide his shoulders are?

Showing open grief went against tradition for Northern men. It was not the done thing to be able to show their feelings; it was not the done thing to breakdown and cry because the man had to be the pillar of strength for his family to look up to. These men had to carry their grief in secret.

Jack relates an incident in which his son exercised his right as a private citizen to carry out some late night security work. "At the top end of the village, a lot of old people live and they were forever getting robbed. So he went up and sat in an old woman's house all night, sat in the chair all night, waiting, and nothing turned up.

So he went to a certain party and said, 'Look, if another one of those houses gets done I'm coming for you, even if you haven't done it I'm coming for you, I'm going to make a job of you, so spread the word, you're the one that's going to get it.' It stopped. Christmas, before he died, when he was shopping with Anna and an old lady wanted a turkey, he said to Anna, 'Keep her occupied.' He went into a butcher's shop and came back and said, 'There you are, mother, there's your Christmas dinner.' They don't know about them things and when he sponsored the footballers and the boxing, things like that."

Pip Wright: Everything what Jack says is said with sincerity and sentiment. Jack continues, "He gave a kid £500 the week before Christmas, he hadn't a penny, he couldn't get the kids anything for Christmas. Viv said, 'There's no kid should get up on Christmas morning without presents, give me it back when you've got it.' That's the way Viv was."

(Author's note: Pip Wright was the man who Viv gave the money to.)

Rob Bell & Peter Donnelly: Hazel: "He saved Rob Bell's life." Jack takes it up, "If Rob knew that we were here, he would…" And just as quick as he had started this sentence he moves fleetingly to another matter. "…Wor Viv bumped into him (Peter Donnelly) in the Fish Bar in the Green Market, he was crying to wor Viv saying, 'Di'vent hit me.' Viv said, 'I'm not going to hit you, don't worry.' (See next chapter.)

You see, the trouble is…" Jack takes a breath before saying the next part of his sentence as if it is releasing a great burden from him to be able to say this to someone, maybe for the first time, "…he couldn't be a bloody gangster at all, he was too soft.

You get these that lend you money and if you don't pay it, it's doubled and then a good thumping and then you get a leg broken the next time, he was too soft.

Mind, when he kicked off, if he had a fight, he could go, there's nobody ever done it yet…" Jack reminds himself of the present situation of his son's absence by saying; "…well they'll never do it now. He was hard, that way it was good, but the other way; he was as soft as claggy taffy (claggy toffee). He was as easy for a hard luck story…" Hazel adds, "He could cry like any other man." Jack continues, "…he was as soft as clarts that way."

Viv Graham & Lee Duffy's Parallel Lives

We talk some while about police corruption and what really went on within a certain situation, but alas legal reasons stop this being written within here, although it is logged and at the right time, if there ever is a one, it will be revealed.

Inspector Peter Durham: Jack talks of Inspector Peter Durham, "He tried all ways to get our Viv. When Viv came out of prison, they were following him in the car and taking photographs of him. They went around the town (Newcastle) and followed him all over and he just used to go, 'All right, lads,' but the surprising thing is, what a hell of a lot got on with him. From what I've heard, all the jumpy jacks are back in the town on the happy baccy and the stuff now and people won't go back in to the town. People are just petrified, where at one time you could go and sit and have a good night out with nothing to worry about."

Stephen Sayers: Hazel gives her account of meeting one of the Sayers family, "I met Stephen Sayers when our young Viv (their grandson) was poorly in hospital, he was a gentleman. I couldn't get over him; he was at the hospital at eight o'clock in the morning when I walked into the general. He said, 'I'm sorry I've met you under these circumstances.' Viv was still in prison and they'd let him out, so he come to see little Viv."

Jack clarifies how Stephen Sayers was out of prison before his son, "They got two years and our Viv got three. So they were out, but he was at the hospital to see the bairn. They were all friends then." I explain that Viv was used as their ammunition then so that they could say, 'Well, this is our guy.' Karen, Viv's sister, throws up something that says it more succinctly, "Using him as a minder."

After his prison sentence, Viv went his own way. Jack explains, "Wor Viv was always a loner though, I mean if somebody said, 'I'll fettle Viv Graham!' He would jump in the car and he would go to that place where this bloke had said what he was going to do, 'Where's so and so, I'm here?' 'He's not in.' 'Well I'll be back tomorrow night.' Where

160

they take teams now! He didn't need that sort of backup. He would go in and he'd never been to that place in his life and wouldn't know the bloke from Adam, he had no fear."

Manny Burgo: Viv got on with people and Manny Burgo is mentioned as an example, Jack says, "They had a fight (boxing as amateurs) and Viv braed bloody hell out of him, because his old man said to Viv, 'You did that to my son.' There were two of the judges sacked through that fight; they gave it to Manny Burgo because he was the English Amateur champion.

Viv never boxed for years and he was finished with the boxing, but he still had the fight with Manny. Viv had not fought for years, he won the Northern ABA championships in 1977, and he had three fights in the one night down South Shields to win it. He then went to Denmark to fight, he was in Liverpool and he got a frozen shoulder and he got beat. He just concentrated on weight training and running, but you know what happens once you start hanging about with lasses, training's out the window.

Jack mimics a woman speaking, "You think more of bloody football than you do of me." We all laugh! "You know what they are like. So he just pursued weight training."

Hazel says something very worthy of being mentioned, "He was never in trouble with the police as a teenager, never. He (Jack) used to say to Viv, 'Burgle anybody or rob them and me and you are finished,' you know." Jack confirms this, "I said if you ever come in here and have been doing a house or drugs, that's me and you done."

Jack is a down to earth guy and calls a spade a spade; Viv used to seek advice and looked up to his dad. Jack is the sort of man who speaks with a matter of fact manner and immediately puts you at ease with his baritone Geordie twang.

(Author's note: You may wonder, at the way Jack speaks, why I have not tidied his dialogue up? (As demanded of me by some of those interviewed in other chapters!) I prefer to read dialogue with regional dialects as opposed to the Queen's English. Hopefully this dialogue will lend itself to reflecting the northern atmosphere of England to our southern friends and others around the world.)

On the way Viv would seek advice from his father, Hazel says, "He used to come here on a Sunday morning after he'd been to the nightclub. We used to always have loads of company and he used to say to everybody, 'Right, I want to talk to my father, everybody out!' It didn't matter who was in."

Hazel continues, "In fact, when this came out about Viv, I didn't even know anything existed, we can't say." Jack helps out and is quite honest in what he says, "We didn't know half that went on, that was his business. He was a man for himself, you make your bed, you can lie in it. What ye de is your business, but as I say, drugging and out dodgy like that, I don't agree with, I've never agreed with it. As I say, he's a man for himself and we don't know half nor quarter of what he did or didn't do down there." (Newcastle)

Karen offers her support in this, "I always thought he had two separate lives because me and Martin started socialising with Anna and him. We started going to the town and nightclubbing, we used to get the feeling he didn't want us down there."

Martin takes up on what Karen says; "Obviously anything could kick off at anytime where he was, so obviously it was for our safety as well." Jack speaks with wisdom when he interjects with, "It's a different ball game doon the toon. They can buy you at one end of the street and sell you at the other end."

What about when Viv wanted to relax? Jack: "We used to go shooting at Haydon Bridge, everything just seemed to lift off him, I don't know how you explain it, but it was like waking up on a Sunday morning." Hazel: "He delivered a ferret, he sent it by taxi with a note! 'I love you dad, here's a present for you.' It was a live ferret! The poor man." (The taxi driver.) Jack tells of how Viv sent the ferret to him,

The Grasshopper And The Squirrel

"There were some kids knocking a ferret around the street and he gave them £2. He said, 'Here's £2, I'll buy that ferret off you.' He then said to the taxi driver, 'Here, take that, here's the address, give that to my father.' The brother-in-law's still got it yet. He sent it all the way from Wallsend."

Hazel confirms Viv's love of animals, "He always had hens, we've still got his two dogs here. We've got his Alsatian, Max, and the Labrador. I bought it in 1989 when he went inside. I had got him a pup." Jack adds, "She didn't know what to buy him, so I said, 'Why don't you get him a Labrador to go shooting?' I said, 'I know who'll have to look after it and to feed it.' But I didn't mind."

When he got Buster he also got the Alsatian. He said, 'I'll give the Alsatian to my father; I've still got the two down the garden. There were lads with pigeon lofts out the back and when he was young he used to get squealers, little 'uns, off the lads. He had about a dozen or more. We used to put them in a cardboard box and put them in the wagon and get away over to Whitehaven and I would let them out.

Viv would say that they had got back at such and such a time. They were just pets, eh man!" Jack is full of these sorts of nostalgic stories and I can picture all of the things he describes and the sentiment that is expressed in jack's voice, what pictures must have been flying through Jack's mind when he said 'eh man.'

Karen is Viv's younger sister and Eric, 42, is the older brother. Viv was a middle child, which might explain his caring ways. Jack talks of how he has an aversion to reporters and he says, "That fettled me with television and reporters when he did that on the Thursday night and on the Sunday morning I saw the headline, '£2m Drug Baron', I said they are not worth a bottle of pop. And then the Cook report, they tried to make wor Viv out as bad as them that done that manageress up in Manchester. I said it wouldn't have been as bad if that's what it was about, but it had nowt to do with security, protection, drugs, drinking it was just a sham. It made him look like…"

Viv Graham & Lee Duffy's Parallel Lives

The Cook Report: The trouble the 'Cook Report' caused for the Graham household is nobody's business. It is not for me to bandy about publicly the private arguments the Graham's have had with certain other people over the items raised in the 'Cook Report', but I will say it has a lot to answer for in terms of misrepresentation of people's opinions.

A Cook Report researcher telephoned Gillian Lowes asking her if there were any changes to her circumstances. They wanted to ascertain any new developments.

Had they known the trouble that was caused by their show, well...

Jack expresses his anger, "If I had been a stranger and I had seen that on television I would say, 'He must be a wicked pig, him!' People that didn't know Viv would say he was nasty, but it had nothing to do with the programme, but the buggers stuck it in about protection.

So when I seen the Cook Report and I knew that things were wrong within it, I then wondered how many more Cook Reports are wrong and have been twisted to make them look worse than what they are?

If I was walking along the Quayside and a little bairn fell in the Tyne and I dived in and got it out, there would be a little bit about that. But if I walked down the Quayside and picked a kid up and hoyed (threw) him in the river, there would be headlines this big," says Jackie while holding his hands feet apart.

"I mean, murder, rape and anything like that they make as gruesome as possible to sell papers."

(**Peter Connelly**: Author's note: A publican, Peter Connelly, said that a Cook Report researcher had called into a pub he had and said he wanted to put cameras in the corners of the bar. Peter asked 'why' and the researcher said, 'Because you're going to have some trouble in here.' Peter said 'Not in this bar I'm not'. He told them in no uncertain terms where they could where to go.

This stage-managed TV documentary seems to be based

on the Jerry Springer show. Hype and sensationalism create TV audiences and prime time TV is big money. No doubt Roger Cook has balls as big as King Kong's in respect of him having courage to pursue those that he was asked to, but his team are the ones that are responsible for putting him in these positions and ultimately he has been used as a means to them getting what they want, TV viewers.)

Paul Ashton & Billy Robinson: Jack is asked about Viv's apprenticeship days as a doorman. Jack: "He was as green as grass when he started at the Hedgefield."

Hazel disputes this and says, "It was in Burnopfield, the Travellers Rest."

Jack continues, "He started working in a number of pubs, as the person owned three, and he went through to Whitemare Pool (South Tyneside) and he ended up at Finnigan's bar in Gateshead. That was where Viv had the fight with Paul Ashton. The fight went on up the road for about twenty minutes.

They reckon Billy Robinson stepped back to see what wor Viv could perform like. He played with Ashy for twenty minutes around the car park and Ashy was shouting and bawling at him to stand still so he could hit him. Viv was just bop, bopping, he was like greased lightening.

Then he went to work at Wheelers, on the Gateshead side of the Tyne Bridge, just before you go over on the left-hand side; it's closed down now.

(Author's note: Wheelers has now been demolished to make way for new development near to Gateshead Quays.)

He was with Billy Robinson then. The problem was, Viv was from the sticks and the townies didn't like this. They would say, 'Where's he from?' 'WHAT!' A lot of them had the idea that no one was going to come in from the sticks and do anything to them sort of thing."

Jack is asked where the turning point came in the transition of 'Viv from the sticks' to 'Viv of the town'. Martin interjects to offer his view, "As things progressed, he just became more popular." Jack: "More and more tried to down him. He won, and he won and he got his name more known and more known in the pubs and the nightclubs. The more that had a go at him the more he beat. His name just spread like that, you know."

Hazel talks of Viv's childhood about when he had run-ins with his peers, "I used to fight his battles, Viv wouldn't fight." Jack offers up a story about Viv's childhood, "He fought out there with young Stubsy and Stubsy was knocking hell out of him. I said, 'I'll bloody murder you, lad, for letting him do that to you, give him some back!'

I used to take him to boxing and he took to it like a duck to water. He had four things going for him that very few fighters have got, I mean street fighting. He had speed, he had the wind, the stamina and he had the hitting power.

Put them on that street or a football field and phew! They just couldn't put it together, they don't know how to use their hands, and they depend on just strength and weight. You can be as strong as a bull, but if you're not fit once you start puffing and panting then you're finished.

You're fighting some bugger and you start puffing and panting and he's still going strong! It's time for you to reverse because you're going to get a tousing. Viv knew how to hit and the weight training gave him the strength. He put four down in less than four seconds. Four blokes in the bar, Anna's dad come up to Viv and said, 'I was just going to give you a hand there, Viv.' Bump, bump, bump, bump! Four left hookers and they didn't get up! Mind you, I'm not just saying that because he was my lad."

What were Viv's fears? Hazel: "You know something, he was the most scared person of the dark. He was petrified, petrified!" Jack says with laughter in his voice, "He would come in through the night, to go out the room he would open that door, put that light on and there's a switch to the top of the landing, he would put that light on. He would fly up the stairs and get a hold of his bedroom door and hoy it wide open. Then he'd knock the switch on and go in.

One night I said, 'Oh, Viv, feed them dogs, son'; 'Aye,

right you are, father.' He would go out the back, and I would sneak out of the front door and sneak down the garden, it was pitch black! He would shout at the dogs, 'Howway!' I would go, 'Urghhh!' The tins and the food would go up a height and he's back in here like a shot." We all break out into spontaneous laughter at the thought of this and luckily for us we are all on the same wavelength to be able to enjoy a moment of nostalgia.

Jack talks of when he and Viv went shooting and how good of a shot Viv was. I know what you will all be thinking or generally thinking, but do not. Viv was from the countryside and their way of life is different. A double-barrelled shotgun does not hold the same fear for these people as it would for a city dweller looking down the barrels of a sawn-off.

Game pie and salmon were things that people took for granted in rural areas, shooting, hunting and fishing is their way of life.

Hazel describes how when Viv passed a pub called the Golden Lion he would say, 'I'm home.' He would say this to all his mates that brought him up in the car.

Hazel talks and looks across to Viv' sister, "She seen him a few days before he died, didn't you, Karen? She said, 'What's wrong with your face today?' He said, 'Oh, I'm just fed up, Karen; I'm on my way home, I'm sick of paying bills. Viv had just bought a house at the time."

We talk of the Gateshead Angel (the Angel of the North) and about an article that appeared in the Telegraph, which depicted the people of Gateshead as being thick for having the Angel.

This sort of bombastic approach unseats all what the Northerners have fought against for many years. Hazel says, "It's horrible." Jack adds, "I think it's a waste of space myself. The people of Gateshead had no bloody choice in the matter. It was the council that made the decision."

Whilst on this subject, Viv's artistic ability is enquired of and says, "I think he was a bit thicker than me when he was at school, wasn't he?" Bear in mind the tone of voice jack has when he says this, he is not condescending or patronising himself or Viv. It is not said in a disparaging way, but simply to show lack of artistic ability.

Jack: "It was only in my last three years at school that I picked up and I think Viv did the same. Viv was obsessed with strength. He started with a bullworker and when he was working, he would put six more bricks in a hod than anyone else and it just went on from there." Martin: "He always covered his body with a big shirt, he didn't go around with his chest hanging out." Jack: "He looked far bigger stripped than he did with his shirt on."

Mickey Conroy: I use the opportunity to go off at a tangent on the subject of Viv without a top on. Viv had a fight on the Quayside with Mickey Conroy and he tore his shirt off like the hulk. Jack: "The way I put it down to is down to these old cowboy films, the gunslinger. There's always somebody wants to take your reputation. Well as he went on his reputation just grew and grew and more blokes tried to take it off him. He wasn't like a bully."

Viv used to hold his head and say to himself, 'Why is that man trying to have a go at me?' Jack: "Viv would say to me, 'I was sitting there having a quiet drink and another one kicked off.' I would ask him if he won and Viv would reply, 'Oh, aye! I've knacked him, you can't even go for a quiet drink, there's always somebody wanting to have a go at you, man.' He used to go out with Anna and they would say, 'He's on his own, we'll get him while he's on his own.' He just got the reputation as a fighter and you've always got somebody to tell you what they think of you."

What about the fighting over the insurance payouts? From what Jack says it seems that money has been the key issue for a number of people and it has cut through Jack's heart so much so that he says, "I'm only pleased the grand-bairns stayed with us on a Friday and Saturday night long before all of this happened. I've done it for donkey's years, otherwise the buggers would be saying 'They're just getting the grandbairns in to see if they can get in to any money.' But they cannot say that because the bairns have been staying long before this insurance wrangle."

Jack is not favourable as to which of his many grandchildren stay, sometimes they have had five or six there on a Friday night. Hazel says something that could be the answer to what has kept their spirits alive, "It is our grandchildren that have kept us going, we look after Karen's and Martin's children because they work. Our Viv's two boys come down and Eric's oldest boy doesn't come down because he's too big. But we always have five of them, don't we?" Hazel looks to Jack for his confirmation to which he says, "Wey aye. We wouldn't have it any other way. Viv and Dean used to live only a stone's throw away, but now they've moved further away they come on a weekend."

We talk of Viv's commitments to others and how he had to be in a number of different places at one time. Jack: "Viv passed his driving test first time and he was a crackerjack! He wanted to be here before he got there." Jack says this in the best possible way with no malice intended, Jack expresses everything succinctly and he has a sense of humour that comes across without him even realising how enthralling it is to listen to him. I get the feeling he could call the Royal family to their face without offending them, as it is not within his nature to hurt or offend anyone.

Jack: "If he was going along the road he would say, 'I've got to get past him, he's too slow!' Not doing out daft, no, not stupid risks, but he had to be away and that bloody thing he had, like, it would catch pigeons, man." We discuss the car and Jack says matter of factly, "It wasn't a big old Mercedes or a fancy BMW it was just a Sierra Cosworth. It had a 2.9 injection engine in it. It was a flying machine, there was nowt swanky about it."

Viv's heroes? Hazel: "Just his dad, he worshipped his dad, nobody else." Jack is overcome with embarrassment and says in a low tone, "I never heard him." What he means by this is that Viv did not openly say soft namby-pamby things. But the point is taken about who Viv looked up to. Jack continues, "He liked the film 'Zulu', he watched that over and over again, it's a cracking picture, like."

Hazel says, "He loved home cooking, you know, and he used to get me to do a spotted dick pudding, put it in the cloth and dish and he used to say to me, 'Now, mother, how long does this take to cook?' And he used to take it back with him to Daisy Hill, in Newcastle, and cook it down there. Christmas cake, I think everybody in Daisy Hill had a Christmas cake off me, scones, pork pies, I think I kept Daisy Hill in them. The minute they came out of the oven he would pinch them."

Viv's grandmother stayed at Jack and Hazel's home for about five years after her husband died and eventually she got a little place nearby to her son's home. Viv had great reverence for older people.

Hazel: "Viv's was obsessed with his nanny, wasn't he?" Jack: "Viv would take her all over in the car, up to the dam and down the coast. My mother would sit on a clothesline and go to hell and back if it was a ride out. I used to say to her, 'I'm going to Keswick tomorrow with the wagon.' Her parents belonged over there in Maryport. I used to go over, take her up and get her in the wagon."

How did Martin get on with Viv? Martin: "Viv did little pranks on me like throwing buckets of water out of the window. It must have been when I threatened him," he says jokingly.

Martin used to train at a place called 'The Hut'. Jack: "It's just a hut, there's no running water or nowt like that, just up the steps, a door, in, benches and weights and all the local lads go in there and train. You would just come home and have a bath or a shower after a session in there. It's got a brick foundation with wood sides. When it first started off it was the St Johns Ambulance Brigade base.

When they started the weight training away, they asked if they could use the bottom end of the hut, the other end was all stretchers and that sort of thing. Then the St Johns

The Grasshopper And The Squirrel

Ambulance just sort of seemed to die out, nobody went to it and the lads took it over and paid the council a rate. It's been there for twenty odd years now."

Indeed, 'The Hut' is still there and an unbelievable sight, the sort of place that those seeking the eye of the tiger would train in, if they were hungry enough for that sort of thing! It is full of menacing looking weight training machines and other machines of self-inflicting torture. The facilities are few and it is the sort of place you would expect to see a regiment of SAS officers queuing up to get out of!

I am sitting looking at a family that is recollecting all sorts of stories about Viv. The fear that was first there upon my arrival had been long gone and here the barriers had been broken down. I still see them all in my mind's eye and my recollection is of a warm friendly family that had been short changed by the media and had not been given a fair crack of the whip.

Hazel: "Our Dean (one of Viv's sons) and I have a great understanding, we confide in each other and we talk for hours, he tells me everything. If he's got problems he tells me." It is mentioned that Dean had private counselling, would it have been just as good for him to have a sit down with his grandma' and granddad? Jack: "Yes!"

Reverend Mark Jackson: Officiated at Viv's funeral. He said, 'Things have been said that maybe shouldn't have been." Hazel: "He was a marvellous little man." Jack intervenes: "Do you like vicars, do you, do you like churches?" This question takes me aback slightly, as it is not easy to answer someone who has been through so much pain as Jack has. I mention I know a priest who goes to see Newcastle United play and he has a pint of beer at times. Jack: "He'll be a Catholic, is he?" I reply that he is and Jack says, "I knew bloody fine well he was!" Everybody laughs at this, but Jack remains in a semi-serious mode and says, "I'm an atheist, me. I'll tell you bloody well straight, but the Protestants; they are two faced, the vicars. But the old Catholic father, when I was at Saint Joseph's, he used to go down every day to the Townley Arms and have two pints."

Harry Thompson & Father Conaty: The talk of religion prompts a changes of subject matter to the matter of Harry Thompson who died from a stabbing incident. Hazel breaks our laughter when she strikes a serious note and says, "You know, Father Conaty brought our Viv's name up in Harry's sermon." Jack relents and says, "Aye he did."
(Author's note: The tragedy that struck the Connelly family is just as bad as that what the Graham family suffered at the loss of Viv. The lives of Viv and Harry were lost to needless violent acts. Harry was the brother-in-law of Anna Connelly, Viv's fiancée.

Harry was killed whilst pursuing the recovery of items stolen from his home in a burglary. He went to the home of those he suspected and a fight ensued in which he was stabbed and later died from his injuries.)

What advice could the Graham's give to anyone considering pursuing making places safer for others, like Viv had tried? Jack: "Leave it alone because now it's a gun in life, it's not like me and you going outside and that's the end of it. They'll stab you or shoot you or get a team up or baseball bat you. There's nowt like that now, you cross somebody and there's a team out the next bloody day looking for you or they cross you and you get a team out looking for them. I think a lad now had far better mind his own business because he's not going to win no battles; there are too many druggies.

This bloody druggie business, I mean they're out there mind, they'll stab you in the night and when they wake up in the morning they wouldn't know they'd done it. You haven't got to be a big bloke; you can be six stone nowt. You can put a knife in somebody or shoot somebody just the same as somebody seventeen stone can do it. You see, a lot of these bouncers just look at a man. I know of a man (name withheld), he's married and got a baby, he says, 'Jackie, it's bloody crackers, man, you don't know when you're going to get a knife in you or...' This is what I mean!"

The Grasshopper And The Squirrel

What drives people on to become a doorman and a trouble-shooter of other people's problems? Jack: "Well, the doorman, the majority of them, have got backup in a club and when they leave a club most people don't know where they come from. At the same time it beats working for a living.

If somebody said they were going to do something to wor Viv, he wouldn't get a team together; he would go and sort it out himself. He never went with teams all over the place.

That's just the way he was, he had no fear of anybody, he never carried a weapon. He never had a gun, a baseball bat or a knife, he just had his fists. If anyone had pulled a gun out on Viv he would have stood his ground and tried to talk."

Paddy Leonard: Jack is asked about Viv consulting him over an offer of work that came from Tenerife. "I told him to keep away from it. I said, 'Just stay clear of it.' Viv was wanted to do their fighting.

Not only that, I says, 'There's bloody guns and all sorts over there. It's not worth it, you stop home.' I mean when you're twenty odd or thirty you never think you'll get to sixty, you're afraid of nobody and you never think what's going to come off. I didn't want him to go and he never went."

(Author's note: The man, who allegedly made Viv the offer, I am told from another source, was Paddy Leonard. Viv was asked to get involved in timeshare protection rackets. Andy Winder was from Darlington and he ran a modelling agency, but decided that he wanted a piece of the cake.

He went into timeshare in Tenerife and he paid dearly for it. He was involved in a knife fight and died. Jack was right to advise Viv to stay away from such things that Paddy Leonard asked him to get involved in.)

Higgins Security: "Higgins Security, they were from Birmingham, they wanted Viv to go and see them. I told Viv to let them come to him," said Jack.

All of those people that Viv helped and made money for are described by Jack, "They weren't friends, they were hangers on, he was a moneybox for them and a minder for them, he got the money from the doors on different jobs and that's all he was. What I mean by that is, he got them jobs, he looked after their jobs for them. That's the way I mean he was a moneybox, because if anybody wanted a lend of money he would lend them it. Any trouble and he would go and sort it out for them. That's all he was to them, a moneybox."

Robbie Warton & Rob Bell: Hazel says about Viv's genuine friends, "Viv had two genuine friends, Robbie Warton and Rob Bell, they both keep in touch, they come up here every so often, they are genuine people."

It seems from talking to Jack that he seems more worldly wise than most people in Newcastle are, it is asked how he acquired this wisdom? "I was as thick as a chip at school, me, lad."

Hazel interjects, "You did the doors, though, when you were younger, you did the local dances." Jack plays it down by saying, "It was just the local dances, there were no nightclubs then! Chains out of the collar and that sort of thing!

It was not as bad as now, you had broken bottles, chains and flick knives, but this drug business set it all off. Then you were hoyed out of the pub at ten o'clock. And you come out of the dances drunk. Now you get some of them in a right state, drinking all day and night and they are on this bloody stuff. It's a different ball game in the town."

Hazel may well have pinpointed something that attracted Viv into his profession, "He did it for the money, there was no money here for him. He hated going out at the finish, though. He would sometimes just stay in."

Jack defends Viv regarding people calling him a doorman or bouncer, "He wouldn't stand at doors, it got to the point that if he looked after a place then he didn't need to be on the door. Those on the door would say, 'Mind, Viv Graham looks after this place, kick off somewhere else, like.'

Viv suffered migraine, which he got from his mother. She suffers terrible with it. He used to take Paracetamol like a child eats smarties!"

Was stress a contributor to these headaches as well? Hazel: "Definitely, stress brought it all on. Eh, I mean at times it was terrible. When he got that abscess and they said he was filled with steroids, what a load of cod's wallop! There wasn't a bit of steroid in his body. They said that about the steroid thing around about the time of his funeral."

Jack: "I said to Viv, 'Why do you need that for, I'd rather be fifteen stone or fourteen stone or ten stone of muscle and bone rather than be eighteen stone of bloody water, it's like carrying two stone of bloody tatties on your back. One minute they're sixteen stone then they're nineteen stone."

"There was a time he had no neck, his stomach hung over his trousers and you ribbed him something rotten," says Hazel looking at Jack. He takes the story up, "He stopped doing the running, he was just concentrating on the weight training. I used to say, 'Bloody weight training aren't you? You want to get on that field outside the house and get running again,' 'Aye, father, I'm going to, get some of this off.' 'Well you want to then, you'll meet a young Viv Graham, mind,' I said."

It was mentioned that Viv always used to say that he would meet someone bigger and stronger. Hazel: "That's his dad's saying." Jack: "I used to say to him that there's always somebody that's going to be bigger and stronger than him or younger than him. 'Bigger, stronger, better.' I used to say, 'It doesn't matter if you live to be sixty, you cannot beat a 20 year old or a 30 year old.

Sometimes there's always somebody coming up, if you're never defeated then there's a time in your life when there's a young 'un who is good enough and fit enough to beat you because you're getting too old.' So I say's, 'You either beat somebody that's better than you, there's always somebody in the world that's better than you somewhere, it doesn't matter who you are. Just look at your boxing. The best in the world can get beat. If you keep on with it then the older you get there's a young 'un coming up and he beats you.' It's a fact of life."

Jack airs his views on the press coverage relating to Viv, "How can the press prove he was a £2m drug baron? Another thing they had in was that he was going over to Amsterdam every weekend for drugs, he only went there once when he went with Mary, Anna's Sister. The reason was that Harry, Mary's husband, worked on oilrigs and he had two weeks on and one off or something like that and the oilrig was near a holiday resort.

Harry said, 'Instead of me keep coming back home, have a weekend in Amsterdam.' Harry's wife went over with our Viv. Harry, his wife and Viv spent the weekend in Amsterdam, that was all there was to it.'

I mean, where's the proof of it that he was active in drug dealing? A solicitor said you can say anything you like about a dead man, he's dead so he cannot argue the fact." The saying 'dead men tell no lies' is a poignant thing to mention here.

Jack talks about stories in the newspapers of bent vicars, which we all break out into laughter over, everyone will recall seeing a story sometime in their life about such a thing on the front pages of national tabloids.

Jack: "Another thing, I don't know how these film stars when they go in and out of places and they're sticking cameras in their faces, I don't know how they don't kick off. It's bloody serious the way that they hound people, like coming out of courts, I would stop all of that."

Hazel: "We had letters put through the door saying, 'We wrote nice things about Viv, if you'd only talk to us,' and things like that. I went to the graveyard and photographers were following me there! I used to go before eight o'clock in the morning to keep out of their road. I used to do all sorts to keep away from them."

Jack: "I opened the door one day and they were there, the television that was. I had to go to the inquest and two of them were in the street and they took my photograph, it was too late to stop them."

The Grasshopper And The Squirrel

Hazel: "Anna's had them sitting at her table and she just thought they were loads of friends coming in. They asked her had she found somebody new?"

Jack talks more on the ecclesiastical side of things, "If I had my way I would sack every vicar, Catholic father, rabbi, mothers, every religion and sack them all.

There's been more bloodshed and murder, bloody religion, in this world than anything else.

My second wish, I would fetch Guy Fawkes back and give him all the bloody gunpowder he wanted.

My third wish would be that Britain would have a ruler with bottle that would stand up to the rest of Europe, we don't want to be told by them what we can and what we cannot eat, what we can do and what we cannot do. See what I mean.

On top of that, all of those asylum seekers, as soon as the boat come in I would turn it around and say, 'Back to where you belong.' Some of them are parasites living off us.

If there were no religion then there wouldn't be any Catholics and no Protestants and there would not be Catholics and Protestants fighting in Northern Ireland.

You wouldn't have Moslems and Sikhs fighting, everybody would be one, everybody would be the same."

Hazel says to Jack, with surprise in her voice, "Do you know something, I've never heard you talk as much in months, I'm pleased Steve and his chaperon have come tonight. It's done you the world of good."

What Hazel says here has shown me that Jack has been withdrawn in the past over the tragic loss. I see before me a man that could run for election in any office of the local council or parliament, subject to Guy Fawkes not turning up.

His orations are comparable with speeches given by most good talkers and dare I compare him to the late great Sir Winston Churchill in the way he can hit the chord of things. Although his Enoch Powell 'Rivers of Blood' speech might need toned down!

Terry Scott: We talk about Terry Scott, an associate of

Viv's, who was there just seconds after Viv was shot. Jack says, "When it happened, Terry said, 'I'm your son.' I've never seen him from that day to this. He just started to move in Viv's circles in the latter part of Viv's life and wasn't a mate of Viv's for years and years and years."

Jack: "When I went into that house, I just had to get out. (Anna's home) Seeing that picture on the wall of the little girl having her communion, that did it for me."

Hazel: "Viv could have a fight with someone and then shake hands, even with Stuey Watson, he made friends and he was invited to his birthday party, but he wasn't a party lad. He was dead old fashioned."

Jack: "On a Saturday night he would got to the Railway pub in Walker, quiet, he would have a nice drink." This indicates Viv was not a party animal and he much preferred the quietness of what could be considered old men's bars. We talk of a whole mish-mash of things and as they come they are here for you to look over.

Michael Sayers: We talk of Michael Sayers and Jack says, "He did say he had some trouble with Michael Sayers. Hazel: "But no word of a lie, that Michael Sayers pulled into the yard one Christmas and gave us a Christmas card and £100 when Viv was in jail." Jack: "Everybody's all friends, but if you fall out you can fall out, can't you? So you're not friends anymore"

What about Viv enjoying the odd bet or two on the horses? Jack: "I said, 'You're crackers, man, put it away and salt it away.' I asked Viv if he'd heard the story about putting his money away for a rainy day. I said to Viv, 'Have you ever heard about the grasshopper and the squirrel?' He said, 'No, what's that, father?' I said, 'The squirrel gathers all the nuts and it hides them all over the place. The grasshopper just jumps about and enjoys itself.

The winter comes, the grasshopper has got nowt to eat, but the squirrel's got all its nuts to eat. You're not going to be thirty all your life; you're going to get to forty, fifty and sixty. You can't keep this game up at that age.'

He would say, 'Aye man, father, I'm not bothered about when I get to that age. I'm living now, man!'

Rob Owen: When Viv used to go the boxing matches with Rob Owen, 'Red Corner, blue corner? £25 on the red corner.' He didn't know what that kid was like; he hadn't a clue what they were like. He was just laughing and couldn't care-a-less about what happened tomorrow, live for today and let tomorrow worry about itself.

Well ye bugger, he was 34, but he had a good life. He had a good last ten or so years. Well, see, when I think back as well, I worked all my life and an insurance bloke came around and he said, 'Get a pension out for when you retire?' I said, 'Get away, I could be dead next week, lad. What good's that to me?'

We won the pools at work in a syndicate. They said, 'Buy a wagon, man.' I said, 'When I park this wagon up tonight, I forget about it until tomorrow morning and if there's out goes wrong with it then he's got to fix it. I want none of that, I could be dead in five years time.'

It's come and it's just went as the years went on, it was all spent, but when I was older it's like what I said to wor Viv, I mean, maybe if I had of invested that money or joined a pension scheme I would have had a good pension. I said the same as Viv and he was just doing the same stroke."

Hazel told me that as long as Viv's dad was around that he would not have married anyone, as his relationship with his father was more important to him. I can see this, as it was his father he worshipped and loved, it was he who Viv confided in and asked his opinion on certain matters. Viv did not leave it to chance for anyone else to advise him. (Author's note: Since this interview took place there have been a number of settlements by insurance companies and there is no further argument as to who has a claim on Viv's estate, as it has been settled via legal means.) **Many thanks go to Mr & Mrs Graham and family for this contribution.**

Gentlemen Prefer Guns

Whilst out in Newcastle for a night out on the town on 22nd August 1988, Robert Bell was involved in some trouble when a fight broke out in the Bigg Market area of Newcastle. About a dozen people were involved in a fracas that led to three arrests by police for drunkenness and public order offences.

It has been alleged that one of the people involved in the trouble was Peter Donnelly, 24, who became involved in a fight with Bell over a woman. Another story was that, allegedly, Bell had stepped in to break an argument up that Donnelly was having with one of Bell's friends and Bell got the better of Donnelly, police were called and broke the fight up.

Donnelly, it is claimed, went home and changed his blood-ied clothes. A good few people witnessed the trouble. Maybe when Donnelly went home he intended to stay there, but changed his mind because he felt the need to keep face over the fight that he and Bell had.

When your macho image is spoiled then it has to be won back, if such a thing is important to you. Some people might say, "Let it drop, it's not worth it." They would leave it at that. The fight ended and should have been left at that, but revenge can eat a man up.

Donnelly may have taken a disliking to being outnumbered and thought it unfair of Bell to step into someone else's fight and take sides thus giving that person an unfair advantage over him.

Weapons were brought into play to even up the situation. Bell was a formidable opponent to anyone by virtue of his power and size. Donnelly was no match against this although he was of a mind to somehow get even.

I can tell you from a meeting that I had with Peter Donnelly, also known as 'Gentleman Peter Donnelly', some years ago, which was not in connection with this book. Peter said that Viv had called at his trailer home (caravan) and for some reason or another trouble started whereby Viv had lost control and humiliated him by giving him a good hiding, which Peter told me his family witnessed at the Glassworks site (name of the caravan site), in Leamington, just outside of Newcastle centre.

In retaliation for this attack on him by Viv, Peter further alleged to me that he went with a gun and found Viv in a Newcastle restaurant, he pulled the trigger and the gun failed to go off. This story was told to me without prompting. I was told, prior to meeting him, that Peter was an animal. How far from the truth this was, Peter acted with the gentlemanly conduct of a cavalry officer. I do not judge people by how other people portray them, 'Let he who is without sin cast the first stone.'

Whether Peter was telling me the truth or not, he came across as a really helpful person in terms of what I was talking to him about at that time. There is no need to patronise people such as Donnelly, as there is nothing to gain or lose, I tell it like it is. Judging by Donnelly's demeanour it was obvious that he was not a person easily rattled or shaken by things that could or had happened to him.

What made him flip on the night in question is anyone's guess. He is alleged to have returned to the Cloth Market, in Newcastle, armed with a gun and a carving knife. What had incensed him and made him so mad that he threw caution to the wind in carrying out the alleged violent attack in which he did not care if Bell was killed or not?

His mental stability had been breached and he was really pissed off at someone. Obviously I cannot ask Donnelly what caused him to flip, as he was acquitted of all of the charges due to lack of evidence, and for that reason he would have no wish to incriminate himself further by leaving himself open to renewed charges or a civil action.

It is further alleged that Donnelly had an accomplice with him, who was never identified, when he returned to the Cloth Market looking for Bell just after midnight. Bell was in Santino's, sitting at a table with Viv and others when violence flared up.

Donnelly's accomplice stayed at the front of Santino's restaurant, armed with a large knife, while Donnelly walked in and went towards Bell. Patrons of Santino's thought it was about to be robbed by a pair of late night villains.

Bell, though, in his own later admittance, knew that Donnelly was coming for him and his feelings can only be described as sobering when confronted by Donnelly pointing a twelve bore at his face from a range of only a few inches.

A size eleven fist moved faster than an eye could blink and took hold of the shotgun and Viv's powerful arm twisted it from Donnelly's grasp like taking candy from a baby. To do this must have taken a split second decision and Viv's boxing reactions were brought into play.

Viv detested the use of weapons in a fight, which was easy for him to profess considering his pugilistic abilities. No doubt what caused him to grab the gun was his anger at such an effrontery to take place in view of these late night diners.

Viv proceeded to smash the gun off the nearby wall. All hell had broke loose and the unknown man standing guard brandishing a knife had now come forward and held the knife to the stomach of Bell's younger brother, Ian, 21. Someone brought a chair crashing down over the knifeman's head and that put him out of action. Bell and Donnelly, somehow, ended up in the back alley of Santrino's. In the ensuing fight, Bell was, what seemed to be at the time, mortally wounded from being stabbed in the shoulder and heart. Donnelly had meant to do the business and would not be content until he had done the job he came to do.

The heart being a pump, when punctured still pumps, it squeezed blood out through the puncture wound like a fountain of red Italian wine. Viv was on hand once more for a second time when he threw a punch that was to break the jaw of Donnelly.

Viv could see the amount of blood gushing out of his friend's body and was so incensed that he lost control and lifted up a beer keg and smashed it off Donnelly's body. Viv took off his top and stemmed the flow of blood from Bell's wounds while they awaited an ambulance.

(Author's note: An interesting analogy can be compared to how Lee Duffy also suffered a fatal injury to an artery in his body when David Allison killed him with a knife. Duffy's blood flow could not be stemmed even with the use of clothing. Yet here, Bell survived a similar injury. At the time of Duffy's death it was also claimed that he had been in the company of Donnelly.)

A total of three times, Viv had to be congratulated in saving Bell's life. Without a shadow of doubt without Viv being there, Bell was a dead man for certain! The first time was when Viv snatched the gun away from Donnelly. The second time, when he set about Donnelly stopping him from completing the job and finally when he stemmed the flow of blood from Bell's wound.

How ironic it would be that a number of years later it was to be Viv's turn to be fatally wounded in a back street and he too was held in the arms of fellow trouble-shooter, Terry Scott outside of the Queens Head pub.)

Viv did not receive a bravery award or a commendation for this heroic action or any other recognition. Had this been any local ordinary citizen or a police officer then they would have been nominated for a bravery award and festooned with medals and plastered all over the front page of the Daily Bugle.

Viv was a known hard man, therefore such awards would only be seen to help bolster his reputation so it did not seem to matter. It was accepted that it was all in a day's work for Viv to be involved in this sort of incident. Maybe now you can see how he was looked on in a different way. What would have been hailed as an act of heroism for other people was accepted as normal everyday occurrences in the life of Viv Graham.

He had feelings just like anyone else, just because he was a powerful man and his exterior did not ever crack in public it did not mean he was not an ordinary human capable of emotion. The ordeal must have been just as daunting to him as anyone else, the difference being that he could react quickly with his disciplined boxer's mind for fast problem solving.

Later on, Bell was to recollect that it was four men and not two who had entered Santino's with guns to get them. This may have been bending the truth somewhat, but the man deserved some leeway due to his injuries that put him in hospital in a critical condition that at times was touch and go as to whether he would pull through.

As a consequence of this near fatal injury, Bell lost his builders business. Viv made a statement to the police, obviously with a view that this could be a murder case if Bell did not last the night.

Bell was eventually recovered enough to make a statement, as did his brother Ian. They named Donnelly as the attacker. Donnelly was remanded to prison to await trial and it has been alleged by one of his associates that an offer of some £15,000 was offered to Bell if he did not give evidence against him in the forthcoming trial.

(Authors mote: I must point out that this is only an allegation and not to be accepted as fact but you the reader are advised to reach your own conclusions in private from the events that were to happen after this allegation. Since this mater is unlikely to be brought before a court of law it remains conjecture. Sworn affidavits confirming what is said herein have been promised if civil action is instigated against me for making these claims!)

Bell, allegedly, accepted the offer, as he was on the road to recovery from being at death's door although it was a long road and that night would always be in his mind and in his nightmares. The £15,000 would help soften the blow that the loss of his business had caused him.

The charges that were put to Donnelly were: attempted murder, wounding with intent, possessing a firearm without a certificate, having a firearm with intent to endanger life and having a firearm in a public place. If Donnelly was found guilty he could be sure the keys to his cell would be thrown away for fifteen to twenty years if not, maybe, even life imprisonment!

Bell had a sudden attack of post-traumatic amnesia; he could not remember what had happened or recall who had attacked him! Bell had particularly named Donnelly in a statement made to police, yet here he was in a state of forgetfulness. This amnesia thing was contagious, as it also caused the memory loss of his brother Ian who said that he was unable to identify the man with the shotgun or his brother's attacker.

Viv was giving evidence and was cross-examined in court, but amnesia had also struck him, he too had no idea as to the identities of the attackers. He said that he lied to the police about the identity of Peter Donnelly who he had named in a statement made to police at the time of the incident who he claimed had inflicted a near fatal knife attack on Bell.

This must have been music to the ears of Peter Donnelly who had pleaded 'not guilty' and was standing in the dock with his fingers crossed.

Regardless of what amount of money was going to be allegedly paid to Bell by Donnelly, it would have been highly likely that Viv would not have named Donnelly in court as the attacker.

Since Bell had recovered it was not going to be a murder wrap for Donnelly. There was a difference in giving evidence in a murder hearing, but Bell had recovered from the stabbing and Viv had his reputation to think of in terms of becoming known as a grass.

The jury, not surprisingly, acquitted Donnelly and found

him 'not guilty' of attempted murder. He was further cleared of the remaining charges that would not have looked out of place to a Beirut Freedom Fighter.

Donnelly was to walk free from court. There you might think the story ends, not just yet though. As Donnelly left the court he caught sight of Viv and made gesticulating hand signs to him, indicating Viv was a 'grass'.

Donnelly left the area and went to a traveller's site at Hull where he stayed for some time; self-exiled for fear of a reprisal that would have been accepted as fair retaliation because the alleged 'promised' £15,000 cash had not changed hands and Donnelly had done a runner. In time, Donnelly returned to Newcastle and became involved in a number of other criminal activities.

Donnelly had 'cocked out of the deal' and whatever reason he had for this is sure to be plausible, as he was well known for his word being his bond. Not for no reason was he known as 'Gentleman Peter Donnelly'.

While in the Fish Bar public house, Newcastle, it has been suggested that Viv came across Donnelly some months after the Bell stabbing incident. Donnelly, on seeing Viv coming towards him, allegedly broke down in tears in front of Viv asking him not to set about him. Viv told him not to worry he was not going to set about him.

In a later incident it was alleged that Viv lifted up Donnelly and threw him in to a rubbish skip in Newcastle city centre.

Well there you have it…or just about! I want to finish on the note of John Henry Sayers (known as JHS), the brother of Stephen and Michael. JHS was released from prison after serving a long sentence for robbery. He wanted to set up a taxi company because he had finished with crime and he knew if he so much as farted in the wrong direction then the police would lift him. Which was later to be true in the case of the Freddie Knights murder. (More in a later chapter.)

When representation is made to Newcastle City Council by JHS for a licence to run a mini cab company, the police attend, the council have a war cabinet and reject it. So what I want to know is this, how come a convicted fraudster can run a security company and be paid from North One and Newcastle City Council and continue to draw money from a publicly and European funded project?

Peter Donnelly appeared before Newcastle Crown court in a long firm fraud case that involved a Welsh slate company being ripped off to the tune of £23,000. In a sophisticated fraud he hoped to escape payment.

Donnelly's past convictions were for dishonesty, burglary & resisting arrest, Section 18 assault (18 months imprisonment), theft, road traffic offences, driving convictions, drink driving and fraud.

Glen Gatland defending in the fraud case told the court: "Mr Donnelly is employing over 40 people, his VAT, Tax and National Insurance are being paid. In a VAT check, the VAT man came up with nothing in the company. He arranges contracts. The offence was committed 22 months ago and his business is very successful and Mr Donnelly makes an offer of full compensation to the slate company and to pay prosecution costs if given a suspended sentence."

Mr Gatland even went so far as suggesting to the judge, Judge Crawford QC, that the sentence on Donnelly be deferred for three months. Judge Crawford said, "People can't buy their way out of prison!"

Councillor Tony Flynn, head of Newcastle City Council, was asked what he thought of such a company (DH Security) being run by a convicted felon and his reply makes for interesting reading:

'The company...would be unlikely to meet the Authority's criteria for inclusion in our standing list of contractors which the authority would allow business to be conducted with. However, the development on which the company has been employed is a complex one, being managed by a consortium of partners in the form of a joint venture agreement between the City Council...'

Gazza Goes Down

"Viv has always been a friend of mine. When visiting Newcastle I would sometimes come across Viv when he was in Macey's and I would stand with him and have a few drinks (as a friend, not as my minder).

Viv asked me if I could get him a signed football, as I was playing for Newcastle at that time. I was happy to oblige.

I was devastated by news of him being killed (as I would be about this happening to anyone I knew)."

GAZZA
Newcastle, Tottenham, Lazio, Glasgow Rangers,
Middlesbrough & England

Gazza's soccer career has brought him riches beyond any normal Geordie boy's belief. Who would have guessed that when he was playing football for Gateshead based Redheugh Boys Club that he was aspiring towards international stardom on the hallowed turf of Wembley?

Gazza agreed to grant an interview exclusively to the author of this book about a nightclub incident that led to him suffering further injury to his already damaged leg in September of 1991.

From the moment Viv passed away, that was the minute the press started rubbing their hands for a big payday. The Newcastle Journal ran an article on 3rd January 1994 that was so outrageous that no journalist could even put his or her name to it. The space where the journalist usually has their name had in its place, an anonymous 'By Journal Staff' heading.

The article started as follows: *'Murdered doorman Viv Graham was today blamed for an attack, which almost wrecked Paul Gascoigne's career. A friend claims the 17 stone father of three was the mystery man who punched the Lazio player to the ground as he visited a Newcastle nightclub.'*

The article went on to quote from this supposed friend of the dead Viv Graham: *'With friends like that who needs enemies?'* As it turns out Viv did not have many friends not unless you could count hangers on as friends. *His real friends were people who had very little physical prowess.'*

Why the press accused Viv of the attack on Gazza no one really knows? The article went on.... *'Claims that Graham was responsible for almost crippling Gazza came just hours after the shooting. The attack at Walker's nightclub in Newcastle came just before his £4.8m transfer from Spurs to Lazio...'*

After Viv's murder it was only a matter of minutes before the press went into action. News travels fast! But this story had taken over two years to surface?

A good friend does not go about telling lies about a dead friend! Now that Viv had been physically assassinated they could go ahead and finish the job by morally assassinating his character.

More lies came in the same article when a supposed ex-bouncer associate of Viv who went unnamed said: *'Viv couldn't stand the thought of someone as famous as Gazza coming to Tyneside with his own minders. As far as he was concerned Newcastle was his town and he was top dog. It was as if he was losing face and had to make the point at least to other guys that he could reach anyone he wanted.'*

Can I now ask you, the reader, to go and get a large pale or bucket so that you can be throw-up in it after reading that load of garbage?

Such sensationalism is usually left to national newspapers to spoon feed the news hungry public, but they do tend to put a bit of research time in to such news items, as it does help lend some credibility to it.

Here is a supposed friend of Viv's spilling the beans in a local newspaper just hours after his supposed friend has died from gunshot wounds! Nah!

Let us all laugh together, one, two, three: 'Ha, Ha.' All the doormen have gone into hiding on the night of Viv's murder fearing that they could be next on the list. Then a few hours after Viv's death, out of the woodwork pops this fellow friend who suddenly blurts out a story about Gazza being set about by Viv? Nah!

Viv would not have minded anyone coming in to Newcastle with their own minders, as it would have meant he could have had a day off with his feet up on his favourite couch watching videos with the kids.

The article is examined in further detail and the supposed associate of Viv goes on to say: *'I'm no angel and I know how to take care of myself, but there are plenty of blokes harder than me who would have given Viv Graham a wide berth.'*

The 'I'm no angel' bit sounds familiar and was used in another article attributed to a well know journalist. That fact about giving Viv a 'wide berth' is very true, but the fact of it was, people did not have to give Viv a wide berth. It is not something likely to be said by a friend about giving Viv a wide berth; nearly all of the doormen in the city were friendly towards Viv in a loose sense of the word 'friendly'.

The 'friend' had, according to the Journal, admitted receiving a jail term for supplying drugs. That explains it then, he was off his head on cocaine and just said anything. Taking the word of a junkie is very dangerous, especially if the story was paid for!

To finish off this piece, we might as well look at what this 'friend' of Viv's finally said: *'I don't think Gazza knew why he was punched but it was Viv showing the rest of the hard cases in town that he was frightened of nobody.'*

Gazza is having a social night out on the town, can you

just see Viv being intimidated by the presence of a man he revered and held in high esteem? He would have been over to him in a flash, seeing if he was enjoying his night out.

The assault on Gazza took place inside of Newcastle city centre's Walker's nightclub, which took place after he and friends had been to watch Newcastle United FC play against Derby County at Saint James' Park. They made their way, via a few pubs, to Walker's.

Gazza's leg was already recovering from ligament trouble and along with another fellow player from Tottenham FC , who was also recovering from ligament surgery, they had hoped to finish off the night of what had been a pleasant day out by visiting a nightclub in Gazza's native North East.

Gazza was able to tell me in full detail exactly what happened so that it would once and for all end the speculation about the attack made on him in Walker's nightclub. "It has been claimed that an attack made on me, in September 1991, while I was in Walker's nightclub was carried out by Viv. This had been reported in the press as having happened because Viv '…couldn't stand someone as famous as Gazza coming to Tyneside with his own minders.'

I didn't go anywhere with Viv in Newcastle and when visiting Walker's I was in the company of a fellow footballer who played with me at Tottenham. We were, both, recovering from ligament trouble. In the company were some local friends and my brother.

I can say with certainty that Viv did not attack me nor was he present when the attack took place. Viv found out about the unprovoked attack on me and telephoned my good friend Jimmy on his mobile. Jimmy passed on Viv's concerns, which were meant in a protective way. Whilst I appreciated his concerns I passed a message back to him that I wanted the matter dropped and Viv respected my wish. Jimmy was not there with me as my minder, he's my very good friend.

People were bitter about me leaving Newcastle at that time so I stopped visiting Newcastle and invited Viv to visit London for a night out and a drink with me. This didn't happen, but the invitation was always open."

There you have it direct from Gazza, no twisted words or lies from a dead man's associate or friend. Gazza did not need to go to the trouble he did in putting the record straight. He understands the grief this must have caused Viv's parents. Viv idolised Gazza

The injury that Gazza suffered in the nightclub attack caused a fracture to his right knee and he was whisked off to the top central London Princess Grace hospital.

In the meantime, the police were trying to identify Gazza's attacker, but word had got back to them that Gazza wanted the inquiry dropped and he was not pursuing a complaint of assault.

Strangely enough, nobody witnessed anything of the attack on Gazza! Bouncers on duty saw nothing, staff saw nothing and Gazza would have been the last to see anything. The attacker made a cowardly move in which he got right up to Gazza, and from behind him, he called out Gazza's name. Gazza turned around and he got it right on the chin, knocking him to the ground!

Some people thought the attacker was a man called Michael Sayers, but it was not he. It would be easy to blame him for this attack while he is locked away serving a twelve stretch for demanding money with menaces, after all it was his ex-associates that blamed him for the attack!

The man who carried out the attack cannot be named for legal reasons. Two reliable sources have come up with the same scenario, one that had direct contact with the man who carried out the attack.

The attacker was in prison on unrelated matters when he bragged about the attack. He claimed to be off his head when he attacked Gazza. He talked big about how he ran over when Gazza had his back to him and then shouted at Gazza and then threw a punch, unbalancing Gazza, knocking him to the ground. His crazed attacker jumped up and down on the sprawled out Gazza! The attack was over as fast as it had happened and the man ran off into the crowd. Gazza was left with further damage to his already damaged knee!

The perpetrator of the attack was not a big name, just a nobody who fancied having a go at Gazza. Where were the nightclub's bouncers whilst this was going on?

The regional manager of First Leisure, which owned Walker's, made inquiries, but came up with fresh air when it was claimed that no one had witnessed the attack.

This book is about stopping any potential future Viv Graham causing their family and friends grief. "It's just not worth it, leave it," how many times have you heard that said when two people are confronting each other with a display of bravado? Every city is carrying a potential disaster waiting to happen to anyone of the same standing as Viv. From Glasgow, Edinburgh, Newcastle, Sunderland, Leeds, Liverpool, Manchester, Birmingham, Cardiff to London, they all have their own large as life or mini Viv Graham.

You can have the biggest set of muscles in the world, but flesh cannot compete with a bullet or a knife attack! Viv was not with Gazza when this unprovoked attack happened, but you can be assured that if he were then the attack would not have taken place.

Viv and Gazza shared some common characteristics, both are misunderstood, both were brought up in caring communities with a mother and father to lend support if needed. They gave money to just and good causes and were/are spontaneous in their combustive natures when faced with sensitive issues. Both could be considered to be the new age man. Viv thought nothing of vacuuming the carpets at the home that he shared with his fiancée, Anna. Gazza would think nothing of grabbing a camera from his young adoring fans and reversing the situation by taking a shot of the fans that had called at his home when he lived with his parents.

Celebrities and underworld figures have always had an affinity of fighting to get where they are. There is always some nefarious figure lurking in the background of a Hollywood style venture. The Kray family was, maybe, the first in this country to bring together celebs and underworld figures. Suddenly they were in the limelight as much as the stars they had hired and they themselves became the celebrities! They could have gone on to different things and could maybe have ended up as film producers.

It can be said that most underworld characters and celebrities have one thing in common and that is usually having an outgoing character. The trait of being an extrovert is shared amongst both criminals and superstars. That particular trait is what helped them get in to trouble or stardom in the first place!

Media fame comes in all forms, famous and infamous. Both only being distinguished from each other by the front-page headlines to show which side of the criminal/celebrity fence the person came from.

One minute you can be a celebrity and the next minute you can become an infamous celebrity...just like Gary Glitter! You can be catapulted in to the status of a famous person like Will Young or you can be catapulted in to oblivion like Michael Barrymore!

Viv was a nobody, and then he became an infamous somebody by virtue of newspaper headlines. Just before he was murdered he was bordering on the threshold of becoming a minor local celebrity. Media fame is a law unto itself, you can work for fifty years to try and make it big on the screen or stage with no results. Then along comes the media bandwagon and if they like what they see then that is it, big time stardom after that! Get the right people in the right places to say the right things and you are in.

That is what happened to Viv, people who were already established in his field of excellence (security) put in the right word and he was elevated from country boy to city man. He still had to earn respect, but he was halfway there and well on to his way to riding the tiger's back.

Anna Connelly talks about the Gazza incident: "Look at that with Gazza? That was a load of crap. Viv never even seen Gazza the night he was attacked. Viv had a football signed from the Newcastle United team. David Roche an ex-Newcastle player got it for Viv."

Another incidence of violence involving Gazza happened when he had been on a night out in Newcastle City centre in July 1991. Gazza was out on the town with his sister. A drunkard bumped into her causing some concern for her safety. Being the good brother, Gazza came to the defence of his sister and ended up being charged with a double assault on two men.

What else could Gazza do, what would you do? Whatever the answer, it ended up with Gazza facing criminal charges because one of the men decided to press charges because he thought he could get an earner out of it on the back of the publicity that would go with it. It is believed the matter fizzled out to nothing.

When You Lose It Completely

Having seen the damage Lee Duffy could inflict on someone with his bare fist we move on to compare the iron fist of Viv Graham.

Within the space of a few days, Viv had been a witness at an attempted murder trial, been shot at by a masked gunman and now here he was in court to face charges of GBH (grievous bodily harm).

The charge stemmed from an incident in February 1988, and here he was in May 1989 standing in the dock wondering if it was all going to end. He faced a custodial sentence, but his "guilty" plea had cut some ice with Judge Angus Stroyan.

The judge heard how Carl Wattler was rushed to hospital for emergency surgery to remove a large blood clot at the base of his brain after he was found lying unconscious outside of Baxter's pub in Newcastle. A scan had shown that an operation was needed at once otherwise he would have certainly died.

Carl Wattler was subsequently left with nerve damage that caused blurred vision in one eye and headaches as well as him being left with a limp. After the operation he had spent quite a bit of time in intensive care as well as having to be put on a ventilator to do his breathing for him.

The assault arose out of it being alleged that Mr Wattler had not finished his drink off quick enough when asked at closing time. Viv had acted a bit hastily in this instance and he put his hands up to the attack, whereby Viv punched Mr Wattler in the mouth.

What happened after that is somewhat unclear, as it was said that there was a confrontation in the street after this when Viv went to lock the doors.

Inquiries into this incident allege that what actually happened was that, yes, there certainly was a confrontation in the street outside of Baxter's.

Mr Wattler was apparently getting the better of Viv when a friend of Viv's who was working the door with him intervened and struck Mr Wattler across the head with an iron bar! This would account for the damage Mr Wattler sustained in the attack.

Wherever possible it is not the intention to glamorise Viv's life or to write things to make him look better or worse than how the public held him in their eye.

No communication has been made with Mr Wattler so as to seek his side of things, apologies to him if he reads this and finds it somewhat different to his account of the events herein. After all, it is Mr Wattler who was the victim of violence.

The sentence imposed on Viv was rather light and he could think himself lucky. He received an eighteen-month prison sentence, suspended for eighteen months, and a £500 compensation order to be paid to his victim, which seems a rather paltry amount in relation to the damage caused?

It would mean that if Viv should become involved in any further trouble and be brought before the court again within the eighteen months he could have the remainder of that sentence added to any other sentence given by a future court. That, you would think, would be a deterrent to most people.

From all accounts received it has been discovered that when Viv hit someone he would use an amount of force in relation to the victim's size. Should they become knocked out he could, at times, catch them in mid fall before they hit the ground stopping them receiving any further injury. Maybe that was after this incident of Mr Wattler receiving such horrendous injuries.

It was a close call for Viv! Just imagine how different things would have been if, say, the injury to Mr Wattler was fatal due to the blood clot not being discovered by the hospital surgeon. Viv would have been banged up for a few years and might have still been alive today due to the change of circumstances. It seems that when Mr Wattler's life was saved by emergency surgery it may have sealed Viv's fate.

Carl Wattler would have had to be dead for it to have enough effect on Viv's life to make him change his ways and thus altering the course of future events.

Fate took a U-turn and decided to pull Wattler back from the brink of death's door and the "what if" scenario mentioned above would not come into play.

Viv, it is claimed, always warned rowdy people three times to behave themselves; maybe it was this incident that caused him to be like that.

Viv was a hard hitter and in an incident when he was out with his family in a Newcastle nightspot he decked four men in the space of a few seconds. The damage he could do was awesome!

His slow and fast twitch muscle fibres were of the right combination to be fast and powerful in the same punch. One of the men he decked was as powerful as Viv. They apparently came into a nightspot wearing rigger boots! One of the men ordered a drink and said, "He's paying," nodding his head in the direction of Viv. This was the one out of the four who did not know Viv!

What happened next is in another chapter relating to Peter Connelly and confirmed by Viv's father, Jacky Graham. It shows the power and speed of Viv who was one of the world's most powerful naturals at fighting with his fists that Mother Nature had ever invented.

I leave it to you the reader to decide if Carl Wattler was hit by an iron bar or only by Viv's fist. Viv went on from Baxter's to work in Cats.

Under the 'Club Doorman Registration Scheme' that was later brought in it would have barred Viv from working the doors after he had a criminal record for violence.

They Call Him Viv

The man who really holds the main keys to the riddle of what made Viv tick is Peter Connelly, the potential brother-in-law of Viv.

Sid Henderson: Peter started by saying, "And you never ever got a chance to talk to his headmaster I suppose, did you?" Peter looked sharp, and he was sharp. That question put me on my toes! "Sid Henderson," I replied. That let Peter know I was aware of who Viv's former headmaster was.

Hussein, Andy Webb & Julie Rutherford: Peter asked if 'Hussein' and Andy Webb had been interviewed. "They were really close to him," Peter said. Andy was not sought for an interview due to it being believed that Viv thought he might have had a soft spot for a woman called Julie Rutherford. (One of Viv's former lovers.)

Viv always blamed Andy for being the father of a child that Julie had conceived whilst Viv was in prison and Andy had been driving Julie to visit Viv. Viv put one and one together and came up with three, as he himself was actually the father of the child!

Peter says, "He (Andy Webb) came here and he was crying, and he asked if I would take him across to Viv's graveside and he knelt there and sat there for an hour crying, showing his feelings."

Andy, a former Mr Great Britain body sculpture winner in the heavyweight division a number of years ago with interests in leisure facilities around Newcastle, was no wimp and for Peter to have witnessed such a huge man giving his emotions an airing would have been witnessing a true friend

Peter was closer than any friend of Viv's, he was nearly a

relation and obviously that put Peter in a status that automatically elevated him above that of a friend.

"People would get in contact with me to ask Viv if he would come and look after their pubs. The breweries would say, 'Get in touch with Peter Connelly, he'll see his brother-in-law, maybe he can sort something out for you?'

We did it in a fair way. We didn't say, 'Either you give us this,' or 'Pay us X amount of pounds and I'll look after your pub.' All the publicans drank with me in this pub and if they had a problem they would come to me. If you had five or six characters in your bar and they want to make it into a loud bar, noisy bar and start effing and blinding and swearing then other people aren't going to use your bar so the trade was dropping off in some of the pubs."

(Author's note: It was common knowledge that even the police passed on Viv's name to those in need of his assistance and advice about security.)

What would make these people come into a bar behaving in such a manner? "It would probably be their local bar, it would be close to where they lived. Lots of the pubs in Walker and Wallsend (areas in the East End of Newcastle) were all getting lots of trouble. A particular publican asked if I could bring Viv down. The troublemakers were pissing in glasses, urinating at the counter. They weren't great big hard people.

When Viv first came on the scene they didn't realise his capabilities, they didn't realise how big and powerful he was until he got up to them. I seen it on one occasion where a guy said, 'Peter, I've had enough of this.'

There was a particular family in the Walker area of Newcastle who weren't hard, but they were a bit crackers! They are a known family, I know them and get on with them, but Viv was working for the publican. I couldn't say, 'Viv, don't give them warnings because I know them.' He always gave them three warnings. You got a first warning, a second warning and then after the third warning you had to be clipped.

This particular guy used to cause trouble in quite a nice pub in Walker called the Stack and he went in and got a hold of this man and within seconds, and this man was a big lad as well, the pee was running down his legs. Running down his legs! So! Even though the manager was a little bit frightened to say anything at the time. The next time the lad came in, the manager threw the lad a packet of pampers, everybody started laughing at this man who was supposed to be a tough guy, that was one.

Then we would go on to another bar called the County. Viv would say, 'What can you afford?' He didn't say, 'I want £100!' He would say, 'What can you afford?' And the reply was, '£50 a week, Viv. I wont miss £50 a week. If I get rid of these two particular people then this bar will pick up again.' So Viv went behind the bar and started pulling pints in the bar and started serving people as if it was a family pub, his pub!

It was, 'A pint of Guinness, Viv.' Viv was laughing away and carrying on. 'A pint of lager, Viv.' And these people stopped literally point blank and never went back in the bar again.

The atmosphere was different in the pubs, the nightclubs and the social clubs. He didn't drink you know?" Peter says this with some admiration on behalf of Viv. "He only drank orange juice and occasionally a Guinness, if you ever bought him a Guinness he would get really happy and enjoy himself. You could have a good laugh with him, it was great and everybody was happy.

I got a phone call from a Bass publican; it was a pub off Norham Road up in North Shields. This landlady had been petrol bombed, she had a child on the premises, she couldn't take much more, but the breweries said they would pay to foot the bill. So obviously then we said, 'Well it's £500, it's a one off thing and we aren't coming up every week.'

We got the address of these people who done this and knocked on their door and they were warned there and then! There was nobody got hit or anything like that and that was the end of the trouble for that publican up until Viv was shot, and then all hell broke loose! Obviously everybody that ever got barred from pubs turned up. There was big parties, everybody went on a rampage, all those pubs got it that night."

Here we have a total antithesis of what the newspapers wrote of Viv being a gangster and a hoodlum. The romantic air of such a man is not good for selling newspapers.

The British are steeped in a history of romantic attachments with so-called likeable rogues: 'Fagin', 'Robin Hood' and 'Ronnie Biggs'. Did the British public really want to see such a romantic figure locked up and the key thrown away?

Even though Peter admits he has a past criminal record of violence for two assaults and GBH he was granted a publican's license. He says it seemed highly unlikely that he would ever get a license under such circumstances. There has been a lot of conjecture as to how it came about that the police granted this application without objection.

This lends innuendo of him being a police informer, he sets the record straight: "I was doing quite well and at that time I didn't hold a publican's license or anything like that. The police asked to see me and I came down. They said, 'Peter, it's come to our attention that you are trying to run a pub and we are thinking about letting you have your own license.' Which I thought was great, but because of my criminal record it was unlikely I would be allowed ever to get a license.

It was ten or fifteen years since I was last convicted. I took the wrong route and mixed with drug dealers, but at the time they were petty. They went in heavy-handed that lot did, they burst into bars and smashed the place up and even took coffins to bars and did horrible and nasty things. I was with that clique for a short time because at that time I didn't have any money."

Peter was asked if the use of coffins being left at pubs was a way of gaining territory for their drug pushers to sell from? "It was mostly about money in those days. It was just before the drugs came in heavy and just before Viv came across here."

Harry Perry: Was it the days just before the end of the Harry Perry era? "Harry was there, it was one of Harry's operations in his time. He was the boss way back then; Harry and me had quite a close relationship then. We were sent in to do the business and obviously they got the message one way or another."

Harry Perry, known as 'H', was considered a forerunner to the pre-Viv days. Although H could use his fists he was said by some people to have a short fuse and could blow for the slightest of reasons. That was way back in the 60s and 70s.

Harry Marsden: In a particular incident involving retired underworld figure Harry Marsden, there was an alleged incident in which H had taken a huge disliking to Harry , a fracas ending up in H being given a bloodied nose. Harry was threatened with being thrown off the Tyne Bridge…and now he's running a successful boxing club in Newcastle.

The main nightclub where most underworld figures met used to be Billy Bottos. All the Newcastle big name gangsters headed there in those days including the Kray's and even Joe Louis!

Jimmy Walker: Times have somewhat changed, but the nostalgia that exists within the North East about such places and names lives on. Peter knew some of the patrons of Billy Bottos and he remembers one in particular. "One of the greatest men that I admired," Peter says, "more than anything was a man called Jimmy Walker. I was at his funeral just a fortnight ago. His father had him fighting three fights a day for a half a crown ($12^{1/2}$ pence) a time, his knuckles were out here." Peter signifies with the use of his cupped hand over the top of the other. "This was a great man and a great fighter in lots of respects."

Where did these fights take place? "These were the bare knuckle days under Pottery Bank, under the bridge, in different places and the Quayside. He met Viv lots of times and Viv loved him.

Viv would sit and listen to some of his stories. And he had the greatest stories in the world to tell. I've always wished that before he died that someone would write a book about Jimmy Walker because his stories were far greater than you could ever say about Viv. There were some belters. I would sit for hours and listen to them.

They cut his legs off three times you know!" Peter indicates the places by pointing to his own leg and saying, "There, there and there. He had fluid in his legs until eventually his legs were off and it was just a body that they were carrying about. He lived through all of that, but died from pneumonia a year later."

Was he a hero of Viv's? "He fought a Dutch man and at the bottom of the plate (winner's trophy) was inscribed: *The man who invented bottle*, which was great because he was, until Viv came along and Viv obviously to me was the man who had all the right bottle in the world and I've seen some awesome things when Viv was fighting!

Denny Haig & The Cook Report: We once got called to a pub in North Shields in which we got paid £200. The man used to have a pub across here called the Queens. When Viv very first came to Newcastle that was the first pub he started to run in the East End of the city and the odd few. Denny Haig was working with Viv at that time." (Denny Haig is from Highfield near Rowlands Gill where Viv originated from.)

Denny Haig was featured in the 'Cook Report' an exposé TV documentary series. Peter goes on to say. "I didn't hold any grievance against Denny until what he did to Jack and I was really annoyed. I know he's quiet old, Denny, about forty odd or fifty, but Jack, to hit Jack! And Jack's never ever harmed anybody.

They all seemed to jump on the bandwagon after Viv was gone, they all seemed to jump on his back and everybody was in his pockets! They'd only ever got money off Viv, he supplied their wages."

It may well have been that Denny Haig was misquoted in the TV documentary about protection rackets. This led to a confrontation between him and Viv's father and all sorts of trouble ending in violence that would have seen Viv turning in his grave!

The televised interview that Denny gave to Roger Cook was cut to shreds and portrayed what Denny had said very differently to what he actually said in one go.

David Lancaster: Peter's ex-brother-in-law was David Lancaster. He was involved in the assault on Stuart Watson inside of Hobbo's nightclub. The whole thing is intertwined and Peter says, "Viv got into the wrong clique and once he got into the wrong clique it was hard for him to get out. They used Viv to get them into Hobo's because they were barred and Viv took them in."

Stuart Watson: A made up story was put to Viv so as to arouse his anger along the lines that Stuart Watson was alleged to have broken the jaws of two young men and had got away with it. Whether or not Viv was told this is conjecture.

Peter says, "You could see by his face (Watson's) he knew what was going to kick off." Peter briefly describes the ensuing three-minute attack on Watson. "Viv slung him about a bit, but Watson never went down, he blocked well and he covered well. You didn't see any photographs of Stuart Watson after it. You didn't see how bad he was?"

Watson is alleged to have said that he was used as a pawn in the game to get Viv. Peter continues describing the fight, "They went on about how heavy he was (Viv) and how he flung him (Watson) about like a rag-doll, this, that and the other. I think it was just his (Watson) jacket was too big for him, it looked worse than what it was; it was never as awesome as that.

There were four tapes, four cameras actually on this fight. You were getting the back before the front; you were getting the wrong sequence. It came out the wrong sequence, not the way the event actually happened. It was nothing, I seen a lot worse than that."

Ray Hewitson: Was a former lieutenant of the Harry Perry camp and had served time in the early 1980s. It was suggested that his connection with Viv had given rise to the drug stories. When Peter had first met Viv, 'Dodgy Ray' was one of Viv's closest friends. They, Viv and Ray, had eventually fallen out. People would say, "Have you spoken with Dodgy Ray?" Ray straddled the past and the future, but with regard to pursuing him about Viv it was accepted that he would have to join the queue of people wishing to be interviewed.

Peter confirms how people would use Viv's name for their own gains, "Any nightclub where people went to, they said, 'I'm Viv's pal,' just so they would get in. They never ever knew him from Adam; they had never ever met the man. You hear some stupid things from people."

Viv was well known in Teeside and he would travel down there once a week to nearby Spennymoor where a once a week rave was held in the Venue, Viv had to show his face. I spoke with the club's DJ who told me that Steve Forrest had taken over the Venue, but its days were numbered as a rave scene.

Peter confirmed that Viv made this once a week trip, as his face there alone would prevent any trouble. "He had to show his face to let them know he was in charge of it." It was put to Peter that Viv might have had contacts in Glasgow, but Peter could not confirm or deny this.

Pip Wright: Viv's generosity, at times, was overwhelming. Pip Wright was a friend of Viv's and Viv gave him £500 on the Christmas day, a week before he was gunned down. Wright was hard up for cash and Viv was generous that way. Peter says, "Some people say Viv bought his own murder weapon." (By this act of generosity.)

Mickey Laing: Wright is brought into the scenario on the allegation that he was close to Mickey Laing. Peter takes the story up from here, "Viv had showed Mickey Laing up a day or two before this (when Wright was given £500 from Viv). In the afternoon, Viv grabbed Mickey and threw him on the pool table, but they were drinking later on.

Laing was close to this Pip Wright. I've never met Pip Wright to this day. I took over a pub a few months ago just before Christmas.

There was a great big brick thrown through the window and it had a note attached saying, 'Put through the window, the next time it will be off your head,' it was signed on the brick, 'Pippy Wright'.

I had never ever met him, but I knew he had got £500, but I don't know what for or anything like that, it was just a favour from Viv."

(Author's note: This story about Viv just about buying himself the weapon that was responsible for his murder must be viewed as an allegation only and there is no inference that Pip Wright had any connection with the murder of Viv. Public opinion at times can be based on strange facts and it is not intended to sway public opinion in any direction.)

Terry Scott: With regard to Terry Scott (Viv's associate who held his head as Viv lay dying on the ground.), Peter says, "I've only seen Terry Scott once since he phoned me from the hospital and said that Viv was dead. I saw him once when I went into a nightclub in the town. It was a nice summer's night and he just sat outside the door with his arms folded and he just looked at me and I walked in. It was just that we didn't have anything to talk about."

Rob Armstrong: What about Rob Armstrong! (One of Viv's closest friends up to a few years before his death.) What I am getting at here is that if Viv had a brother that was just like him in the same way and they worked hand in hand like the Kray's used to or like the Richardson's then they would defend each other if something happened to one of them.

Because Viv did not have this support system there was no continuity to his defence. Therefore although, yes, the Connelly's were as close as he was going to get to a family it was not as though they were blood related.

What about all of those people and his friends? "They were just like rats leaving a sinking ship. They were super hard when he was there, but soon as he was gone they became nothing, they were just weaklings. He was their strength. What was going to happen to them as long as he was there? It was him that was always going to be in the front line, it was always going to be him that was going to be…" Peter talks fast at this point half finishing a sentence before moving on to the next, "…they knew his capabilities and knew nothing was going to happen to them and it was just a free ride for them and there was as many as there could that got on to the band wagon."

Brenda Hickman: Peter is saying that there is no loyalty there and in terms of Viv's mother and father that are not financially sound compared to some of Viv's so called friends who have got money. "Ask Brenda Hickman where's all of these millions then, £2m and there's them (Viv's parents) can't even get the phone on. Viv's car was on the chuckie (HP). They've got a house that any average person's got, they don't own it or nothing."

(Author's note: Brenda Hickman is a crime reporter that has worked for the Evening Chronicle for some years. She covered the Viv murder. And according to one fellow journalist has "everything sewn up.")

Alan Rooney: The Alan Rooney case is talked about. Rooney, 34, (1994) received eight years imprisonment for blackmail. In June of 1993, six months before Viv was murdered, Rooney had heard of a Sunderland publican putting Viv down with insults. For these insults Rooney was prepared to collect in the name of Viv. The sum of £5,000 was demanded and if it was not forthcoming then Rooney told the man that he would be tortured and have his home burned down as well as being murdered. The victim was told that he was acting on behalf of Viv and said, 'He's the man.' (See chapter 10.)

The victim in all of this was a father of three and for the

sake of the children his name is withheld. Had Viv been a real 'up and get 'em gangster' he would have gone along to the man's home himself and done the business for the disrespect he was shown. Viv just laughed it off like the affable man he was. Those that said Viv took liberties with people were proved wrong by this scenario.

Peter comments on this. "That was on the other side of the water, Sunderland. I used to like Alan Rooney, he was quite a funny lad and he came out with some funny things. When Viv was murdered, though, Alan Rooney then tried to twirl it to say he was working for Viv when that happened."

Viv was not into blackmail and obviously had said whatever you are doing has nothing to do with me, but if you make anything from my name do it, but I am not into that."

The Independent newspaper was mentioned and given a good report from Peter, but as for the other newspapers, he gives a cutting criticism of them. Should there be a law to prevent the invasion of the press at such times? "Definitely. As far as the Independent was concerned that was not the case, but the rest of the press I had nothing to say to them.

I was a pallbearer at the funeral and my stepbrother Michael was comforting my sister. The press said that this was 'Peter Connelly comforting his sister', it wasn't even me it was my brother Michael! They didn't even know me or nothing.

Tony Cartlidge: Then I was angry and I did want to say something. I was at the inquest and I said a lot there. Tony Cartlidge who interviewed me in the Close Up North TV documentary did a fair representation and I told him all that I knew."

Gillian Lowes: Peter is asked how Viv found the time to relax? "Taking the phone off the hook for one, he used to love just getting out the road and going somewhere different from people and maybe just him and Anna. I knew that he loved his kids and would go across as often as he could to see them he just absolutely idolised them. There was nothing greater, I was there the day he went to the hospital when

They Call Him Viv

Gillian Lowes gave birth to the bairn, it was a lovely day, he was happy.

He was a great provider for her; he never ever left her short. She always thought there was something there and that he would come back. He was a great man."

What of the stress? "I think Viv took too much on, he was doing far too much. Later on drugs became a big thing and they started coming in. They weren't there at first; they started moving very fast and there were quite a few drug dealers. I didn't realise there were so many drugs about and they all wanted to be in on the nightclub scene. That's where they were sold. The 'E's became popular and different types of ecstasy tablets. Viv was never involved in any type of drug dealing."

Viv had been accused (After he died.) of being a big drug baron; people say there is no smoke without fire. Suggestions of a £2m turnover and racketeering were plastered in enough newspapers to cover the side of any barn door.

Most people will know of someone who is a drug user or know of someone who knows someone who is a user of drugs. Why should Viv be any different in this context? We live in a decadent society. Even President Clinton of USA drawed but, '…did not inhale.' Viv was a naïve person when it came to that side of things, but he certainly did not approve of drugs that were used to get a high. Unwittingly, he may have become involved in some activities that could have been misconstrued.

Geoffrey Tote: A story was related on hearsay to Peter about Viv being asked by Geoffrey Tote in Newcastle's Madison's nightclub to sort some trouble out with the doormen who had allegedly taken his 'E's and his money whilst he was in the toilets.

The Sayers': He went crying to Viv saying that his drugs and money were taken from him. Viv went and knocked the two doormen out and gave Tote his things back. Peter says, "I don't know why he did that, but I heard about it. It was a stupid thing to do, but Viv was like that and he thought he was helping out. They weren't Viv's drugs. There was another girl in who was a big drug dealer who had plenty of money. The Sayers' got involved and beat her and her man up there and then in Madison's. Viv didn't intervene, he just kept out of it. He stood back and didn't get involved in it. Then I realised that there was that many people wanting to sell drugs.

A drug dealer asked Viv for a loan of £500. The man offered to pay Viv £600 back, I don't know if he loaned him the money, but that's the way people went on. Viv had no idea of other people's motives for wanting to borrow money."

Peter must have seen a number of changes in Viv since he first met him up until the time of his death? "He used to love going to the gym for half an hour or an hour, he would use Andy Webb's gym and they would end up having such a laugh. The laughs that went on in the gym you haven't heard the likes of it.

I never ever touched weights, but I was watching him as they put some weights on the bar. It was awesome, the weights they were putting on for him! Off he goes, he was bench-pressing it and it was great to see him doing this and everybody would clap and cheer. Then they would put a bit more weight on and he would just press the weight that nobody could bench press. He used to love it if he could exceed it and get a better weight, he thought it was great.

Each time he was getting bigger, you could see him getting bigger, but then he was getting little side affects. He was complaining about certain things, he was aching and he didn't feel well at some stage. He had an abscess on his leg." Viv at this time was taking steroids and they did not agree with him as they do not (in the end) agree with anyone. Viv gave them up because due to pressure from his fiancée and his father.

Peter says, "Bad temperedness started creeping into it. Viv didn't train as hard then. He didn't have time to train because

212

he was running all over the place. His mobile phone number changed that many times because there were that many people who had his number. You would say, 'Have you got Viv's number?' Then you would pass that number on to others. On my book I've got about five or six numbers for him."

Higgins Security: What about Higgins Security. They were employed, apparently, to get Viv out of a pub he was running, is this true? "They phoned Viv up and asked to meet him and he met them and took them for dinner. They actually wanted Viv to work for them, the Higgins Security Company."

They were called in though a North East pub, a Newcastle pub? "To stop Viv from entry? They couldn't stop Viv from entry!" Not to stop Viv from entry but to secure the pub because a publican called them in? "I knew that he had a meeting and had to go to Birmingham, but he didn't go." I recalled a story I was told, which was that Viv had slapped one of the Higgins crew around and they all left after giving Viv some money.

The other story was that a publican called in Higgins Security because Viv was causing some trouble, they went to see Viv and told him not to go into the pub and Viv complied, was this right? "Viv wouldn't go down (to Birmingham), they offered to take him for a meal and meet him and obviously give him a bite of the cherry, they knew he was the only one up here who could control the doors."

Peter relates how Higgins Security men were controlling the doors of certain places in Newcastle. The men working for such a lucrative company had to abide by the company's wishes, but they were frightened whilst in the Tyneside area. Peter says, "The guys were frightened on those doors, even though Higgins was the company. They were frightened they had to do it. Everybody was going to stick by them if there was a fight, but they didn't. Whoever got hit, got hit, in Viv's case they tried to befriend him because they didn't want to get on Viv's bad side."

Higgins Security is not a fly by night company, they are a

very respected security firm and at times do work hand in hand with the authorities. "It was costing them a lot of money to bring these people up from Birmingham and keeping them in hotels. It was costing them a lot more money than what Viv was getting." What were they brought in for? "I think it was the fact that there was that many getting in for nothing in some of the clubs. They started off in some of the clubs as well as some of the nightclubs, they seemed to get bigger and bigger."

Here we have a reputable company supplying their staff to work the club doors. What was the difference between this company and Viv? Just because one company is registered does not mean it is any better or more above board than an individual employed privately for the same service. Viv was consequently asked to help Higgins's out. "You could see that they wanted nothing to do with Viv when he went to the places. You could see that the fear of the thought of him coming to the places put the fear of God into them. There was never any trouble. Viv didn't cause trouble for the sake of causing trouble sake."

Paddy Leonard & Billy Robinson: What about those people who started Viv off in the game, Paddy Leonard and Billy Robinson. "They all get old, they've lived there lives, they just want an easy life, they just want to retire you see. That's it basically and live their lives in Tenerife."

Alan Malarkey: Viv did some good in his life and supported many sports he sponsored football teams and had a heating system installed into Wallsend boxing club.

"It was for a lad called Alan Malarkey who ran the club, they were a good club who were tremendous in the way of amateurs. Viv used to like to go training with the young 'uns. When they seen him it used to really cheer them up, they thought it was great.

Manny Burgo: "Another thing that was said about what Manny Burgo was supposed to do to Viv in the ring. Manny was around in the amateur boxing scene the same time as Viv. I seen Manny cower away from him, he nearly died when he was caught in Macey's in the town. When Viv caught him he couldn't get out, he shouted, 'VIV! I've come to sort it out.' Manny was more or less in charge of the coast. He didn't ever venture on to Viv's territory, but then obviously Viv got well known. It didn't stop here, it was getting bigger and bigger so eventually these people were getting sick of the people they had paid for a long time and they wanted Viv. They wanted Viv; it was as simple as that. People would say, 'Who's he?' And just about everyone knew him, 'They call him Viv,' would be the reply.

Then he started going into Whitley Bay, Tynemouth and he started getting bigger, pubs and clubs. They felt he shouldn't be doing this because he was cutting them out of a job. Viv would say I'll keep two of your pubs and you can have the rest yourselves." Manny Burgo had come into Newcastle to see Viv to sort the situation out.

Peter continues, "In Macey's, there was him (Manny) and a few of his pals and he had come to try and see Viv. There was something or another said. You've never seen anybody run! Viv was running this way and the other to try and catch him! Manny talked his way out of it and Viv gave him the benefit of the doubt and didn't hit him or anything and this man Burgo is huge.

Manny actually got in the car to drop me off, it was never mentioned again. When Manny ever sees me now he never speaks or anything, he just walks straight past, and mind, I watched him box, but I never rated him. He didn't ever fear me in any way and I wasn't feared of him. I'm not feared of anyone that I've mentioned, I don't fear for Adam.

I don't value life anymore now. It just cut everybody up, he didn't deserve it." Peter's voice goes dry and husky and just a hint that his inner strength is fading shows through the happy go lucky exterior. His point of not valuing life anymore was amplified by a number of people connected to Viv. Viv seems to have been the beacon of light that led these people into another world.

What about these people who made Viv Graham into what

he was. Built him up and put him on to a pedestal and went away and left him there. He had to be Viv Graham on his own; he couldn't be Viv Graham with Billy Robinson or Paddy Leonard? "I think you start to meet new people and new friends. I don't think Viv ever thought to any extreme that things were going to come to him being wanted as badly by different pubs and clubs and even shops. What about the coloured community, he had to go and sort out trouble at the mosque. Viv was asked to help them resolve a situation, which he did.

It could be argued that Viv had no colour bar when it came to money but the fact is Viv had no discrimination against any race or colour. What if Viv was a member of the National Front? Would that make the press happy enough? There were no reports of his do-good actions by the press because it just didn't sell newspapers."

Many thanks go to Peter Connelly for his assistance in helping put the full story across.

The Last Tango

There was a lot of talk of the Duffer and Viv getting it on in a winner takes all fight. We all have fears, secret fears, fears masked by a thin veneer of braveness and fear that just breaks free from its shackles to be exposed for all to see!

I feel that Viv may have harboured a secret fear of the consequences of ever fighting the Duffer. Such a fear was not of meeting the Duffer, but a fear of the consequences of what such a meeting would produce...even if Viv won the fight he would have still have lost his kingdom!

It has been claimed that if the Sayers' turned up with Lee Duffy in tow then Viv was going to be a little bit nicer to them than he would have been without Lee Duffy at their side.

A fight was organised between Duffy and Viv in the Havana club, in Middlesbrough, but Viv did not turn up! But this has proven to be a rumour and nothing else!

The feedback from a second attempt at organising a fight between the two was that Viv thought he was going to be shot and again didn't turn up. Some say he remained at home...sitting on a toilet bowel?

Someone has suggested that Viv had not bottled it, but the two, Viv and the Duffer, actually did meet some time before such a fight was even talked about.

A meeting in a Tyneside pub on a very different matter saw Lee Duffy stand on a table and say, "If anyone wants to question my credibility then question me." This was relating to a man called Craig Howard. Viv was through the bar end of the pub and it is claimed that he never opened his mouth. Of course this was not a confrontational meeting and at that time Viv was not in conflict with Duffy.

Viv Graham & Lee Duffy's Parallel Lives

An underworld character from Teesside said: "No doubt about it, Viv was a very hard man, but I don't think Viv would have beat Lee. Viv was big and strong, but the Duffer had a psychopathic streak that Viv didn't have!

Something the Sayers' might have been worried about was that if Lee and Viv had of got their heads together then they might have blitzed them clean out of the water.

But considering it was going to come off, Lee was permanently up the Mayfair nightclub (Newcastle) all the time, constantly up Newcastle, but Viv wasn't down here.

There were two arranged fights and Viv didn't turn up at either of them! Viv had a few doors up there and Lee went around and taxed a few of Viv's men. He wanted to put it on Viv's toes because he hadn't turned up."

"One Saturday night..." it is claimed by Lee Harrison, "...the Duffer went around the Bigg Market nightspot in Newcastle and knocked all the doormen out, first one pub, then the other one, then the other one and so on.

I dropped him off while he went and done it and he was on his own, I've even dropped him off in Moss Side on his own when he chinned a doorman in a kitchen. Lee was wearing a white rain hat at that time.

When he chinned them in the Bigg Market he said, 'Go and tell Viv I'm here, get him here, go and tell your boss I'm here!' They all ran a mile, including Dodgy Ray."
(Author's note: Craig Howard is the man rumoured to have been one of Duffy's main drivers and it is thought that it was Craig who also drove Duffy around the nightclub doors when Duffy was in search of Viv.)

Tommy Harrison says, "People say Viv wouldn't go (to fight Duffy) because the Sayers' would have shot him. The Sayers' wouldn't have shot him, they were just young lads. When Lee went and knocked Graham's doormen out, where was Viv? If Viv believed he was going into a death trap in an organised fight with Lee and then Lee goes to Newcastle and knocks his doormen out and tells them to go and tell Viv he was there then he should have come, shouldn't he?

The Last Tango

I've worked all the doors, I've fought everybody you want to fight and if a man had of come and knocked my doormen out then I'd have had to go.

That night he went looking for Viv, bang, bang, bang and it cost them nothing. Viv called into my house, as he was passing, but how do you pass.

Viv said to me, 'I'm not frightened of nobody, me, you know. I'll fight anybody.' I said, 'So will Lee, but why? Who's going to benefit out of it, who's going to benefit out of you and him having it off, why don't you two just graft together?'

Viv Graham never came to the Havana club it was just a rumour. A fight was going to be held in a warehouse outside of Newcastle. He came to see me when it was all getting out of hand; it was like the old cowboy thing wasn't it.

I said, 'Use your heads, you've got Newcastle in your hands and Lee's got all of Teesside in his hands. What the hell you want to be running around fighting with other people for, I don't know.'

But Lee had this thing about them (Sayers'). They were going to look after him. I think that was the last tango, he didn't need them. He didn't need any money, he could go into a bar or a pub or a club or a restaurant, they'd invite him into the place.

I'd say to Lee, 'If you can wine, dine, eat, taxis for nothing then what the hell do you want to be going up there for, ham and eggs?'

Lee Harrison says, "I flew to Jamaica and one of the people I bumped into said, 'Where are you from?' I replied, 'Middlesbrough,' and he replied in a broad Jamaican accent, 'You know Lee Duffy, man?' He knew straight away and he hadn't been brought up in England, he was a full Jamaican.

He said, 'I was in jail for a week and he came on to my landing and started throwing everyone over the top of the landing.' At that time Lee's name was bigger in the jail then it was outside."

Others had an interest in Brian Cockerill's fighting power

and two in particular wanted to see a match between Brian Cockerill v Viv Graham.

Brian, the big fellah, explains what happened, "Stephen and Michael Sayers were willing to put £50,000 up for me to fight Viv and if it had of come off then they'd have been able to say, 'We've got a better fighter than you now.' They thought they could manipulate us to their own ends!

I was in a rave club and I was talking to Robbie Armstrong who was Viv's partner and I'd had a fight with a big lad from Stockton the week before, I'd knocked him out and Robbie said, 'Do you know a lad called Cockerill?' Well of course Robbie only knew me as 'Big Bri', he didn't know my second name was 'Cockerill'.

Robbie went on to say that the kid I'd knocked out had offered Viv Graham £10,000 to come and fight this 'Cockerill' guy.

Robbie said, 'What do you think he'll do?' I said, 'I think the big fellah will beat him,' and he went, 'He's that good!' I laughed and said, 'It's me, you daft cunt,' and he said, 'You're joking,' and he couldn't believe it.

About a week later, Robbie said, 'Viv doesn't want anything to do with that fight, you know.' I said, 'What fight?' 'Stephen and Michael put the £50,000 up,' he replied.

I didn't even know anything about it. What they were going to do was put a fight up in a warehouse in Gateshead or wherever it was or Newcastle and they we're going to charge £10 a man to come in and watch it.

They'd done all this behind my back without them even knowing. Robbie was saying, 'The fight's supposed to be next month,' and I hadn't a clue what was going on.

Anyway, I went to Newcastle to see Stephen and Michael, I goes in the nightclub and they'd only done it because they knew Viv Graham was coming in that night, but he never come in.

I heard Viv did a lot of bad things with lads up in Newcastle; he invited Stevie Hammer out and then has a punch up with him and punches him in the face. That, for me, was out of order, you know.

When I was inside with Geordie kids they used to say that he was a bastard for doing that. He'd get you up, get you pissed, put his arm around you and say, 'Let's have our photograph taken,' and then he'd punch them in the face, he was terrible for it."

The name Lee Duffy is raised to Viv's father, Jack. He speaks candidly about this man, "Duffy said wor Viv wouldn't meet him, wouldn't have anything to do with him?"

Duffy came to Newcastle from his manor of Middlesbrough in Teesside a few times looking for Viv so as to have a fight. As you've already heard, he went to a club and beat some doormen up so as to flush Viv out of hiding. Such an act on someone else's territory was seen as a direct insult, 'I spit on your grave' sort of thing. But Viv knew what was being plotted and did right to stay away.

It has been claimed that the Duffer arrived at Newcastle in the back of a van, and as the van was moving through the centre of Newcastle he threw open the rear double doors and shouted, "I am the god of hellfire!"

If such a claim is thought to be true, it certainly shows the Duffer not to have been scared of Viv. It is further claimed that when word got back to Viv he decided to stay at home and switched his phone off!

Assuming these doormen would allow Duffy to do that, doormen would come in from the surrounding pubs to help out in such circumstances.

Admittedly, Viv felt awkward about meeting this man, so it goes. But Viv's father, Jack, feels strongly about this and offers up this explanation, "Not likely, Duffy couldn't brae wor missus. What a load of bloody tripe." It is explained that people wanted Duffy to settle their scores with Viv, but that is only hearsay.

A fight was set up and it was arranged to take place in a warehouse in the Byker area of Newcastle. Viv's reason for not turning up was because he had been warned about certain people who would be there in the crowd watching. Even if he beat Duffy, he thought the set-up would result in him being murdered anyway.

Duffy was simply a pawn in a much bigger game than he could perceive himself to be in. Duffy was a fine strapping lad; he had a similar background to Viv. He had made a name for himself in the Teesside area and could handle himself as well as take a good punch. Both Viv and the Duffer were no strangers to the smell of death; they had both been staring death in the face from the barrel end of a shotgun in their pasts.

Viv was a former associate of the Sayers, this is accepted, but after the Stuart Watson incident that led to imprisonment for Viv, he always blamed the Sayers for being the cause of that.

He knew he had been used like a clockwork mouse and after finishing his prison sentence for the assault he went solo.

His territory in terms of being a trouble-shooter for publicans was off limits to just about everyone who intended to cause trouble, and that included all of the crime families in Newcastle.

Viv was the thorn in their side and a plan was needed to oust him from his position of authority of stopping drug dealers from entering his patch in the East End of Newcastle.

The Duffer was the only real hope for the dealers of ousting Viv, as there was no one else in Newcastle capable and even if there were then they would not want the unenviable position that Viv held.

They had to go head hunting outside of the area in their recruiting drive for someone who stood a likely chance of winning a fight against Viv.

Lee Duffy was the answer, he had been having a bit of a hard time of it in Middlesbrough because it seemed no matter where Duffy turned there was someone out to get him. He was offered the opportunity to take over things in Newcastle, but there was just one little problem, he would first have to beat Viv in a fight.

The Last Tango

If Duffy had been successful in having a fight with Viv and just supposing there was an outside chance of him beating Viv, then the tables would have eventually been turned on Duffy by his hosts. How long would it have been before Duffy decided he was going to have it all for himself!!!!

Duffy would have become ambitious and would have become a threat to those that had brought him in for their own gain. Full circle and what goes around comes around.

Looking at the other scenario where Viv definitely beats Duffy, it would not have been as cut and dried as that because there was a faction just dedicated to getting rid of Viv at any cost!

He would have been killed at the proposed fight anyway. Viv had turned lemon and people were starting to see him in a different light to that of being a pub and club trouble-shooter.

Viv would have been either killed while fighting Duffy by some knife or weapon attack on his back from the spectators or shot dead at the end of the fight. Viv knew this!

They would have been over Viv like gremlins, access to the East End of Newcastle was needed at all costs even at the cost of people's lives. Nothing mattered to these people. Viv had a family and friends, but in the end friends soon leave the fold, leaving relatives to grieve on their own.

Viv and the Duffer never did get to meet in battle. The two gladiators with huge reputations were simply reduced to two small pieces in a much larger battle...drugs!!

Russian Roulette

There are two stories as to how Duffy met his death; I'll give you the one you have probably read of in the hundreds, if not thousands, of column inches of newspaper articles and features that have been written about it. I do not intend to rehash those features so I will move through it as quickly as possible. What follows is the official version of events, and as we know 'official' versions differ a great deal from 'real life' events!

August 1991: David James Allison killed Lee Paul Duffy on 25th August at 3.30am outside the Afro-Caribbean Centre, in Marton Road, Middlesbrough. As a result of what is claimed to have been an argument in the centre, both men became embroiled in a fight that took place outside of the centre.

February 1993: Allison, 26, of Overfields, Teesside, claimed he feared Duffy might have a gun when the pair fought and he said he swung out a knife that was handed to him during the fight because he feared Duffy was going to kill him.

Allison said that he'd seen Duffy with a gun on previous occasions. Once Duffy, Allison claims, pulled out a gun in August and did not say or do anything. He believed Duffy was playing mind games with him.

At the trial, the jury heard how Allison had told police: 'I had to fight on; I was fighting for my life.' What is true is that when Allison said that he and Duffy had clashed several times in the past it ended up in him being given a good hiding in Blaises (Blaze's) nightclub, in Middlesbrough.

Duffy gave the offer of a fight to him in the Afro-Caribbean Centre and Allison, not wanting to appear a coward, accepted. Allison claimed Duffy said to him: 'I'm going to bust your head in and kill you.' After that they started fighting and Duffy overpowered Allison and he says: 'I thought my head was going to split again. I thought he was going to kill me.'

Allison broke free and he was handed a knife, he says: 'He came lunging at me; I was exhausted at the time and just swung out with it. He backed off saying, 'I'm going to kill you, you've stabbed me'.

I used the knife to protect myself, to hurt him, to win the fight. If not, he would have come after me, used a knife or used a gun.'

Allison's particular use of the phrase '…to hurt him, to win the fight' is usually sufficient in terms of what the court would deem beyond 'reasonable' self-defence since self-defence is not a defence for hurting someone, needlessly. On the basis of the words Allison had incriminated himself with, it looked likely that the least finding against him would be a one of manslaughter.

Self-defence is the 'minimum' use of force required to defend yourself or your property from the real threat of an injury or further injury or even death. Using a knife to 'hurt' someone or to 'win' a fight with is NOT self-defence!

The court was told by Allison that he was in the wrong place at the wrong time when Lee Duffy decided to pick a fight with him.

Giving evidence in his own defence, Allison added: 'He put his hand round the back of my neck. I thought about the knuckleduster in my pocket. I thought to hit him with it. Finish it at that and leave. I thought I might knock him unconscious. I would have to leave him unconscious to be able to walk away.

I believed he could kill a person…he was capable of it. He started to beat me up. He came forward at me and threw me to the ground. I landed on my back. Duffy got on top of me. He was braying my head off the floor.

I thought he was going to kill me, I thought my head was

going to split open. The knuckleduster was in my right hand. I was hitting the back of his head trying to get him off me. He was butting me. I bit his cheek. Heard someone say, 'Shiv him!' I now know that means to stab someone.

Then for some reason he was off me? I was helped to my feet by some friends and taken to a nearby wall. When I was against the wall the knife was put in my hand. Someone said, 'Protect yourself!'

I could hardly walk. I did not know where I was. I just wanted to get away from him and go home. I was terrified and semi conscious. I could not let myself go unconscious. He would have killed me there and then. I took him seriously when he said he was going to kill me.

Some people were shouting, 'He's got a gun!' I was terrified. I was confused. Duffy came towards me. He had an object in his hand. I don't know what it was. When he walked forward he raised it. I thought it might be a gun.

There was nowhere to run. I was not in a fit state to run. I walked forward to get on to Marton Road and go home. He raised his arm so I lashed out. I did not aim for any part of his body. I did not intend to kill him. I did not want to cause him serious harm. All I wanted was for him to leave me alone.'

Later that morning, Alison visited Middlesbrough General Hospital, where he found out the shocking news that Duffy was dead!

The court was told by Allison how he had met King and Neil for drinks in Middlesbrough town center at a pub and then they went on to the blues party, getting there shortly before Duffy arrived with some Geordie friends. Allison later described them as 'gangsters.

The prosecutor, Jim Spencer QC, at the murder trial, which took place nearly 18 months after Duffy's death, said: 'Allison had been drinking for 12 hours before the fight, while Duffy, known as Teesside's top dog, had taken ecstasy tablets and cocaine.

Seconds representing each man had separated the pair into

corners and when round one came to an end they had a minute's rest.' During the course of the fight Allison had a knuckleduster on and used this to his advantage and when Duffy spotted metal in his hand he said: 'You cannot even do it with metal in your hand.'

In defence of his actions on behalf of Allison, David Robson QC told the court that Allison was trapped in the car park and, believing Duffy was armed with a revolver, only acted in self-defence. 'He was like an animal in a cage; if there was an evil supreme in Middlesbrough it was Lee Duffy. Allison was the rabbit in the trap.'

David Woodier, a prosecution witness, told the jury that Duffy had punched him senseless two weeks prior to his death for no good reason.

The jury was given a graphic description of Duffy's last minutes. Woodier went on to say: 'Duffy enjoyed the fear people had of him.' (Maybe he should have been a defence witness!)

He went on to describe how Duffy had come into the Afro-Caribbean Centre looking 'stoned and wild eyed,' and he agreed with the defence QC, David Robson, that Duffy had 'poisoned the atmosphere' of the previously jovial and happy feeling in the place.

Duffy was then meant to have entered the club, telling people to 'move' and to 'get out of my way, now!' Woodier went on to say that he could sense something was going to happen and that Duffy had approached Allison, saying: 'Do people think we are going to fight?' With that he saw Duffy walk outside and Allison followed him.

Woodier said he went out about five minutes later and described how Duffy and Allison had a hold of each other in a sort of lock. 'I noticed Lee had his top off and was bare-chested. David Allison was covered in blood. Both seemed to let go of each other at the same time. Allison looked tired and worn out. At that stage Duffy was jumping about looking really fit, like a boxer.

I heard Duffy say to Allison: 'You had to use a

knuckleduster, but you still couldn't put me away.' Allison answered: 'When it comes to bullies like you I have to use something.' Duffy seemed to get very angry. He picked up a bottle off the wall and said: 'You know what I'm going to do, don't you?'

Duffy brought one of his arms round holding the bottle. Allison seemed to move to one side and pointed his arm out in a sort of roundhouse move. Duffy was facing him. That blow struck Duffy towards his left arm.

Straightaway Duffy put his arm across his chest and said: 'Get me to hospital, I'm dead.' There was blood, a lot of blood! I saw his jeans turn red.'

David Robson QC asked Woodier some leading questions that should have in normal circumstances, with a diligent prosecutor in attendance, been objected to.

> David Robson: *'Allison did not go out to terrorise people in the way Duffy did?'*
> Woodier: *'No.'*
> David Robson: *'Lee Duffy had the town terrified, didn't he?'*
> Woodier: *'Yes.'*

Was the judge awake at this point, because such leading questions are not allowed in court? Even the judge can intervene in such cross-examining, but he did not?

I cannot understand what the prosecution were doing by using Woodier as a witness, he did nothing other than help the defence?

Alongside Allison were Richard Ralph Neil, 20, charged with assisting Allison to get away from the scene and Lee Robert King, 25, charged with attempting to pervert the course of justice by dropping the knife down a drain, both denied the charges.

During the course of the trial, various witnesses who were either friends of Duffy or Allison gave evidence. John Fail, Duffy's friend, told the court: *'Allison was staggering after Duffy had banged his head on the ground and nutted him several times.'*

Russian Roulette

An acquaintance of Allison's, Adrian Boddy: '*At one stage, Duffy picked Allison up in a rugby tackle and smashed him to the floor.*

Allison just stood there staggering, I never saw anything in his hand. Allison had swung several punches at Duffy, but failed to make any contact.

It was after one blow which did land under Duffy's armpit that Duffy shouted he was dying.'

On behalf of the police, Dr Alistair Irvine, a police surgeon, examined Allison after the fight with Duffy and confirmed that the injuries Allison had received were consistent with having spent some time on his back during the fight and that the injuries to his head were consistent with having it banged on the ground several times.

Dr Irvine also testified that there were also indications of blows to his face.

Questioned by the judge, Angus Stroyan QC, Dr Irvine confirmed that such blows could have caused a concussional effect and would have caused a significant jarring effect to the head.

With regards Duffy's wounds, the Home Office pathologist, Dr John McCarthy, described Duffy's injuries, which had included two stab wounds, one to the back which did not nor could not have proved fatal and one to his armpit which severed a main artery (axillary artery) causing Duffy to bleed to death within minutes! With regards the stab wound to Duffy's back, this will be reviewed later.

An early morning telephone call at 8am alerted David James Allison Snr to the state of affairs involving his son and Lee Duffy. In a phone call to his father Allison said: '*I think I've killed Lee Duffy!*'

When Allison pleaded with his father to get his clothes from a garage rooftop he agreed to do that.

Mr Allison Snr appeared on behalf of the prosecution and he told the court that his son was crying when he called him and he told his son to give himself up to the police.

Allison, a scaffolder, rang back some $3\frac{1}{2}$ hours later at

11.30am saying he'd give himself up at his aunt's house.

The reason Allison gave the court for having the knuckle-duster in his possession was because Duffy had threatened him the day before the fatal stabbing. Prior to that, the knuckleduster had sat at his mother's home for some years.

Q: When is a gun not a gun? **A:** When it is not there.

You've read that Allison claimed someone shouted that Duffy had a gun, and it was claimed that Duffy had held something aloft in his hand and that Allison may have been concussed.

A surprise exhibit was produced in court, namely a Smith and Wesson .38 revolver said to have been found near the scene of Duffy's fatal stabbing!

Blues party DJ Saidhu Kamara told the court how a gun (miraculously) 'fell' from a black leather jacket which he found near his DJ box at the Afro-Caribbean Centre after the fatal fight. The jacket, he said, was similar to one that Duffy had been wearing earlier that evening! What a coincidence!

On finding the gun, Kamara said he had hidden it in a nearby derelict house and then proceeded to bury it underneath a rosebush at his girlfriend's home. How generous of him!

And just as remarkable as that story was, here is an even more remarkable story! Somehow, magically, Joseph Livingstone, a friend of Allison's had found out about this hidden gun that was buried beneath a rosebush!

As a consequence of this bizarre find, Livingstone approached Kamara saying that the solicitor, James Watson, representing Allison would like to see the item in order to help with his defence at the trial. Such good timing!

A forensic scientist, Michael Hammond, gave testimony to the court that Duffy had consumed a massive amount of the drug Ecstasy and that blood samples taken from Duffy's body had revealed a high concentration of metabolised cocaine and traces of alcohol.

Mr Hammond went on to say that the amount of Ecstasy in Duffy's body was two micrograms per millilitre, which is an extremely high level of the drug and in some cases that concentration could be life threatening.

The court was further told by Mr Hammond that high doses of Ecstasy could produce anxiety, paranoia, symptoms of psychosis together with mood swings and violent irritability. He advised that cocaine could have a similar effect, including causing aggressive behaviour. The combination of the two would make each more effective than one on its own.

It would seem that the circus had come to town when a host of witnesses were brought forward to testify to Duffy's gun totting exploits. Witnesses testified that Duffy:

- He once held a gun to taxi driver Arzur Shan's head in a bizarre game of Russian roulette! He spun the chamber after putting one bullet in to it, fired at the taxi driver's head ordering him to drive 'faster', but the gun never went off. He then he pulled the gun away and fired it again, this time the gun went off, putting a hole through the taxi roof! This was done to impress someone who was with him.

- Often played a game of one-man Russian Roulette in front of Karen Pitelem in her Thornaby home with a revolver loaded with one bullet. He would say, and believe, that he was 'invincible' before pulling the trigger a number of times as he held the gun to his head!

- Played three-man Russian Roulette with friends, one man bottled out of it and on the third pull of the trigger Duffy fired the gun at the wall and the gun went off!

- Duffy had asked a DJ in a nightclub to dedicate a record to Allison and continuously waived a gun at him while the record played.

- Fired a gun into the wall of Karen Pitelem's house when he was visiting as an unwanted guest in order to frighten her.

- Fired a gun off in Middlesbrough's Havana nightclub.

Forensic evidence, though, showed that Duffy had NOT been in contact with a gun on the night of his death. Which of course dumbfounds any of the testimony given by the DJ, Kamara.

Duffy had earlier assaulted a man who tried to save his life. Stephen Pearson was thrown backwards and grabbed by the throat in an unprovoked attack by Duffy.

Later on, Mr Pearson saw the fight leading up to the stabbing and chased after the fatally wounded Duffy as he ran in various directions shouting for help.

Mr Pearson took his T-shirt off and used it to try and stem the blood spouting out of Duffy's armpit wound. He tied a tourniquet and helped place the mortally wounded Duffy in to a car that had been flagged down. Immediately prior to this, attempts were made to flag a taxi down, but it had driven off at speed.

When it was Lee King's turn to be represented, his defence counsel, Jamie Hill, told the jury that they had to be sure he intended to pervert the course of justice when he disposed of the knife. Mr Hill said: 'He had just seen his friend Allison having his head pounded on the floor and suffering considerable injuries at the hands of Duffy. It must have been a fairly fraught experience for Lee King. He must have been fairly shocked.'

Earlier, Richard Neil had pleaded guilty to unlawful possession of the lock knife, but he too denied assisting an offender when his counsel, Ian West, told the jury: 'There is not a shred of evidence that what Neil was doing was assisting an offender.'

King was found guilty of attempting to pervert the course of justice as a consequence of him trying to hide the killer lock knife by dropping it down a drain. Charges against both Neil and King of assisting an offender were dismissed. King received 150 hours community service for hiding the knife. His previous criminal record showed he had form for violence when in 1995 he was jailed for 18 months for assaulting an off-duty policeman.

Russian Roulette

Allison was acquitted of murder and walked from the court a free man. Allison punched the air when a not guilty verdict had been returned after two hours of deliberation at the end of an eight-day trial. Allison: *'I'm all right, I'm not sad about the verdict anyway.'*

Quite poignantly, Lisa Stockell pointed out that the jury had been swayed by all of the violence and she went on to say that too much of Lee's past was brought up in the trial and not enough about Allison. By law, none of the accused could have their past brought up, but Duffy had his character unceaselessly attacked!

Duffy's mother, Brenda, and Lisa both burst into tears when they heard the verdict. Brenda Duffy: *'Lee would not have wanted his man to go down, even though I would like his head on a stick in my garden.'*

Some claimed that Duffy led a charmed life in being able to avoid so many attempts on his life, but in reality it was Duffy's upbringing that helped him avoid this sort of occurrence.

An unremitting tirade of attacks on Duffy had caused endless injuries to his body, which was riddled with lead shot! Was this a charmed life?

Viv Graham had to be just as diligent as Duffy in terms of being aware of attacks, but he was not. With Duffy it was only a matter of time and a numbers game as to when he was killed. Viv had less to contend with than Duffy in terms of assassination attempts, but his lack of inbuilt survival instinct was his Achilles heel!

Someone like Duffy parading around Tyneside would have been a force to be reckoned with and had he of teamed up with Viv, as he did with the big fellah, Brian Cockerill, for a short period then maybe he would have had the whole of the north sewn up.

Their kingdoms have been broken up into smaller estates run by lesser mortals than Viv and the Duffer. Factions that keep a low profile find safety in numbers, no more is there a big name for them to throw up as weapon of defence.

Since the days of the Duffer the incidence of violence has actually increased!!!

No More Good Times

This set of events relating to Lee Duffy's death is based on fact. To every story there are two sides, you have read the other side in the previous chapter. This side of the story should make the whole of the moon visible to you. (*The Whole of the Moon* was Duffy's favourite song.)

There are many flaws to the previous chapter's submission. Many people have been interviewed in relation to the death of Duffy; many people have spoken, but only with a guarantee of anonymity for them. That is how it must be; if someone confesses something after being given this guarantee then the guarantee remains in place.

Credibility must be maintained otherwise word would spread like wildfire that Richards did not keep his word.

Confirmation was sought to confirm that Duffy and Allison (nicknamed 'Buck weed') did in fact have a conflict going on between them. Had it been found that no such conflict existed then it would have meant all of those people standing up in court and particularly Duffy's killer, Allison, were lying when they told of a running conflict that Allison had with Duffy.

But, indeed, there was a conflict between Allison (Allo) and Duffy. At a mutual friend's wedding, John Graham, Duffy and Allo had a bit of a set to, but nothing too ferocious had happened. Years previously they had a fight and from other accounts they had regular skirmishes with each other.

One night, Duffy was in the Havana when some friends from Hartlepool met up with him, they were ferried by taxis to the blues in Princes Road where the first attempt on Duffy's life had taken place some eight months earlier. Duffy pulled up in a black cab with some others and he invited some of the men into his cab, saying: 'Jump in here with us.' From there they went on to the Afro-Caribbean Centre in Marton Road, which was at about 3.15am. Fifteen minutes later Duffy would be dead!

Outside of the centre stood Stephen 'Morph' Reed, mortal drunk! He was put into a cab and sent home by one of Duffy's party. It seemed that this night was to have a calamitous effect on many of the people present, as if though something sinister pervaded the place.

That night in the centre, a man called Fields had given a letter to someone to pass on to Allo. That person is rumoured to have been Mark Hartley.

It was claimed that Hartley approached Allo, who was up against the back wall, and he was seen to pass him the letter in question. On seeing Hartley approach Allo, Duffy went over and said to Hartley: 'What the fuck are you talking to that rat for?'

Allo at this point looked like a frightened mouse, but he still argued with Duffy and he was heard to say to Duffy: 'Do you want it, do you want it, do you want it?' What Allo was doing at that time was taking a knuckleduster from his back pocket and slipping it onto his hand, which falls in line with what Allison admitted under oath in court during the subsequent murder trial.

As the knuckleduster was slipped on, Allo had obviously given some thought as to what he should now do.

In reply to Allo's earlier question of, 'Do you want it?' Duffy replied to Allo, 'Yeah, I do! Get outside and I'll give you it.' Duffy was then heard to say to Allo: 'Don't be getting the fucking knife out, don't be getting the fucking knife out!' Duffy did not know it was a knuckleduster at that time and during the fight he thought it to be a cosh of some sorts.

As the Duffer and Allo got outside, the doors were shut! At first nobody saw what happened, they can tell you this, they can tell you that, but nobody other than the few present from both sides saw anything that happened...apart from a third party who saw everything!!!!!!!!!!

That person was able to give an accurate account of what really went on. The following information is based on an eyewitness account, which is NOT guesswork – it is fact!

Duffy took his top off, note that he was not wearing a leather jacket. That is very important to remember so keep it in readiness for what will be sprung on you later.

Duffy was wearing a T-shirt, it was a summer's night, he is proud of his body and he does not want anything as cumbersome as a leather jacket on when he is going to a blues party, given that, yes, he did take Ecstasy that night then he would have been far too hot to even consider wearing a leather jacket.

At no time did Duffy even have a leather jacket under his arm and at no time did he ever leave this invisible jacket with an invisible gun in the pocket draped over a chair near to the DJ box in the centre.

As soon as Duffy's top was off, Allo run at him and punched him heavily on the head with the knuckleduster. Duffy grabbed him, threw him to the ground and straddled him. Allo received numerous head butts followed by having his head smashed off the ground by Duffy.

The Duffer then started to pull Allo's head towards him to head butt him. Allo was trying to bring his hand over the top to hit Duffy with the knuckleduster. At this point Duffy was heard clearly to shout: 'You can't even beat me with a cosh,' because he thought the knuckleduster was a cosh. This is the point where the people who were temporarily locked in the centre started coming out.

The eyewitness saw Lee King slip by Duffy; he came round the back of Duffy and stabbed him in the back while Duffy was sat on top of Allo. The party who relayed this information saw the knife blade catch the light, like a torchlight flash, before it entered Duffy's flesh.

This fits in exactly with what Allison testified to in court: 'Then for some reason he was off me. I was helped to my feet by some friends and taken to a nearby wall.' This accounts as to why Duffy was off Allo in a shot, what other reason would Duffy have had to get off Allo?

Duffy had been sufficiently injured by the stabbing attack to his back to warrant him jumping off Allo. The court did not apply sufficient time to this particular wounding.

If the court had studied it in detail then they would or could have assumed then that Allo already had the knife in his possession and had carried out the attack on Duffy's back with it or that a third party, the man found guilty of possessing the knife, had in fact inflicted the injury. Richard Neil had pleaded guilty to unlawful possession of the lock knife.

But none of these scenarios was what had actually happened! This is what happened:

The fight was broken up, but at first no one would act to do that. One of Duffy's aid de camps (second in command) got in between Allo and Duffy and pulled Duffy off, he slipped in between them and put his arms tight around Duffy's midriff and pulled him up, not unlike the Heimlich maneuver applied when someone's choking on something stuck in their throat.

Remember, Duffy had been shot twice some months before this and he had a bad limp due to the state of his knee and foot, each damaged in different attempts on his life. (Half of Duffy's foot was blown away; there was a hole that had to have grafts.)

What happened then was, Duffy sat on a wall and he said: 'You can't even fucking beat me with a cosh.' Then Lee King passed Allo the knife. This is in total contradiction to Richard Neil entering a guilty plea to the unlawful possession of the lock knife that inflicted the fatal wound.

The reason why King could not take the wrap for this was because he already had convictions for knife attacks and it would not have gone well for him had he been found guilty of possessing the knife.

Imagine if it were King on this charge of possessing the knife, the judge would have come down on him like a ton of bricks. You can see now why King did not want to have anything to do with having possession of the knife.

Duffy had not made any spontaneous complaints about pains in his back because he was in a fighting mode and the adrenalin rush would have warded off the initial pain. A stab wound does not initially give a feeling of pain it is only afterwards.

Allo came towards Duffy with the knife in his hand and one of Duffy's men got in between him and Allo.

A clear picture was developing of what was going to happen. Someone was heard to say: 'David, put the knife down. David, put the knife down!'

Allo then did a roundhouse move with the knife, as was said in court, and shouted at the man in between him and Duffy to 'Fuck off!' With that, Allo went at the man and it hit him in a similar way that it was to hit and kill Duffy seconds later, but it only nicked the man's skin under his arm and twanged off the his shirt, whereas in Duffy's case it was to go in to an artery and fatally wound him.

Allo then went straight for Duffy, who picked a little plastic drink bottle up and he was pretending to throw it, and Allo did a similar roundhouse move as he'd jut done on the man intervening, the knife entered deep into Duffy's flesh severing a main artery.

Duffy immediately put his arm down and said: '*Fucking hell, Allo, you've killed me. This one's serious.*' As Duffy turned to run, Allo ran after him and was seen to stab Duffy on the side of his leg, it is thought to have been Duffy's right leg.

Duffy ran a matter of only twenty or so yards from the scene shouting for people to help him. A big fight took place and it is rumoured that Peter Donnelly was amongst them and they ran off leaving Duffy nearby on the ground. Mistakenly, in a previous, it was advised that it was Peter Donnelly who was in the taxi with Duffy when he went to hospital this is now known not to have been the case.

What had happened was, Duffy had brought a group of Geordies into town and people were saying they were 'Geordie Gangsters' and it was like a time bomb waiting to go off. But once the kingpin, Duffy, was taken out then they did not give two hoots about the Geordie Mafia, it didn't matter who they were because they were out of town.

The minute Duffy was taken out of the equation, they all steamed into them. Although Duffy was seen regularly with the Sayers' of Newcastle there is no certain proof that they were there that night. There were about twenty people fighting in the street. The Geordie Mafia, without their main piece of artillery (Duffy), got a good kicking from Lee King and the others.

Duffy at this time was sat up in the street shouting for help, his life blood pumping out of him like a fountain and as it hit the floor it made a clapping sound. *'Help me, someone help me,'* was Duffy's words. A crowd had gathered around Duffy and shouts of 'Die' were heard!

A taxi, as already mentioned, came in to view and it was flagged down, it promptly did a U-turn and left the scene. The driver has not been traced, hopefully he is not a reflection of what taxi drivers are like in Middlesbrough!!!!!!!!!!

A passing car was stopped, the driver's name was John Smith (his real name), and at this point it is clear that the man who flagged the car down was Mark Hartley. Whatever he said to the driver it worked and he allowed Hartley to put Duffy in the back of the car. Duffy was now flat out on the ground, lying face down and in a state of shock with scarlet coloured blood squirting feet high in to the early morning air.

As Hartley struggled to get Duffy off the ground, a crowd of some few hundred had gathered, as if watching some free for all gruesome horror show. One gallant person, Stephen Pearson, stepped forward from the morbid crowd and said he would help.

He freely admitted that he did not like Duffy, but he still helped, many are called few are chosen. Hartley took hold of Duffy's top end while Pearson took hold of Duffy's legs and put him in to the passenger side back door of John Smith's Mk III Ford Escort car. Duffy's head was behind the driver and his feet were bent up across the back seat. Hartley jumped in the front passenger seat, another man ran and jumped in the car to get out of the way of a man he had earlier been fighting with.

Hartley was seen to be on the obstructive passenger's knees in the front of the car and was seen to lean across tending to Duffy, who by all accounts was still alive.

The driver set off to hospital as fast as he could and as the car went through the hospital gates, Duffy took his last gasp and is believed to have died!

The paramedics went through the motions and still applied electric shock to stimulate Duffy's dead heart back to life. An hour or two later, it is claimed that Peter Donnelly and another two Geordies turned up at the hospital.

Lisa, Duffy's girlfriend, was called on the phone and she says that Mark Hartley told her that Lee had been stabbed! When she enquired as to how bad it was, Mark is said to have told her that he didn't know.

Lisa, her mother and stepfather, Terry, turned up at the hospital and there they saw the lone figure of Mark Hartley outside of the casualty department.

Lisa ran up to Hartley screaming, 'I WANT TO KNOW, I WANT TO KNOW?' 'He's dead, Lisa,' came the reply and with that Lisa became hysterical.

An astounding fact exists, why is it that that Mark Hartley was not called as a witness in the subsequent murder trial??

The prosecution could have subpoenaed Hartley; his testimony would have altered the outcome of the trial as well as the fact that another party was not called. At times it makes you wonder who actually designs such trials?

From start to finish, it is believed that both the prosecution and the defence assisted in the end result.

Inside sources say that Hartley was arrested at the hospital when he refused to make a statement to the police. He had asked to leave the interview until the following day, but the police immediately arrested Hartley on suspicion of murdering Duffy. Of course this was merely a holding method employed by the police in order to keep a material witness in their grasp!

At 3.30am, Duffy was killed! At 3.31am, the police had a call to say there had been a road traffic accident (which fits in with the fact that Duffy was lying in the road) and at 3.33am, the police received a telephone call to say Allison had killed Duffy!

The police were already aware of who was responsible for Duffy's death; they just wanted someone to finally finger him. In the end, Allison fingered himself, even though he fancied taking off abroad somewhere.

Again, inside sources say that Hartley was asked to touch one of three names presented to him while he was held in police custody; one of the names was 'Allison'.

The person who had called the police told them everything, so holding Hartley was just a callous act and by leaving him covered in Duffy's blood whilst in the cell shows the callousness of the police in this inquiry.

The holding cells were to see the arrival of Allison at 2.20pm that afternoon and, unbelievably, Allison was put only a few cells away from Hartley, both men were only yards apart and could so easily have spoken to each other! This is often a ploy used by the police in the hope that if their captives talk to each other then they might learn something.

There is forensic evidence to support the fact that Duffy was NOT armed with a gun and also further witness evidence to support the fact that he was not even carrying a knife at the time of the fight or just prior to the fatal fight.

The Smith and Wesson .38 revolver, so bizarrely and dramatically discovered in a cock and bull story was an outlandish invention that it came close to being a fairytale.

The club DJ, Saidhu Kamara, told the court how a gun 'fell' from a black leather jacket which he found near his DJ box at the Afro-Caribbean Centre after the fatal fight. Well, what a coincidence! Then he says he goes and stores it in a derelict house, yawn, yawn. After that he buries the gun underneath a rose bush in his girlfriend's home. The case is rested on that particular story and Mr Kamara wants to think himself lucky he was not charged with perjury.

(Author's note: Witness evidence gathered for this book is first class and should anyone think of pursuing a civil action against me then you had better remember that in such cases there is much less burden of proof needed to secure convictions resulting from civil evidence. I would submit this evidence and of course any judge presiding over such a civil case would be compelled to refer the matter back to the criminal courts, which would be the case by time I finished off my defence of what is written here. Believe me, I do not write such things lightly.)

Yes, King had dumped the knife down a drain, but had the truth come out that he was in possession of the knife and that he was the one to stab Duffy in the back then it would have probably made a bigger story than Duffy's death.

Richard Neil took the wrap for passing Allo the knife when in fact it should have been King who was charged with this, as well as the fact that King should have been charged with wounding Duffy with the knife and this would have seen him also being charged with murder in a joint venture charge alongside Allison.

Double jeopardy used to be a rule whereby once the law courts had acquitted you of a crime then you could not be tried for that same offence, even if you later confessed to it or if the police discovered new evidence. The Criminal Justice Bill, which was announced in the Queen's Speech in June 2001, did away with this 800-year-old rule. Now you can be tried for the same murder twice!!!!!!!!!!!!!!!!!!!!!!!!

Since the advent of DNA evidence and improved forensic detection it would seem a logical approach in making the court system just as fair for the families of murdered loved ones.

Finding out that the accused went on to make a confession that they 'did it' after they had been acquitted is an insult to justice. Lord Mackenzie of Framwellgate is quoted as saying: 'I have always said that a wrongful acquittal was just as important a miscarriage of justice as a wrongful conviction.'

Killers are getting away with murder and in particular the case of Billy Dunlop who was acquitted of the 1989 killing of single mother Julie Hogg, 22, from Billingham, Teesside after a jury twice failed to agree a verdict.

Dunlop strangled and then mutilated pizza delivery girl Julie's body and then hid the body underneath a bath. Three months later, the police handed Ann Ming the keys back to her daughter's property. What the police had missed in the domestic property was soon discovered when Ann Ming made the grim discovery of her daughter's body…beneath the bath!

But Dunlop later confessed to a prison officer that he had carried out the murder and as a consequence was charged with two counts of perjury, which he pleaded guilty to and received six years imprisonment.

Julie's family successfully campaigned to have the double jeopardy rule changed in order that Dunlop can be tried again for the murder…time will tell?

In a macabre twist to the Duffy killing, it would seem that the lives of those involved in the killing were fated as if though Duffy reached a hand out from beyond the grave in a gesture of revenge.

Lee King, the man who stabbed Duffy in the back in that fateful fight with Allison, was blasted to death on 28th January 2000. His body was discovered, in Penistone Road, Park End, Middlesbrough, with shotgun wounds to the head and back. Keith McQuade, 45, was remanded into custody in September 2001; some eight months after the murder investigation had begun.

February 5th 2001 saw the start of the murder trial in which King, 32, is described as a man with a reputation as a womaniser; this is an important fact to remember! McQuade denied the charge.

"McQuade stuck a sawn off shotgun into Mr King's back in a Teesside street in the early hours of the morning and blasted him through the heart at close range. As his rival lay wounded, McQuade reloaded and shot him in the head at close range," said James Spencer, prosecuting.

King had a one-night stand with an ex-lover of McQuade's, Lisa Piercey, 25. After this he called her a 'slut.' Mr Spencer said that McQuade had told a friend that Mr King had made a fool of him over the woman. McQuade said that King told him two nights before he was killed that he had slept with McQuade's former lover. McQuade told the court that King had said to him: 'You are not bothered about it, are you, because I was round there that night? She's a slut anyway, isn't she?' McQuade said he replied: 'She's got three kids to three different fellahs, it's got nothing to do with me.'

Mr Spencer told the court that McQuade had said: 'He told me about sleeping with Lisa and said she was only a slut. I told him, "You don't need to do something like that to me," and I pointed the gun at him. He said, "You won't do something like that to me," and he walked away. I shot him once in the back and then in the head.'

It was alleged that McQuade had acted out the killing afterwards to two friends, telling them that King had turned his back on the gun saying: 'You wouldn't dare!'

McQuade told the court that King had invited him to take part in an armed robbery on a crack house in Kensington Road, Middlesbrough; this was planned for the night King was killed. He went on to say that King had arrived at his lodgings in Kenilworth Avenue, Park End to collect some tools he had hidden in the back garden. King then produced a sawn-off shotgun, which was wrapped in bin liners at which point McQuade told King that he wanted nothing to do with the robbery.

When King's body was found, he was clutching a knife in one of his hands and there was a bag containing two balaclavas. This was McQuade's defence that King had organised the proposed crack house robbery.

They both left the lodgings together and went in opposite

directions and the next day he heard that King had been shot dead. When asked why he thought witnesses had evidence against him, McQuade told the court that he believed that prosecution witnesses were involved in drugs and had plotted with each other to tell lies.

A prosecution witness told the court that McQuade had left a friend's house carrying a holdall in which it is alleged to have had the sawn-off shotgun that was used to kill King. A mechanic, John Johnson, known as 'Car Jack' told the court that on 28th January 2000 he was working in his garage when neighbour Peter Heeran walked in and he was saying: 'Keith Needs a lift, urgent.'

Mr Johnson said he drove McQuade to a nearby mutual friend's home and ten minutes later on his return he heard emergency vehicle sirens. A while later, Mr Heeran called in to the garage and told him that Lee King had been shot. Mr Johnson went on to say: 'Heeran said to me, "It served him right, he was trying to get me shot." I told him that I did not want to know anything about it.'

The jury found McQuade not guilty of murdering King. Nearly to the exact day in the same month on the eighth anniversary of David Allison being acquitted of murdering Lee Duffy, similarly, Keith McQuade was acquitted of murdering Lee King, the man who had stabbed Duffy in the back.

Just as Duffy was stabbed in the back, similarly, King was shot in the back and as is claimed, if true, King was lying on the ground mortally wounded (just as Duffy was) before the next gunshot blasted him in the head, which in a macabre way fits in with how Duffy was stabbed twice. (Although it was also suggested that Duffy was also slashed on the right leg.) For each stab wound Duffy received, King had received a gunshot blast as if from invisible hands from beyond the grave.

The other twist in the tale is that the woman involved in this was called 'Lisa', the same Christian name as Lee Duffy's girlfriend, Lisa Stockell. As much as Duffy's mother, Brenda, said that her son would not have wanted

Allison to go to prison for what had happened then neither did McQuade go to prison and just like Allison, he too was acquitted – scary or what?

Just when you think that is the end of the twist to the tale, it is not. Keith McQuade faced his first murder charge in 1993 and was discharged of that murder when the charge collapsed. Magistrates in Teesside refused to commit him to trial for the shotgun murder of Kevin 'Rico' Richardson.

The court ruled that there was insufficient evidence. Remarkably, McQuade walked from court a free man in the same year as Allison walked from court a free man when he was acquitted of Duffy's murder. King was murdered on the same estate where Rico Richardson was killed.

After McQuade was acquitted of King's murder, Detective Superintendent Adrian Roberts said: 'There is not a shred of evidence to implicate anyone else associated with the investigation, or to suggest a new inquiry. We will not be looking for anyone else.'

In an even bigger macabre twist to this tale from the unexpected, you will recall that King was murdered on 28th January 2000. Two days later, on 30th January 2000, Beverly Reynolds, 31, a mother of three, was found hanging by a piece of wire around her neck from a loft hatch…she had killed herself!

Scaffolder David Allison, 32, found the body of his girlfriend who had returned home on her own earlier after rowing with Allison on a night out in Middlesbrough. It is claimed that she wanted to stay out longer while Allison wanted to return home. Beverly, though, retuned home first by taxi after the row, she had to smash the glass of the door to gain entry because she did not have a key. Her children were staying overnight at relatives so when she entered the house she was alone.

Dr Jeremiah Murphy spoke at the inquest held in January 2001, he said he was treating Miss Reynolds for depression due to domestic stress and said that she had twice taken overdoses of Paracetamol.

No More Good Times

On 31st January 1991, three men burst into the home of Lisa Stockell and forced a gun into her mouth in order to find out where her boyfriend Lee Duffy was. Nine years to the day (nearly) on 30th January 2000, tragedy strikes again, but this time against the man who killed Duffy!

Already Lee King has suffered a horrific gangland slaying and now Allison has been put in the same position as lone parents Lisa Stockell and Carol 'Bonnie' Holmstrom. Duffy's three children are fatherless and now the three children of Allison's girlfriend are motherless!

Just as you think it can get no worse, it does! Beverley was rumoured to be having an affair with Lee King and it was two days after King's death that she committed suicide. You have already read that she and Allison were arguing earlier in the night and that she was being treated for depression due to domestic stress, it all got too much for Beverley and it is rumoured that she thought that if King was taken away from her and she could not have him then Allison would not have her.

The devastation this will bring to Miss Reynolds' children is mind numbing! For a child to lose a parent to death is distressing, no one can doubt that and just as Lisa Stockell and Carol Holmstrom had to try to come to terms with the loss of their children's father then it would seem that Duffy is as vengeful in death as he was in life.

When the police arrived at the tragic scene in Allison's home in the early hours of Sunday it was PC Timothy Lowe, the first officer to enter the house in Ormesby, Teesside, who gave mouth-to-mouth resuscitation to Beverley.

PC Lowe told the inquest that he could hear Allison downstairs and he seemed very distressed. 'He became more and more agitated, passing from anger to violence. He went in to the kitchen and smashed a chair and threw a radio cassette in to the sink. He kept throwing himself about the kitchen. He was saying, "Who will tell the kids? What am I going to do?" He caused damage to numerous items in the house.' The coroner for Central Teesside, Michael Sheffield, recorded a verdict that Beverley killed herself.

If in some way there is a connection to Duffy in all of this tragedy then we are likely to see further tragedies connected with those involved in what happened on the night of Duffy's death.

Violence attracts violence and as Duffy once said: 'Those who live by the sword die by the sword. Further tragedy struck when Kevin Howard, who had once fought with Duffy also hung himself. Another friend of Duffy's, Docker, was blinded when a car battery exploded in his face and a close friend of Mark Hartley also committed suicide in 2001.

Duffy also used to say: "Treat good people good, treat bad people bad." Many people saw him as a Jeckyl and Hyde character, but he was an adaptable person and has been described as speaking the language of the street and the language of the jet set. Someone said, "Duffy spoke fifteen languages," meaning he could communicate in the language of violence or the language of business.

You could take him to tea in an old people's home and he would be most respectful, but put him in a blues party and he acted accordingly, he wore his heart on his sleeve.

People connected to the death of Duffy, and that includes all of those who conspired to pervert the course of justice by telling lies and assisting in some way or another, will have a propensity to carry on in this way and it is sure to catch up with them.

Investigations in to when Duffy was shot in the first murder attempt at Princes Road revealed that this was carried out in a similar fashion to the way Viv was murdered. In Duffy's case, the hit men stood in a dark alleyway and shouted him over.

(In Viv's case it was a car that was parked in a dark alleyway and from within it they shouted something at Viv to attract his attention so as to get his body square on so he could be a better target.)

Duffy though, unlike Viv, had seen the gun that his hopeful assassins carried. This is the difference between

No More Good Times

Duffy and Viv.

On seeing the gun, Duffy turned and went to run backwards, which given his speed and power would be as fast as some people could run forwards. He jumped behind a car and they opened fire only managing to shoot him in the leg, Duffy had escaped death by the skin of his teeth! They were trying to take him out; they were not giving him a warning!

The second attempt on Duffy's life, as you now know was in an illegal blues party. Three of them walked up to him, Duffy seen them and tried to slip around them in the darkness of the blues. He tried to work his way towards the door, but they caught him before he could get out. Duffy instinctively knew they were out to kill him.

One of them pulled a shotgun out of his long coat; Duffy instinctively grabbed the barrel of the shotgun and started fighting with his would be killer. While he was fighting the gun from him, one of the other two had a crowbar and started hitting Duffy over the head in the hope that he would let go of the gun.

To prove this is true, the records would show that Duffy also had quite a few stitches put into the back of his head. At no time did the hired hit men push the gun downwards – this was a full-blown hit meant to kill Duffy! While Duffy was fighting with the gun, one shot went off and missed, which again supports the shoot to kill story.

When Duffy was in hospital, he had photos in his possession of the so called 'professional' hit men along with all of their names and addresses written on the back of each photo.

In an update on two of the accused, Marnon Thomas and Leroy Fischer, both now 41, in the second murder attempt on Duffy's life, these two made an attempt in 1999 to pursue Cleveland Police Force for compensation for 'malicious prosecution' in a High Court action. Both petitioners claimed damages from Cleveland Chief Constable Barry Shaw following their acquittal in 1991 of involvement in a conspiracy to shoot Lee Duffy.

Lawyers representing Birmingham men Thomas and Fischer called the Crown prosecutor for Teesside, Keith Simpson. Mr Simpson has denied being involved in any deal to grant immunity to Ria Nasir, one of the suspects. The High Court - sitting at Teesside – was told by Mr Simpson that any such deal would need approval at a much higher level than himself.

Ria Nasir had been questioned in connection with the shooting by police treating the case as attempted murder when intelligence reports suggested that some of the men involved in the shooting were seen at or near Nasir's home.

Teesside solicitor Keith Leigh, who represented South Bank woman Nasir at the time, had told the High Court that he had been involved in 'striking a bargain' with Detective Supt Len Miller with the aim of having all charges against her dropped if she co-operated with police investigating the shooting. Mr Leigh claimed Mr Simpson was present for part of these discussions. What a pity Nasir had not kept her side of the bargain in this alleged deal! It would have meant some sort of justice for Lisa Stockell who, along with another female, was a witness as to the identities of two men involved in this crime.

Nasir's lawyer also claimed he witnessed her - who he said had a drink problem - being interviewed by officers in Middlesbrough police station while under the influence of drink, drinking brandy and with a bottle of brandy close at hand. He told the court: "She was not being interviewed under caution, she was not at risk. I was perfectly happy to let the police conduct the investigation as they saw fit."

Mr Simpson told the court that all he had done was to offer the police advice. He said: "I was there to advise the police about the prosecution rather than the investigation."

He had recommended no action against Nasir on the basis that the only evidence against her was an informal unrecorded conversation between her and the then Detective Inspector Ray Mallon and this could not have produced a realistic prospect of convicting Nasir on charges relating to the shooting.

Cross-examined by barrister Peter Johnson, for the Chief Constable, he said that on the evidence submitted by the police to the CPS - which included that of Nasir - he was satisfied the charges brought against Thomas, Fischer and others were 'appropriate'.

Both Marnon Thomas and Leroy Fischer lost their case for a frivolous claim when Judge Michael Taylor said: "Whatever shortcomings in the investigation that the case had thrown up - they did not affect the central issue of malice. The claimants had maintained they had been wrongly prosecuted as a result of identification evidence provided in a deal struck between police and South Bank woman Ria Nasir at a time when she was herself a suspect in the case and known to be 'unreliable' as a witness."

Judge Taylor gave judgment in favour of the police and said the decision by Detective Superintendent Len Miller to drop potential charges against Nasir in exchange for information from her was a "totally justifiable" gamble, taken at a time when the investigation was "up against the buffers."

In an outright attack on Thomas and Fischer he said: "It was clear that those directly involved in the shooting were from outside Teesside. With almost all the potential witnesses coming from the criminal community, there was little chance of co-operation in finding out their identities."

Judge Taylor added that while it was not his role to decide whether the claimants themselves were involved, it would have served the public better to have convicted several people prepared to use a shotgun in a public place rather than have one woman in the dock.

Fischer, who at that time was serving a five-year sentence for robbery started shouting abuse at the judge and police officers in the court and continued as he was led away to the cells.

Chief Superintendent Miller was delighted with the outcome and said: "I'm pleased the judge supported our decision to take a risk in an effort to catch the people responsible for the shooting."

In another prison letter from Duffy: *Manny Burgo (boxer) was in the blues last weekend, Allo and some lads were working themselves with Manny, so he knocked 3 or 4 of them out, or so I have been told. (Hope it wasn't Allo.)*

A letter dated April 1991 written from HM Prison Durham, Duffy writes: *Lee Harrison has been up to see me, well he actually done my head in, teasing me about the Havana, etc. He was at the courts yesterday taking the piss out of the police and generally making a disturbance, you know what he's like, he makes me laugh, he's off his head. I know this is going to sound daft but in a way I have been glad of the break from it all really. Living too fast, too long, it burns you out. But I could think of a better place to take a break like. (Ha, Ha.) But having said that I've had some brilliant times with you and the lads and I wouldn't change my lifestyle if it meant no more good times like we've had.*

Tommy Harrison

"When Lee was fighting with 'Allo', that wasn't Lee fighting, he was as high as a kite, he was drunk, they were on Champaign, Russian Blacks and he hadn't been to bed for two days. He'd been on Charlie (cocaine) and his reflexes were gone. I don't think that would have happened if he wasn't under the influence of drink and drugs."

Detective chief Inspector Brian Leonard

"There is always someone trying to put their head up and take the place of someone like Lee Duffy because they have seen him get away with it so much. But if there is a lesson to be learned it is this: if you get involved in drugs, violence and bullying you may come to a sticky end."

Detective Sergeant Ray Morton

"It is the end of an era. Many people have tried to emulate Lee Duffy, but they failed."

Viv No More '94

Viv left the Queen's Head public house 6.05pm on New Year's Eve 1993. Viv was making the short walk back to where his powerful Ford Sierra Cosworth car was parked in Border Road. The 'Cossie' had become his pride and joy when he replaced his BMW with it. It was a self-bestowed award he had furnished on himself that reflected his near celebrity status. The boy from Highfield near Rowlands Gill just outside of Gateshead had nearly made it and here was the proof.   The shiny burgundy red Cosworth reflected the sodium streetlights off its gleaming metallic paintwork. A lone soft toy monkey hung from the rear view mirror as if like some lucky talisman warding off evil.

The cigarettes and dog food Viv had just bought from the corner shop that were carried in his brawny hands signified the things he loved in his life, the cigarettes for his fiancée, who he worshipped, and the dog food represented his love of animals. Here he was on New Year's Eve thinking of the ones he loved and on his way back home to them.

Viv wished the shopkeeper "Happy New Year" and they shook hands. There would not be any late night revelling for him because his fiancée, Anna Connelly, was not feeling too well. Anna stayed home, knowing her beloved Viv would soon be resting in his favourite position, which was with his feet up on the couch amongst those he loved with the phone off the hook and a video playing. Beneath this seemingly rose tinted picture of serenity there were some complicated issues within Viv's demanding life.

Conflicting thoughts may have been going through Viv's head. He had just received a death threat over the phone whilst he was in a pub where he had been passing time with friends and acquaintances. "It's for you, Viv," the manager of the New Anchor pub said as he passed Viv the phone.

"I've just had a death threat," Viv said, as he kept his innermost fears hidden - it did not do to show this lot his real self! But, a part of his fear shone through like a shaft of light escaping through a hole in a dark cloud on a sunny day. A few of those present had caught a glimpse of what they thought was a slight change in Viv's composure, but it did not do to let him know they could see this.

Viv was the man and no one messed with him! There was no one capable of doing him and, anyway, he was always getting death threats. This one was probably just from some upstart waging war over the phone because they knew they could not do anything physically in a one to one fight. What did Viv have to fear? These threats, after all, were ten a penny and it was probably just another wind up like all the previous threats had been. As far as Viv was concerned, it sucked.

Anyway, Viv had more important things on his mind, he had just telephoned his secret lover, Gillian Lowes, and he told her he would be calling her at midnight to wish her a happy New Year. There was not a day that went by when he did not have her or their two children on his mind.

It was a busy time of year and Viv would be in demand as usual, as there was always some 'troublemaker' ready to cause upset at the drop of a hat. Viv was on call 24 hours a day, 365 days of the year.

Complacency has to come in to it somewhere. Whereas at one time he was sensitive of his own security, but now he had become too relaxed and lethargic where his safety was concerned. He had forgotten the lesson that he was taught in 1989 when he was shot at outside of Manhattan's. This, as well as the trouble he had in Santino's restaurant, should have kept him on his toes...all forgotten! Watching too many videos created his vision of being executed gangland style by a motorcyclist riding alongside his car!

Alarm bells should have started ringing when he received

that threatening phone call! The dread of something happening must have given him a brief feeling of shock, but he had faced this before and his adrenaline just did not pump like it used to do at the beginning of his career.

Viv could camouflage his feelings and, anyway, it was soon masked by all the other thoughts of what he had to do, it became a haze in his mind. Tomorrow he would be seeing his secret love, Gillian and his kids? This seemed more important to him than thinking of when a strike would happen against his life…"live for today."

This was a time of year to relax, de-stress and hang out with friends and that is what Viv was doing. He had been in the Anchor pub since 4.15pm

Then he walked only a matter of a few metres away, into the Queens Head, which he eventually left at 6.05pm and from there he called into a corner shop. People were making their way to a nearby bingo. "Nah!" Viv must have thought to himself, "No one's going to be daft enough to do anything here." Soon he would be cocooned in the womb like safety of his beloved Cosworth and be back home in a flash to devoted Anna, she would soothe his stressed out headache away.

Within a few seconds of leaving the corner shop, Viv was at the side of his car. The keys were in his hand; it was dark! Viv's fear was of the dark! He is now in sight of the killers! (Stated to be two and later stated to be three.)

Something to Viv did not quite look right, but he could not quite decide what it was, his mind was not thinking as straight as it normally did. That was it; the window on the car door was broken! (No, not the broken window diversion technique!) A car pulled out from the nearby dark alley, something was called out to Viv! In a conditioned reflex, Viv turned to look.

BLAMH! Bullet number one was fired from a range of only five meters as the .357 Magnum handgun blasted out its first of three bullets. A flash followed by fiery pain milliseconds later was the first indication to Viv that he had been shot! The gunshot had telegraphed to those in earshot that something ominous was going on by its eerie echo!

Viv's instinctive reactions were swift! Before the first bullet had completed its journey through his thigh, having entered from the outside, his hand shot down so fast between his thighs that it beat the bullet exiting that particular leg. The bullet nicked the edge of his hand before continuing its blood-splattering route in to the inside of his other thigh and exiting out of the outside! Viv's legs were no longer responding to what his brain told them to do!

BLAMH! Bullet number two ripped apart Viv's lower abdominal area before exiting out of his side, leaving organs in his muscled torso fatally damaged beyond repair! Haemorrhaging was so bad that nothing in the long term would have saved Viv. A hole the size of a melon was visible in Viv' side!

BLAMH! Bullet number three was fired at Viv when he was down; it had not fully made contact with him. The bullet, it is believed, may have struck the ground and ricocheted off the solid surface, fizzling over Viv's back, where it left a visible line on his body. This was not a shoot to maim attack; it was clearly a shoot to kill attack! The reason being, that once Viv was put down by the first shot then that would have been it, but it was not, they shot again and again! And drove off at a deathly pace!

Viv summoned up what was left of his strength and started to crawl back towards the High Street he had just left seconds earlier. The shopkeeper ran out to see what had gone on. Viv was crawling his way towards the pub he had only just left some minutes previously. The injuries that were obvious to the shopkeeper, who wished to remain anonymous, showed that the bullets had passed straight through him leaving open wounds that were identifiable as having been unmistakably caused by gunshots.

Twenty-five meters away was the Queens Head pub. Blind instinct must have been the only thing leading Viv back the way he had came. Only this time it was a crawling, bleeding, dying Viv that was seen through the window from inside of the pub by Terry Scott who was an associate of Viv's. Terry ran out to Viv without concern for his own safety, although unknown to him the two killers had left the area when they sped off in the stolen blue Ford Escort.

As Viv lay there bleeding, he pulled his shirt down over his main wound as if signifying one last act of neatness. Viv said, "I can't let them see me like this. Terry, I'm going, I'm going." Terry leaned his tall powerful body over Viv to help him up to his feet; he could see there was a lot of damage to Viv's body; he could do little to help! Terry cradled Viv's head for a while, what a sight that must have been!

From the Rubaiyat *of Omar Khayyam*

Awake! For morning in the Bowl of Night
Has flung the stone that puts the stars to flight:
And Lo! The hunter of the East has caught
The Sultan's Turret in a noose of Light

Dreaming when Dawn's Left Hand was in the Sky,
I heard a voice within the Tavern cry,
"Awake, my little ones, and fill the cup
Before Life's Liquor in its Cup be dry."

And as the Cock crew, those who stood before
The Tavern shouted - "Open then the Door!
You know how little while we have to stay,
And once departed, may return no more."

Now the New Year reviving old Desires,
The thoughtful Soul to solitude retires.

Peter Connelly, Anna's brother, arrived at the hospital, the scene that greeted him must have looked like bedlam. He was moved by the amount of people he saw.

Terry Scott was running around venting his frustration out on the walls with punches that would have floored Mike Tyson.

Anna Connelly, Viv's fiancée, managed to see Viv, if only briefly, he said he loved her.

The doctor knew there was not any hope; Viv could not have survived the gapping hole in his side!

Jack Graham, Viv's father, said to Anna that his son would pull through, but Anna somehow knew that the gapping hole in his side just would not allow him to continue living due to the severity of the damage visible, it was to be the end of Viv's life.

Viv suffered a massive heart attack. How could the doctor tell a highly agitated group of relations, friends and associates who packed out the hospital waiting area that the man they had all willed to live was dead? Viv's body was placed in the recovery room where visibly he looked quite normal, but in fact at this stage he was dead! Later on that night, when things had calmed down, at 10.20pm Viv was pronounced dead after being formally identified by his father, but in actual fact he had died some hours earlier.

The unlit blue Ford Escort, registration number G668 DTF, had been in the area for a while before finally being dumped in Simonside Terrace, Heaton, Newcastle. Some ten to fifteen minutes after the murder, the car was torched. A later report was that a woman had nearly been knocked over by a Blue Ford Escort in Debdon Gardens, only a matter of a minute away from Simonside Terrace.

Detective Superintendent John May (now retired) was in charge of the murder investigation. There were actually two independent witnesses to the incident and they put a blonde woman as being across the road and then after Viv was shot she was put as being near his body as she went across the road towards the shop.

The getaway car had been stolen earlier in the day from Durham Road, Birtley, near to Chester-le-Street, between 2.30pm and 3.30pm. It was also discovered that telephone calls were made to Viv's home that day asking where he was, as well as similar telephone calls being made to the two pubs Viv had visited that day.

The word soon spread around Newcastle that Viv was dead. In certain quarters, champagne bottles popped their corks and the toast was, 'Viv no more '94.' Doormen refused to work, as they feared that they would be next on the hit list. The whole city of Newcastle's nightlife came to an abrupt stop as doormen walked out in fear or sympathy.

The police made a number of key arrests, Darren Arnold, Karen Young and her father, Brian William Tait, Alan Jackson, Alan Wheat, Michael Sayers and Lee Watson.

Karen Young had to move out of the area because hate mail and smear campaigners disrupted her life. Her role was alleged to have been a distraction to Viv somehow and that was the reason she was arrested. Police believed they had witnesses strong enough to testify in court that she had some involvement. Karen was kept in custody on two occasions for stringent questioning, but she stood her ground and used her right of 'no reply' that was applicable at that time.

Alan Wheat was no longer wanted for questioning, Watson, Sayers and Mr Young were fully questioned and released. Karen Young, Darren Arnold, Alan Jackson and Brian William Tait were eventually told by the CPS that there was no case against them.

The Crown Prosecution Service had to consider the following, the car used in the drive by shooting had been stolen from Birtley and the area it was stolen from was beside a gym that was allegedly used by a female stripper whom Darren Arnold was having a relationship with.

That was the connection they were trying to prove. It seemed too coincidental and too convenient that the car was stolen from Birtley nearby to a gym.

A witness had given a description to the police and that description matched one of those arrested, but because of the fear of reprisals the witness suffered from nerves and could not go witness if called upon. There were other witnesses, but they were considered to have too much of a criminal record to be able to stand cross-examination. This gives rise for concern, as a key prosecution witness in the multi-million pound Freddie Knights murder trial (Leeds crown court - June to September of 2002) was also a suspect in the Viv Graham murder investigation! Killer Watson's criminal record did not seem to be a stumbling block for the CPS in this case!

After Lee Shaun Watson, 32, pleaded guilty to the murder of Freddie Knights, he went Queen's Evidence against Dale Miller, 38; Edward Stuart, 39; Michael Dixon, 39; John Henry Sayers, 38 and Anthony Leach, 37.

One witness who helped give information for the Viv murder inquiry was David Glover Jnr. He eventually stood trial for the kidnap/torture of Billy Collier. It was alleged that in return for the police speaking up for Glover to the court that he would go witness in the Viv Graham murder trial against those he had named. Unluckily for him and luckily for those he was to have gone witness against, he was found guilty and received a 10½-year prison sentence. Glover then refused to go as a witness for the police.

Glover had previously said to the police that he knew of a safe house that was used by the killers, which formerly belonged to the father of Stephen Craven. (Serving life for the Penny Laing murder.) Someone had gone to view the flat and had a key cut, so the story goes. It made an ideal hideout as the place where the car used in the Viv murder was dumped and set fire to. (Across a field from this bungalow.) Glover had mentioned that the car had hit a wall and left a scrape of blue paint on it and allegedly the police found this, Glover's story sounded plausible.

The payment, allegedly, for the hit on Viv was a bag of cocaine! Viv was no longer around and what the police had to consider was who would be trying to make a take-over bid because they initially thought that it was another heavy outfit vying for power of nightclub doors. That was not the case and the power vacuum could not be filled, although a feeble try was made.

Viv No More '94

Sharon Tate on Viv's murder

"With his uncanny knack of being able to spot a pinhead of trouble starting in the darkest of nightclub corners, then on the night of his death when a gun was aimed at him, Viv must have been in a world of his own. It was even suggested that he had been spiked in an effort to slow his reactions. I just can't fathom that out, not for the life of me. Viv was told if you ever go to your car and your tyres are down or your windows are out, get away from it."

Anna Connelly Says:

"If I could say something to those people who killed Viv it would be this, why did you want to kill him? Why didn't you shoot him in the legs and make him a cripple? Why use a gun so powerful as that? They tell me just the force of that bullet is enough to kill you. A .357 Magnum didn't need three bullets. Why didn't you just get out and just break his legs because what did he ever do to deserve this? There are millions of guns a .22, but why did they pick that size gun. I knew that if they shot and they missed, Viv would have been in jail today for murder because he would have killed them."

Gillian Lowes on Viv's murder

Gillian she said it was frightening to be involved with a man that could be injured or even dead at any time and that she knew people would always want to have a fight with him, but she did not think he would get murdered and maybe one day he would get out of it all. She knew Viv was not invincible, but the way his life suddenly ended had shocked her. The problem was that Viv did not carry 'fear' in his dictionary of words; he just did not know the meaning of such a word. She said that she hoped that if the person is married or has a family that their family has not ever got to go through what her family went through and that they may not have known the consequences of what they did and she said that she did not know if they wanted to kill Viv or warn him off.

Viv Graham & Lee Duffy's Parallel Lives

Peter Connelly Says

"After I had heard about it, I just wanted to walk, I was crying, I just wanted to walk and keep walking. Suppose I walked to London and I walked back and someone would tell me that he was all right. That's what I felt like doing. We didn't really think about who did it at the time, it was more or less the next day we said that somebody knew. There had to be a 'Judas' amongst them."

£15-20m Murder Trial – Who Pays?

A murder that I believe holds the key to discovering the killers of Viv Graham is the unsolved murder of Paul Logan: two men murdered Paul **Logan**, 25, the pizza delivery driver from Shotley Bridge, two nights before Christmas 1993, seven days before Viv was murdered? It is claimed that the same two men responsible for this murder could also be responsible for Viv's murder.

Joe Marshall, a convicted gunman, gave evidence to the police naming the alleged killers of Paul. Further claims are that £5,000 was paid to the two men to beat Paul up - the men went too far and accidentally killed Paul!

The Geordie Mafia underworld has it that one of two killers is definitely a heavyweight informant who gets away with selling drugs under the watchful eye of the police while it is claimed that the second man is said to have served a term in prison for offences of violence. To date, neither man has been charged in connection with the Logan murder.

In a twist to the tale, PC Jeff **Hunt**, 33, received a three-month prison sentence for misconduct as a public official following an arson attack on a van belonging to Hugh Logan, father of Paul. The man responsible for the petrol bomb attack, Keith Suddick, 36, was jailed for carrying out the attack in Shotley Bridge. Help supply information on this murder or any other murder: **Crimestoppers, run by civilians. Freephone: 0800 555 111**

The bigger they are, the harder the fall! High-ranking criminals are seemingly falling over themselves to be as helpful to the police over the Viv murder as they can...but only in order to receive more lenient prison sentences when caught for serious crimes!

Viv Graham & Lee Duffy's Parallel Lives

David Glover Jnr gave a statement to the police about the Viv murder, but it was a statement of pure invention designed to help him get off with his dastardly crime of kidnapping and torturing small time criminal Billy Collier. Glover had high hopes of going as a supergrass against the Sayers brothers of Stephen and Michael. By blaming them for the Viv murder, he anticipated that he would walk free from court for his own vicious crime. Glover ended up being found guilty of the kidnap and torture charges (ten years imprisonment).

Glover's hopes of an acquittal had been dashed and as a direct result of this he became stubborn over his invented murder statement. At Glover's torture trial, the then Detective Chief Inspector Felton put in a statement (known as a 'text', see stills section) to the court on Glover's behalf, confirming that he had been working as an informant for Northumbria police since September 1992 under the pseudonym of Adrian Scott. Glover's job was to gather information about the Conroy family and others.

Later on, the promoted Superintendent Keith Felton explained that Glover had said things in relation to the Viv murder, but that Glover was not right in the head and he could not be believed. After Glover was imprisoned, he still made a bid for further help in having his sentence cut. Here is a précis of what Glover told two visiting police officers, DC J Bower and DC A Trotter, at HM Prison Birmingham on Wednesday 22nd February 1995 at 1.30pm:

Glover was shown by DC's Trotter and Bower a video recording of Sackville Road, Newcastle upon Tyne. Glover indicated an area of bungalows in the street stating that the murderers of Viv Graham had gone to one of them after the killing. When asked how he knew this Glover said, "I drove the getaway car."

When asked what exactly he meant Glover said, "I drove the getaway car after the shooting." When asked who did the shooting he said, "Michael Sayers."

Glover was asked to tell the story of his involvement from the beginning and gave the following story: -

£15-20m Murder Trial - Who Pays?

He stole an old, blue Escort from Birtley from a car park near the baths. He took it by jiggling the locks. He was with Michael Sayers at the time and they drove to Heaton, in Newcastle parking the car somewhere in Sackville Road.

They arranged that Glover should collect Michael Sayers later that day. In the middle of the afternoon Glover collected Sayers in the stolen car and was directed to various places looking for Viv Graham. Sayers said he was going to shoot Graham in the legs in retaliation for some ongoing dispute. They went to Graham's house but his car was not there. They then drove around Wallsend and discovered Graham's car parked in a street off the High Street next to a flowerbed.

Glover parked the stolen car in a back lane with a view of the back of Graham's car and Sayers walked over to Graham's car and smashed the driver's window. Glover stated that he saw the hazard warning lights flashing and assumed the alarm had been set off. He could see that Sayers was walking up and down the street where the car was parked. Then he heard three shots fired, looked and saw Graham on all fours beside the car. Sayers ran back to the stolen Escort, got in and Glover drove off.

Glover stated he was directed which way to drive, eventually arriving at a back lane somewhere in Heaton. He torched the car and both he and Michael Sayers were picked up by Stephen Sayers and Tony Leach in a burgundy Shogun vehicle.

Glover stated that Sayers had used a .357 Magnum, which was grey in colour, which he kept in a shoulder holster and always carried. He stated he believed Sayers was high on cocaine at the time and that they both believed Graham was only wounded.

It was pointed out to Glover that all of the details of the murder had been well publicised and that he had not told us anything about the way the shooting was carried out that could not have been read in a newspaper. He was asked if he could give any details which would add credence to his story. He said that during the getaway drive he hit something, damaging the front of the car and that he believed the car was a woman's because it had a box of tissues and some furry toys in it.

He also said that he had a tape recording of Michael Sayers bragging about the shooting. This had been recorded without Sayers' knowledge at a Karaoke night in a Newcastle pub. Glover claimed to have the tape in safekeeping, but would not disclose where. He also said that there were other things he could say that would convince us his story was true, but that he'd save these until a later time.

At the time Glover gave this account he was in a restraining body belt having previously self-inflicted injuries on his wrists and damaging his cell. We pointed out to Glover that in the circumstances any further conversation held on the subject would be with his legal representative. He stated he would be happy to repeat his account and give further details of the incident in an interview in the presence of his solicitor Mr Harrison. He was informed that we would arrange to interview him at the earliest opportunity convenient with his legal representative. At 2.20 pm that day the visit with Glover was concluded.

The nearest Stephen and Michael Sayers had got to shooting anyone on the night of 31st December 1993 was shooting a game of pool. They may well have bragged of shooting Viv, but it served their purpose in having people believe they could have carried out such an attack.

The Paul Logan and Viv murders, according to anonymous police claims, compare to each other due to the same MO (modus operandi) being used. *Both Logan and Viv were lured away from their locations they were at just prior to the murders by means of a telephone call. *Probability that both victims knew their assailants. *Each murder was for revenge and because of this, Northumbria Police are aware that the same assailants could have killed both men some few days apart. *The assailants' propensity for violence is well known to Northumbria Police.

On 20th September 2000, the murder of small time

£15-20m Murder Trial - Who Pays?

Newcastle drug dealer Freddie Knights, 38, is particularly relevant in terms of revealing how low those higher echelons of the crime world will stoop to when breaking the biggest taboo there is to break within their circle …becoming a supergrass! Within the underworld, this is act of betrayal is classed as being in the same ranks as a paedophile. So when someone becomes a supergrass, you can bet all you want that they have not done so out of the goodness of their heart!

Supergrass and self-confessed underworld killer and drugs dealer Lee Shaun Watson, 32, from Gateshead headed the gangland style hit on cocaine dealer Knights. Scar faced Watson had hoped to get away with the hit when he heaped the blame on the unsuspecting John Henry Sayers. (Also known as JHS and John Henry.)

John Henry had only been released from prison a short while after serving eleven years of a fifteen-year prison sentence for what has been claimed was his masterminding and taking part in a £350,000 daring robbery.

After his release from prison, John Henry had made a concerted effort to go straight, but his application to set up a taxi business was blocked by Northumbria police who objected to him holding an operator's licence needed to run such a business.

John Henry is considered to be one of the most poised and unruffled underworld figures ever to come out of Newcastle. Facing such a setback for John Henry was not considered a defeat, but merely a temporary hold on his intentions to go straight. Clean cut and clean living was part of John Henry's ethos; he abhorred the use of drugs and did not even drink alcohol.

Northumbria police still considered John Henry to be their 'number one target' and set about, in a most unremitting way, of maintaining surveillance and updating intelligence reports on him. Unruffled by this renewed vigour in the way he was targeted; John Henry continued seeking out ways to make an honest living.

When Freddie Knights was cruelly gunned down and

killed on his mother's doorstep in a shotgun attack, it was to be the start of a £15-£20m murder inquiry that was to see psychopathic Lee Shaun Watson, the self-professed joint second in command to a criminal outfit he called the Firm, turn supergrass!

It was on 13th October 2000, only matter of weeks after Knights was murdered, that Watson was a passenger in a car driven by Dale Miller when it went through a red traffic light, a passing police car gave chase. Both Miller and Watson ran off, when Watson was cornered by the police he had to be hit with a truncheon to disarm him after threatening the police with a lock knife. After being found in possession of £25,000 worth of heroin he was given three years imprisonment, a pretty light sentence?

During his imprisonment, Watson was visited in prison regularly by his junkie girlfriend Vanya Alan who lived in Highfield, Gateshead. During one of these prison visits the police covertly recorded what was said between them via a hidden microphone, this is what prompted Watson to admit to the murder of Knights and invent his outlandish story that John Henry was the boss of the Firm and that three others, Michael Dixon, 34, Eddie Stewart, 39, and Dale Miller, 38, were runners working under him.

During cross-examination by Jonathan Goldberg QC, Watson was asked if the heroin he had been caught with was payment for the hit on Knights? Watson: "No." Mr Goldberg went on to say, "You asked Dale Miller if he would take the wrap for these £25,000 worth of drugs?" Watson: "No." "You asked Miller to say it was his heroin?" Watson: "No." "Do you know a man named Mickey Conroy," Mr Goldberg asked. Watson: "Yes." Mr Goldberg immediately put it to Watson, "Has he anything to do with drugs?" Watson: "I think so."

During further cross-examination, Watson told of how he took his girlfriend Vanya Alan with him when he test fired a shotgun he had bought for £120 and that she had also test fired it in a field. Mr Goldberg asked Watson about an incident on 4th September 2000, which took place only 16 days prior to the Knights killing, when Watson attacked a property at Hardman Gardens, Ryton, Gateshead. Mr Duff for the prosecution: "Kathleen Median, the occupant had a partner who was a supposed drug dealer. When the house was vacated at 12.15pm, Watson ransacked the house. Firing shots from a 4.10 sawn-off shotgun into the headboard of the bed (twice) and shooting out a window and a mirror as well as ripping sinks out. Within half an hour the police called to a house that Watson was in, he was seen to pedal away on a bicycle. Watson evaded capture until 15th September. Further evidence that Watson had been in the property was found in fingerprint evidence."

Watson admitted to being a career criminal and that his earnings from drug dealing, racketeering and pimping netted him £175,000 per year. He admitted that Knights' little empire would have earned the firm £100,000 a year when Knights was ousted from the estate he supplied.

Mr Goldberg to Watson: " I suggest you're a ruthless man and are prepared to shoot someone if you can get away with it?" Watson lied when he replied, "No." In fact Watson had shot someone in the head with a live .22 during some after-hours drinking in a pub. The drug-crazed victim did little more than antagonise Watson! When Watson pulled the trigger, the victim was bobbing his head about and only ended up with superficial bullet-damaged!

Watson: "Once Freddie was shot in the leg I would take over the drug dealing on the estate." When asked, "Mickey Conroy, you knew he dealt in drugs… Did he ever suggest taking over Freddie Knights' estate as far as drug dealing was concerned?" Previously Watson said he knew Mickey Conroy, this time he said: "I don't know Mickey Conroy."

Watson was digging himself into a deep hole! On 8th March 2002, he entered a guilty plea to the charge of murdering Knights; this was in order to accommodate him as a prosecution witness. The remaining co-defendants of Watson had all entered not guilty pleas. So it must have been a daunting prospect for Watson when he considered playing this game of the badly done to hit man. Watson was given break, after break, after break, during his session in the witness box, in all he could not have spent more than twelve hours in the dock over a four-day period! When his girlfriend, Vanya Alan, gave evidence she had admitted that the police had given her something in the region of £25,000 to assist her and her mother in witness protection payments!

Heroin junkie and gang member Stephen Carlton escaped the wrath of the law when he received a healthy payout of £23,000 from Northumbria police and escaped robbery charges when he gave evidence against those that he should have been standing next to. Carlton housed some of the gang members after the killing...yet he walks free?

"Mickey Conroy got Lee Watson to murder Viv Graham after Viv had beaten him up in a fight on Newcastle's quayside," said John Henry from the witness box! A remarkably bold statement that took all aback, but it is thought to have been nothing more than a retaliatory remark by John Henry, which was aimed at a particular man who had stood in a court dock in the mid 90s and had sworn the lives of the Sayers' family away and blamed them for the Viv murder. This tit for tat action by John Henry was deemed to be a disguised two-fingered salute to those concerned.

This certainly seemed to nullify Watson's so-called assisting the police with the Viv murder! Secretly swearing every top crook's life away could in reality be a ploy by Watson to save his own skin! Watson seems to forget that he was a suspect in the Viv murder inquiry in 1994 and when he was in Gateshead magistrates' court on 12th March 1994 he said to the police and CPS: "Why don't you fuck off, you couldn't catch us for the shooting of Viv Graham."

John Henry, as I predicted from the day he was arrested, walked from that court in Leeds a free man...acquitted of all three counts of violence against him. The CPS were said to be banging their heads against the wall over John Henry's acquittal. Certainly, police impropriety, the dubious evidence

£15-20m Murder Trial - Who Pays?

from DCI Bob Pallas and the lies from crazed killer Watson had helped convince the jury of the innocence of not just John Henry, but also of Anthony Leach's innocence,both men were acquitted.

Mickey Dixon was, unbelievably, found guilty of conspiracy to cause grievous bodily harm…9 years. He was the saddest sight to see!! Unwittingly he used a mobile phone he had bought and eventually given back to one of the other unnamed men who was acquitted, he also stole a car! Hope he wins his appeal! Dale Miller, the supposed gunman - not guilty of murder, but found guilty of manslaughter…16 years. Eddie Stewart, admitted his role as getaway driver - not guilty of murder, but found guilty of manslaughter…13 years.

The finale was kept until the very end!! On 2nd October 2002. The Honourable Mr Justice Douglas Brown, a decent sort of judge, vacated Watson's plea of guilty to murder and accepted a plea of guilty to manslaughter…11 years! £20m of taxpayer's money down the drain – who pays??????????

www.johnsayers.com
www.crimethroughtime.com
www.miragepublishing.com
www.bronsonmania.com
www.crimebiz.co.uk

Other Titles

Charles Bronson's Solitary Fitness
***Fitness & Strength *Paperback *ISBN: 1902578120 *RRP £7.99
*100+ Photos *Win £500 Fitness Competition
*Editor – Stephen Richards**

Charles Bronson has served 28 years behind bars, 24 of those years have been in solitary confinement, yet in spite of this he remains supremely fit and strong. What are the secrets to his phenomenal strength and fitness? How can Bronson punch a hole with his bare fist through bullet proof glass, bend solid steel doors by kicking at them, do press-ups with two men on his back and all on a basic prison diet! Without the use of fancy gym equipment, steroids, steaks, supplements or pills you can pack on pounds of muscle, lose weight fast and gain superhuman strength. Did Hercules do steroids, did Samson do pills…think about it. Also contains a little known product that has been claimed to cure cancer! And the secret of looking the same age in ten years time as you do now!

Ramraiders - True Crime
***Paperback *16 Pages mono-stills *RRP £7.99 * Foreword by
Freddie Foreman ISBN: 1-902578-10-4 by Stephen Richards**

The 'Yellow Pages' ram raid gang. £l00m ram raid gang escape totally undetected into Europe, the biggest and cleverest ram raid ever! Bizarre ram raids as well as the wacky and weird. Top ram raiders reveal all about the business.

The ram raid phenomenon was a crime exported worldwide. Spectacular ram raids in the UK, Australia and New Zealand. Police were rendered impotent by the gang's ability to defeat them. £3.5m ram raid gang given a total of 33-years behind bars.

Counter surveillance techniques, getaway routes explored, attempted murder— and more! Prison life uncovered with never before published photos smuggled out of UK prisons showing the true extent of this gang's power right under the noses of prison authorities — drink and drug parties within prison. Prison violence becomes a way of life for the gang that started a crime wave of ram raiding throughout the world — their own story.

Birdman Opens His Mind
***RRP£7.99 *ISBN No: 1-902578-03-1 *Author: Charles Bronson
*Hardback book *Full of his hand drawn colour illustrations**

Colour illustrated adult humour - hardback cover. Bronson's laughing all the way to the crematorium written and colour illustrated by the Poet from Hell. Get one if you can. In Charlie's own inimitable style and in his own words he will make you laugh. Don't get hooked up on the word 'poetry', 'humour' is the word - don't miss it! In limited supply, sure to become a collector's item. Edited by Stephen Richards

Other Titles

Silent Scream

The Charles Bronson story, his own story, his own words
'Autobiography' *Serialised in UK newspaper for five days
*16 pages of stills *ISBN: 1-902578-08-2 *RRP £15.99

The silence has been broken with this best seller. The truth about Bronson's life and his ill treatment by the authorities in penal and mental establishments. He's had more porridge than Goldilocks and the three bears. He's taken more hostages inside of prison than any other UK prisoner. Holds many awards for his art and writing. Banned from the Guinness Book of Records - holds six world records for feats of strength and fitness. More prison rooftop protests than anyone living or dead. Violence, violence and more violence, inflicted on him by the prison service! In Bronson's own words find out what makes him tick and explode. Hannibal Lecter is kids stuff compared to this real life action, full of sex and violence. Given a top review in UK's 'Front Magazine'.

Charles Bronson – 'Sincerely Yours'

*Video Documentary *VHS Format *£15.99 *2? hours
*ISBN: 1902578198 *Directed by Stephen Richards

The one the UK government tried to ban. The one that Jack Straw took Steve Richards to court for. The one that got Richards a three-week prison sentence. Exclusive footage and audio action never ever before seen or heard.

Features: Joe Pyle; Snr., Lord Longford, Andy Jones (owner of 'Crime Through Time Museum'), Tony Lambrianiou, Charlie's mother; Eira first time filmed interview, Loraine; Charlie's cousin, Ray Williams; long time civilian friend of 30+ years, Jan Lamb; 'The Sport' newspaper celebrity pinup, James Crosbie; Scotland's most prolific bank robber, John 'Alf' Lodge; Wales' answer to James Crosbie and that flash showbiz character Dave Courtney and 'Harley', Charlie's gangster dog.

Audio of an actual prison hostage-taking situation involving Charlie! 'The Swellbellys', a contemporary punk band from Scotland perform a song for Bronson ('Caged'). Jim Dawkins, formerly 'Prison Officer Dawkins' used to guard Charlie in HM Prison Belmarsh!

See Bronson boxing in an unlicensed fight, watch a gun fall to the floor of the boxing ring out of someone's coat pocket, as one hell of a fight breaks out. A highly controversial documentary, worryingly, for the authorities. Can be ordered from any bookshop if you give them the ISBN number of 1902578198.

Other Titles

PUBLIC consumer *ENEMY*

'The Amazing little A-Z Handbook of how to complain and Win!'
*You, the consumer, are being ripped off *Paperback pocketbook
*ISBN 1-902578-02-3 *RRP was £5.99 *By Stephen Richards
NOW FREE – YOU ONLY PAY P+P OF £1.50

Police arrest the author and his two researchers for alleged deception after national food and drinks companies complain to the police about the amount of complaints they're receiving! Simply put, it's THE complainers Bible. Don't join Internet companies who claim to complain for you, this book does it all for you, includes legal advice. Repays its RRP time and time again. A must-have for anyone who ever complains.

LEGENDS

*By best selling authors: Charles Bronson with Stephen Richards
*True Crime *ISBN 1902578-11-2 *Hardback *£14.99

Serialised in a national newspaper for four days. Banned by a national chain of bookshops, but can be ordered from any Watersone's bookshop or www.amazon.co.uk. The OFFICIAL Charles Bronson guide to who's who in the underworld and beyond. Legends that Charlie feels deserve space in this A-Z guide of Criminals and those connected in some way to them. Includes a chapter from Manchester's Paul Massey.

Short succinct write-ups. Bronson goes overboard in this book with a universal appeal. Nicknames leave little to the imagination: The Mummy, The Wolf Man, The Human Slug, Semtex Man, The Pie Man, The Wizard, Cannon Ball, Quasimodo, Voodoo Man, The Promoter and hundreds more – all real people. Legendary Scottish Bank Robber, James Crosbie - guest contributor for Scotland's chapter. Foreword by Joe Pyle Snr. Ireland isn't forgotten either. Icons are few Legends are many.

Looking at Life

By the legendary Joe Pyle 'The Hood with a Heart'

*ISBN: 1-902578-09-0 *RRP £8.99 *Full colour photographs &
Illustrations *Foreword by actor Ray Winstone
Edited by Stephen Richards

Take a moment to read this, please, and in doing so you'll help some terminally ill babies at the only hospice for babies in the UK. Some of the hardest men in the UK helped contribute towards this book - some of the softest hearted people you could ever wish to meet. Features inclusions by Gerry Adams the President of Sinn Fein, Sir Elton John, Sir Trevor McDonald, Richard Branson, Mohamed Al Fayed, Lulu, Roger Daltrey, Roy Shaw, Freddie Foreman, Dave Courtney, Tony Lambrianou, Charlie Richardson, Charlie Bronson, Johnny Nash, Frank Maloney and many, many more. Joe Pyle as featured on TV's 'Hard Bastards' and in Blake Publishing's 'Hard Bastards'.

Other Titles

A Sting in the Tale

(Hardback)
*Only Biography ever authorised by STING *RRP £14.99
*ISBN: 1902578-13-9 *Mono Stills *Foreword by Sting

An eye-wateringly funny book will guarantee to have you laughing and in stitches regardless of whether you're a Sting fan or not. Short succinct chapters show the bizarreness of what it's like to have such a world famous rock star as a friend. Written by Sting's closest friend for the past 38 years, the only book to be given Sting's blessing covering his life with the author from their schooldays right up to Sting's marriage to Trudy Styler. Serialised in News of the World, Sunday Mail's Night & Day mag book of the week, Top Review in the Independent on Sunday's Review mag, featured on Richard & Judy show, TV, Radio, Sunday Life (Belfast) - top review, Sunday Sun, Outlandos Web Site (Sting's fan club on the Web)

Insanity

*By the second best selling convict author Charles Bronson
With Stephen Richards *By Blake Publishing
*January 2003 *Hardback *£15.99

Charles Bronson, the UK prisoner, has been imprisoned for nearly 30 years; some 25 of those years have been spent in solitary confinement. Although a number of books, 'Silent Scream' and 'Bronson', have successfully mapped his prison life, this book, written by Bronson in his own words, gives you an insight into his mental asylum life.

Charles Bronson, the only man to have served time in all three of the major asylums in the UK for the criminally insane tells you what it was really like. Ashworth, Broadmoor and Rampton are explored in depth with plenty of prison madness along the way. Sure to be a best seller this book holds absolutely nothing back from the reader. Gory, gruesome and grotesque are the scenes painted by a man certified insane time and time and time again by an anachronistic penal system. For further details please contact John Blake Publishing by visiting their web site: http://www.blake.co.uk

POSTERS

Viv Graham – The Legend
POSTER – A3 SIZE – GLOSSY - £1.99 (UK ONLY)

Charles Bronson's artwork now in poster form
POSTER – A3 SIZE – GLOSSY £1.99 (UK ONLY)
(Two types A & B)

Other Titles

Crime Through Time
*Hardback Book*ISBN 1902578171 *Photo's – 2,000+ mono
*RRP Price - £19.99 *Crime/Celebrity/Taboo Subjects
*550 pages - all gloss coated *Author: Stephen Richards

True Crime book with a difference – based around the exhibits on display at the infamous Crime Through Time museum - The Black Museum, Newent, Gloucestershire.
www.crimethroughtime.com

Hitler's Holocaust – Brutal & Evil Nazi death camps!

Gory and gruesome photos depicting horrific & cruel acts of merciless slaughter will make you shudder and shake in revulsion at the ghastly Nazi show of horror!

Churchill rejected peace deal offered by Hitler's deputy - Rudolf Hess story will rock government!

TV sex symbol shamefully exposed committing acts of gross indecency in a public toilet with another man!

Sportsmen and celebrities exposed performing in perverted auto-erotic sexual acts & bondage games!

Sexual Scandals – Linda Lovelace of 'Deep Throat' fame & Anna Nicole Smith expose their assets!

The barbaric and sickening bloodthirsty sex games of Fred and Rose West – A living victim speaks out!

Sid Vicious – Commando style raid sees his ashes emptied over his murdered Jewish girlfriend's grave

Shocking - Marilyn Monroe on the mortuary slab! Horrendous – JFK's brains blown out!

Night Stalker, Richard Ramirez, taunts you to touch his cursed hand, dare you defy him!

Human skin lampshades, Ku Klux Klan apparel and body cages at the museum are evil, say officials!

Other Titles

Sex, Drugs & The Stamp Scam

*Best selling True Crime Author: Stephen Richards
True Crime Autobiography–Insulted, abused, jailed & blackmailed
*Due for release in November 2003 *ISBN: 1-902578-15-5
*Mono Stills *RRP£14.99

The true story and previously untold story of how a gang masterminded what was said to be a multi-million pound stamp fraud right under the noses of UK Post Office fraud investigators. Royal Mail were said to be losing £1m per day.

This gang stopped the post office being privatised; it is said, on two occasions. The gang were eventually jailed, but not before they had a good run for their money!

An early learning curve for the not yet grown up member of the stamp gang: "Nazi, Nazi, Nazi," was the ongoing chant that became louder and louder with each "Nazi" that the children in the schoolyard were directing at a frightened looking boy seeking refuge by the locked door to the school building – England 1960s.

Violence was becoming a way of life for him: "I'll kill you, you little bastard," the balding man said to the eight-year-old boy as he had his hands grasped around the boy's throat lifting him clear of the floor. As the boy's face turned blue and he made choking sounds he was dropped like piece of hot coal.

Racial hatred in the UK against a white in the 1960s toughened him up ready for the job in hand: A child's fight to overcome racial hatred long before blacks were classed as being racially abused, a turbulent and violent upbringing, the trauma of prison life is revealed within. World champion marshal arts expert hatches plot to blackmail him by exposing his criminal past for his own ends. And his eventual rise from the ashes of a wrecked and plundered life. A story too unbelievable to believe!

The Golden Pen reveals all: A very, very special true crime story from the man with the Golden Pen – acclaimed best selling investigative author and Underworld Expert Stephen Richards. Every word carrying part of Richards' soul, every comma and full stop bearing testament to his efforts. Full to overflowing with violence, sadness, nymphomaniacal romps, sexual fetishes so bizarre they nearly kill those taking part, lesbian romps, wife swapping, underworld drug deals and ultimately the subject matter in question - 'Stamps'.

A story of oppression, racism, hatred, neo-Nazis, love, deceit, crime and a soul-destroying end that will see you shaking your head: Richards will not fail to light up your passions, fuel your anger and leave his mark in the depths of your mind for the rest of your life with this creation. Will probably be the best selling book of 2002, given the true crime content will be too unbelievable for you to believe it to be true!!!!!!!!!!!!!!!!!!!!!

Other Titles

Price List - Reminder

Solitary Fitness	£7.99
Ramraiders	£7.99
Birdman Opens His Mind - Charles Bronson	£7.99
Sincerely Yours (Video) Charles Bronson	£15.99 P & P add £2.00
Silent Scream (Bronson's own words)	£15.99
PUBLIC *consumer* ENEMY - FREE you only pay P+P	£1.50
Legends	£14.99
Looking at Life Joe Pyle	£8.99
A Sting in the Tale	£14.99
Crime Through Time	£19.99
Viv Graham Poster (A3 size – not shown)	£1.99
Bronson - Metal Pen	£1.00
Bronson Bizarre Artwork Poster (A3 size, not shown	£1.99

UK PRISONERS RECEIVE 25% DISCOUNT (Books only)

Total…………………...………………………….......£……

POSTAGE AND PACKAGING

P+P for books/posters/pens/CDs is free in the UK.
(P+P is not free for Public *Consumer* Enemy book)

CHEQUES OR PO PAYABLE TO

'BOOK TRADERS'

WORLDWIDE SHIPPING

• Shipping to Europe add 20% rest world add 50%

ORDERING

• We <u>do not accept credit cards</u> when ordering by post
• Send your payment with order, name and address to:
**BOOK TRADERS, PO Box 161,
Gateshead, NE8 4WW, England**

Pay by credit card on website:
www.miragepublishing.com
Books can also be ordered directly from:
www.amazon.co.uk

Our thanks to ALL the good bookshops that sell
our books, particularly: Waterstone's and WH Smith